Birnbaum's
Walt Disney World ®
without kids

by Pamela S. Weiers

TOM PASSAVANT
EDITORIAL DIRECTOR

ALICE GARRARD
EXECUTIVE EDITOR

CYNTHIA AMBROSE
ART DIRECTOR

DEANNA CARON
SENIOR EDITOR

VICKI L. BLANCHFIELD
CONTRIBUTING EDITOR

TRACY A. SMITH
COPY EDITOR

ALEXANDRA MAYES BIRNBAUM
CONSULTING EDITOR

HYPERION AND HEARST BUSINESS PUBLISHING, INC.

TABLE OF CONTENTS

When to Go 10
The Logistics 13
Getting Around 17
Sample Schedules 21
Special Needs 29

8 PLANNING AHEAD

First things first: Lay the groundwork for an unforgettable Walt Disney World vacation by timing your visit to take advantage of the best weather, crowd patterns, and special goings-on. Learn about the various package and ticket options, how to save time and money during your stay, and how to get around on the World's extensive transportation system. We also provide mix-and-match sample schedules to help you plan your days and nights. And there's a section with additional information for older travelers, people with disabilities, singles, and couples.

Walt Disney World
    Resorts 39
Disney Village Hotel
    Plaza 65
Beyond the World 68

36 CHECKING IN

Whether it's elegant, rustic, whimsical, or romantic digs you're looking for, you'll find them among Walt Disney World's 16 resorts, themed as only Disney knows how. Choose from hotels whose architecture and ambience evoke such locales as New Orleans, Martha's Vineyard, Polynesia, or an early-1900s mountain lodge. We explain the advantages of staying on property and the big draws of each resort (conveniently organized by price). You'll also find recommendations for lodging outside the World's boundaries.

74 THEME PARKS: THE BIG THREE

Enchanting, engaging, entertaining...overwhelming. The Magic Kingdom, Epcot, and the Disney-MGM Studios can rekindle even the most dormant sense of wonder and curiosity. But where to begin? Right here: We've devised some strategies to help you make the most of each day. We've also provided an orientation and map for each theme park; detailed walking tours that highlight the most alluring and amusing stops for adults; and lists of touring priorities that rank every attraction. From "Don't Miss" and "Don't Overlook" to "Don't Knock Yourself Out," we've scoped out the grownup fun quotient.

Magic Kingdom 78
Epcot 90
   Future World 96
   World Showcase 107
Disney-MGM Studios 118

132 DIVERSIONS: SPORTS, SHOPPING & OTHER PURSUITS

Within the 45 square miles of Walt Disney World lie five first-rate golf courses and abundant opportunities for tennis, boating, fishing, and biking. Those who prefer soaking and sliding can head for the River Country, Typhoon Lagoon, and Blizzard Beach water parks. Die-hard shoppers will have a field day checking out our favorite shops. Nature lovers can commune at *Fort Wilderness* and the Discovery Island wildlife sanctuary. Want to give your brain a workout? Sign up for an adult learning seminar or book a stay at the new Disney Institute.

Sports 135
Shopping 152
Other Pursuits 163

174 DINING & ENTERTAINMENT

Here's your insider guide to adult best bets for full-service restaurants and casual eating spots in the theme parks, resorts, elsewhere in Walt Disney World, and off property. We've found an upbeat brunch, (dining) rooms with prime views, cheap eats, sweet treats, afternoon teas, wines by the glass, and only-at-WDW microbrews. After dark, you'll know where to go to hear cool jazz, dance the night away (disco, country, or cheek-to-cheek), find a dinner show or a comedy club, or catch a theme park spectacular.

Restaurant Guide 177
Nightlife Guide 200
Holidays and Special
   Events 214

ISBN: 0-7868-8121-6

Printed in the United States of America

A truckload of gratitude to my fabulous supporting cast of family and friends (especially Michael, Mum & Dad, and Marianne) for their patience, understanding, and tireless support. Ears all around! —Pam

Other 1996 Birnbaum Travel Guides

Bahamas and Turks & Caicos
Bermuda
Canada
Cancun/Cozumel and Isla Mujeres
Caribbean
Country Inns & Back Roads
Disneyland
Hawaii
Mexico
Miami & Fort Lauderdale
United States
Walt Disney World
Walt Disney World For Kids, By Kids

A Word from the Editors

When you stop to think about it, a Walt Disney World guide for adults makes a lot of sense. Look at it this way: How many children do you know who have been there alone? As it happens, Disney has been catering to grownup sensibilities for a long time; the most obvious example is one entire theme park, namely Epcot. And, for true movie mavens, the Disney-MGM Studios is close to nirvana.

Sophisticated resort hotels and restaurants, world-class golf courses, and this year's new Disney Institute, a self-contained resort that offers workshops in everything from music composition to rock climbing, have only added to the allure.

But there's a whole other, more subtle level on which Walt Disney World has always appealed to grownups. We're referring to the little jokes, both visual and verbal, that keep popping up where you least expect them. Take, for instance, Epcot's Cranium Command, which purports to be a journey into the brain of a 12-year-old boy named Buzzy, but interjects sly references to certain human emotions and responses that are way beyond the ken of kids. Somebody, we thought, put those knowing puns and winks in the script just for us.

The editors at breakfast. Eventually, they did get to eat.

More than ever before, Disney's creative efforts are crossing over to the grownup side of the street. Lots of adults, both younger ones ("pre-kid") and older people whose children have flown the coop ("post-kid"), are descending on the parks with needs and notions that are vastly different from those of the parental persuasion.

Clearly, it was time for us to respond—by adding an adult-oriented book to our ongoing series of Birnbaum Guides to Walt Disney World and Disneyland. But what sort of book should it be? We already publish what we immodestly believe is the definitive annually revised guide to Walt Disney World. Anyone who wants the most complete word on everything there is to see and do there is well-advised to accept no substitutes.

The book you hold in your hands is different in several important respects. First, as you may have already noticed from the title page, it was written by one very talented person, Pamela S. Weiers, aided and abetted by the rest of the Birnbaum Disney Guides staff. Pam's distinctive voice, equal parts authority, experience, and humor, makes her the perfect person to lead a tour of this vast enterprise. Second, this book is by no means comprehensive. Rather, it skips the kid stuff and delivers the goods on adult amusements in and around Walt Disney World.

Put another way, this guide is selective in the very best sense. We spent weeks debating which of the attractions, shows, hotels, and restaurants merit special attention by adults. Then Pam, usually accompanied by one or more fellow staffers, would make another trip to Orlando and put everything to the test.

For the most part, these visits were not the sort we would recommend for the casual traveler. Consider the time that Pam and senior editor Deanna Caron made a sweep through 15(!) hotels in one day, looking for the very best adult nooks and crannies. The mere memory of it still sends chills up their spines, as does the recollection of a plunge into River Country's unheated (read: almost numbing) Ol' Swimming Hole one cool January afternoon.

The result is that anything that didn't live up to expectations was bumped from our "stand-out" list to the "good bets" rankings or banished entirely from the selective listings. Attractions that are awash in a sea of kids were simply given short (or at least shorter) shrift. And when we found something that just tickled us with pleasure, we weren't subtle about mentioning it. When you come across more than one reference to the new *Planet Hollywood* restaurant it's because our group of somewhat jaded New Yorkers was absolutely bowled over by the place, and we want to be sure you don't miss it.

Even with research aplenty, we have to fess up to the fact that not one word of this book would ever have seen print were it not for the dedication and talent of many, many other people. To begin, we owe enormous thanks to the people who manage and run Walt Disney World. It is their willingness to open their files and explain operations to us in the most detailed and timely way possible (not to mention letting us—and only us—publish pictures of their parks and characters) that makes this the Official Guide, even though it is, in fact, written by non-Disney employees.

In the listing at right we've tried to acknowledge all of the Disney staffers, both in the parks and behind the scenes, who contributed their time, knowledge, and experience. In addition, we want to extend a deep bow to Wendy Wolfe, Michael Mendenhall, Laura Simpson, Diane Hancock, and Robert Sias for the care and effort they've put into this project. We'd also like to thank our favorite off-site Disney expert, Wendy Lefkon, who edited our guides for many years and is still instrumental in their publication as executive editor at Hyperion.

For their role in the production of this book, we salute Elizabeth Irigoyen and Margaret Casagrande for their typesetting skills, and Laura Vitale, Kieran Scott, and Mark Spoonauer for their keen eyes in reading the final galleys. Shari Hartford, who kept our own cast of characters on schedule, is especially deserving of a nod, as is Susan Hohl, mapmaker extraordinaire.

Of course, no list of acknowledgments would be complete without our founding editor, Steve Birnbaum, who was surely smiling on this project, as well as Alexandra Mayes Birnbaum, who continues to be a guiding light—to say nothing of a careful reader of every word.

Finally, it is important to remember that Walt Disney World is constantly changing and growing, and in each annual revision we expect to refine and expand our material to serve your needs even better. For the debut edition, though, this is the final word.

Have a great visit!

The Editors

We Couldn't Have Done It Without...

Greg Albrecht
Kevin Banks
Beth Brainard
Debbie Carlos
Lana Carnahan
Scott Cassidy
Robin Dickerson
Kristine Dobson
Gene Duncan
Michelle Fisher
Marc Glissman
Dave Herbst
Richard Hutton
Mark Jaronsky
Pam Jorgensen
Keith Keogh
Chris Kurth
Todd Lenahan
Bob Mervine
Rebecca Miller
Lori Oxford-Schott
Robbie Pallard
Amy Sadowsky
Elizabeth Schar
Rob Scheuerman
Deborah Scott
Kelly Slagle
Mary Tomlinson
Brian Walton
Bob Weiers

Planning Ahead

There are plenty of hotels, restaurants, and theme park attractions for everyone at Walt Disney World. So why sit down with a book in hand to plan ahead? Because a little attention to detail beforehand—we like to think of it as shopping for fun insurance—pays big dividends once you arrive in the Orlando area. Just ask the couple who had the foresight to book a table at the ultra-deluxe *Victoria & Albert's* dining room *before* they left home. Or the friends who arrived with admission passes in hand and thereby avoided the ticket line at the entrance to Epcot. Or the golfers who knew about Disney's golf packages and got a coveted mid-morning tee time on the Osprey Ridge course during their Easter visit. Our point: You can't be assured of the vacation experience you want without knowing which of the gazillion ways to enjoy Walt Disney World most appeal to you, and how to go about making sure these potential highlights don't become missed opportunities.

This first chapter not only provides the framework for a successful visit; it establishes a vital awareness that helps the information in subsequent chapters fall right in line. On the following pages, you'll find insight on when to visit; advice on tickets, packages, reservations, and how to save money; information on how to get around the World; flexible touring schedules; tips for older travelers, couples, singles, and guests with disabilities; and a whole lot more. This chapter is a straightforward planner that you'll return to again and again—no doubt with greater purpose than the first time through, when you're eager to learn about Walt Disney World's hotels, theme parks, dining, and nightlife. So go ahead and give it a quick skim if this is your first read, but don't forget to come back.

Experienced guests know the value of plotting their course through the World.

WHEN TO GO

Much tougher than the (rhetorical) question of *if* you want to visit Walt Disney World is the prickly matter of *when*. In addition to your own schedule there is the weather to consider; you'd also like to avoid the big crowds, although you'd love to get a gander at the Christmas parade or that flower festival you read about in the newspaper. You want to experience Walt Disney World at its best. But when?

Weather and crowd patterns are charted here along with other factors such as extended park hours so you can see how possible vacation dates stack up. Timing your visit to meet all expectations may be impossible, but experience suggests certain optimum times. Early January until mid-February, late April through early June, September, October, early November, and the week after Thanksgiving through the week before Christmas stand out as particularly good times to find oneself in the World. Taking things one step further, we like to underline the period from the Sunday *after* Thanksgiving to the week *before* Christmas as the ultimate timing for a WDW visit. This is a chance to savor Walt Disney World during one of its least crowded and most festive times of year. The place is wrapped in wonderful holiday decorations, and there are tons of special goings-on, from parades and parties to themed dinners and stage shows.

Of course, the holiday season isn't the only time that Walt Disney World makes an extracurricular spectacle of itself. The WDW calendar is jammed with festivities and special events, most of which attract major crowds and many of which have the power to make (or break) a vacation. Packages are available in conjunction with some. For information on packages, see the "Logistics" section of this chapter. For more detailed descriptions of happenings perhaps worth timing your trip around, see the "Holidays and Special Events" section of the *Dining & Entertainment* chapter. For now, note the following lineup:

NEW YEAR'S EVE CELEBRATION (December 31): Double-size fireworks; the theme parks stay open until the wee hours; many on-property resorts host celebrations; Pleasure Island hosts a special-admission blowout.

Calling Cue

Unless otherwise noted, all telephone numbers are in area code 407.

WALT DISNEY WORLD MARATHON (January 7): International competitors and first-time marathoners alike lace up for a race through Walt Disney World.

LPGA HEALTHSOUTH INAUGURAL (January 19–21): The second annual WDW golf tournament is so named because it's the first full-field event of the year for women professionals.

SCI-FI CONVENTION (January 20–23): New this year. Science fiction celebs and fans converge on Tomorrowland in the Magic Kingdom.

INDY 200 AT WALT DISNEY WORLD (January 27): New this year. Indy race cars do their stuff on a track just south of the Magic Kingdom parking lot.

PLEASURE ISLAND MARDI GRAS (February 17–20): Crescent City jazz bands and special street performances bring New Orleans' biggest party to Pleasure Island.

PLEASURE ISLAND'S ST. PATRICK'S DAY CELEBRATION (March 17): Pleasure Island gets its Irish up with live music and merrymaking from the Emerald Isle.

EASTER SUNDAY (April 7): A hopping Magic Kingdom hosts the televised Easter parade.

GRAD NIGHTS (April 26–27, May 3–4): Graduating high school seniors take over the Magic Kingdom from 11 P.M. to 5 A.M. in these special-ticket events.

EPCOT INTERNATIONAL FLOWER AND GARDEN FESTIVAL (April 18–June 2): Epcot is abloom with elaborate display gardens, special horticultural tours, and gardening workshops.

FOURTH OF JULY CELEBRATION: Fireworks in excelsis mark the busiest day of the summer season.

DISNEYANA (September): A five-day convention centered on Disney collectibles, limited-edition art, and memorabilia.

What to Pack

- ■ Comfortable walking shoes
- ■ Sunscreen
- ■ Bathing suit
- ■ T-shirts and shorts for day
- ■ Casual separates and collared shirts for evening (jeans are okay)
- ■ Lightweight sweaters or jackets for summer evenings, when air conditioning can be chilly; warmer clothing is essential evening (and often daytime) wear from November to March
- ■ A jacket for men and dress or comparable outfit for women if plans include dinner at *Victoria & Albert's* or another elegant local dining spot
- ■ Any sporting togs and equipment you'll want for tennis, golf, fishing, jogging, or gym workouts (racquets, clubs, balls, golf shoes, and poles are available for rent)
- ■ Lightweight rain gear and a folding umbrella

All in the Timing

Factor the following WDW trends and truths into the equation before settling on vacation dates. For up-to-the-minute details on park hours and any attractions closed for refurbishment, call 824-4321.

■ Shortest Lines, Smallest Crowds: the second week of January through the first week of February; the week after Labor Day until Thanksgiving; the week after Thanksgiving through the week before Christmas.

■ Small to Average Crowds, But Lots of Spring-Breakers: the last week of February through the first week of April.

■ Longest Lines, Biggest Crowds: Presidents' week; Easter week; second and third weeks of April; second week of June through third week of August; Fourth of July; Christmas through New Year's Day.

■ Sorry, Refurbishment in Progress: During less-crowded times of the year, particularly January and February, some of the WDW attractions and water parks are closed for renovations.

■ Extended Hours: Presidents' weekend; the two weeks surrounding Easter; summer months; Thanksgiving week; Christmas through New Year's Day.

WALT DISNEY WORLD 25TH ANNIVERSARY CELEBRATION (October 1, 1996–December 31, 1997): The World marks its silver anniversary with a big shindig incorporating new shows and attractions, and all kinds of special festivities and vacation packages.

PLEASURE ISLAND JAZZ FEST (October): Jazz greats from various eras bring live music to the fore.

DISNEY VILLAGE MARKETPLACE BOAT SHOW (October): Central Florida's largest boat show makes waves on Buena Vista Lagoon.

WALT DISNEY WORLD/OLDSMOBILE GOLF CLASSIC (October 5–8): Top PGA Tour players compete on three classic Disney links.

FESTIVAL OF THE MASTERS AT DISNEY VILLAGE MARKETPLACE (November): One of the South's top-rated art shows.

DISNEY'S MAGICAL HOLIDAYS (November 24–December 19): Decorations, special festivities, and holiday spirit abound in WDW's theme parks and resorts.

WDW WEATHER
Temperature

	Average high	Average low	Mean	Average rainfall (inches)
January	70	50	60	2.28
February	72	51	62	2.95
March	76	56	66	3.46
April	82	61	71	2.72
May	87	66	76	2.94
June	89	71	80	7.11
July	90	73	81	8.29
August	90	74	82	6.73
September	88	72	80	7.20
October	82	66	74	4.07
November	76	57	67	1.56
December	72	52	62	1.90

THE LOGISTICS

SHOULD YOU BUY A PACKAGE?

Travelers who like the idea of paying for their vacation in one lump sum that includes accommodations, transportation, and park admission have a wealth of choices when visiting Walt Disney World. As a rule, these package plans offer some savings over the total cost of the included vacation elements purchased separately; but their real hallmark is convenience—a completely organized vacation with a few perks thrown in for good measure. Some are designed for a moderate budget; others are intended for travelers who want a luxurious getaway with all the frills.

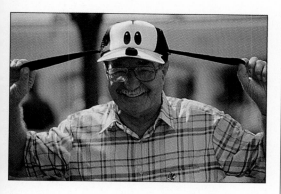

Vacation plans put forth by the Walt Disney Travel Company tempt with such extras as unlimited use of recreational offerings, from bicycles to golf courses; meals at WDW restaurants; and unlimited admission to Discovery Island, Pleasure Island, and the water parks as well as to the three theme parks. Specifics vary according to the package chosen. But WDW's basic package offerings range from the economical Classic Plan to the top-of-the-line Grand Plan. Additional packages are built around the needs of golfers or honeymooners, and still others are tied to a season or a special WDW event. New for 1996 are packages that include airfare. For details on the many vacation plans available from the Walt Disney Travel Company, call 800-828-0228.

The Right Package...

■ Saves you money on precisely the type of lodging, transportation, and recreation you want.

■ Includes meaningful extras (meals at restaurants of your choice or unlimited golf, for example), as opposed to fluff like welcoming cocktails and so-called privileges that are actually services available to all WDW guests.

■ Fits like a glove. You wouldn't buy a pair of gloves that were two sizes too big no matter what the sale price; nor should you buy a package that encompasses much more than you can reasonably expect to take advantage of.

Example: If this is your first visit to Walt Disney World and you have three days to spend, you'll have your hands full just exploring the theme parks, so a package whose main appeal is unlimited admission to other attractions is probably not worth your while.

Alternatively, if you're looking to golf yourself silly, you'll get a lot of wear out of a package that allows for unlimited tee times.

Cost-Cutting Tips

■ **Consider lodging with kitchen facilities to save on food costs.**

■ **Compare lunch and dinner menus at a favored restaurant. The same dishes are often available for less at midday.**

■ **Think about how much time you plan to spend at your hotel, and don't break the budget to stay at a resort packed with amenities you won't have an opportunity to enjoy.**

■ **Consider sharing accommodations with family or friends. There's greater financial power in numbers, and it can buy lodging in spacious villas with kitchen facilities at places such as the *Disney Vacation Club*.**

■ **The *All-Star Sports* and *All-Star Music* resorts offer the least-expensive rooms on WDW property, with rates at *Caribbean Beach, Dixie Landings,* and *Port Orleans* only slightly higher.**

Plans featuring hotels on WDW property are available through Delta Air Lines and American Express Vacation Travel in addition to Walt Disney World itself. The Delta Air Lines packages are noteworthy for their inclusion of low-cost air transportation; for details call 800-872-7786. American Express Vacation Travel options can be booked via the same number.

Packages featuring off-property accommodations are offered by a number of operators, including American Express Vacation Travel (800-872-7786) and Go Go Tours (800-821-3731). Premier Cruise Lines (800-726-5678) and Carnival Cruise Lines (800-327-9501) offer packages combining a Walt Disney World vacation with a cruise. A travel agent can be invaluable in sorting through the possibilities.

Because the value of any given package depends wholly on your needs, we have provided a checklist to help you quickly narrow the choices. If you think you might be interested in buying a package, call for the brochures, then use the guidelines on the previous page to help determine which plan, if any, is right for you.

MONEY MATTERS

The bottom line on cold, hard cash at Walt Disney World is that the kind with Andrew Jackson and George Washington is good at all parks, shops, and resorts. A few other points of interest related to green matter and its plastic counterparts: Fast-food restaurants and refreshment stands operate on a cash-only basis. For all other charges incurred at Walt Disney World, traveler's checks, American Express, Visa, MasterCard, and The Disney Credit Card also are acceptable forms of payment. WDW resort guests who leave a credit card imprint upon check-in may use their hotel ID card to charge meals at full-service restaurants, purchases at shops and lounges, and recreational fees; the hotel IDs are valid only for charges incurred prior to check-out. For information on The Disney Credit Card, call 800-222-1262.

As for banking services, there are several ATMs and two full-service banks easily accessible to WDW guests. ATM locations include Main Street and Tomorrowland in the Magic Kingdom, the entrances to Epcot and the Disney-MGM Studios, Pleasure Island, the Disney Village Marketplace, the Crossroads of Lake Buena Vista shopping center, and the *All-Star Sports* resort.

For full-service banking, there is a Sun Bank branch on Main Street in the Magic Kingdom (open 9 A.M. to 4 P.M. daily; 828-6102) and another across the street from the Disney Village Marketplace (open 9 A.M. to 4 P.M. weekdays, with drive-in teller service from 8 A.M. to 6 P.M.; 828-6106).

ADMISSION OPTIONS

The first thing visitors need to understand is the name game: Disney defines a ticket as admission good for one day only; multi-day admission media are called passes. Once you know this, you're ready to consider your options. Note: For the purposes of this section the term "parks" is understood to mean the three major theme parks. Also, adult admission prices quoted include sales tax and were correct at press time, but may change during 1996. Call 824-4321 to confirm current prices.

ONE-DAY TICKET ($39.27): Good for one-day admission to one park only.

FOUR-DAY VALUE PASS ($130.95): Valid for one day in each of the three parks, plus one additional day at the park of your choice; includes use of WDW transportation. This pass need not be used on consecutive days, and any unused days may be used on a future visit.

FOUR-DAY PARK HOPPER PASS ($141.55): Valid in all three parks for four (not necessarily consecutive) days; includes use of WDW transportation. Any unused days may be used on a future visit.

FIVE-DAY WORLD HOPPER PASS ($189.15): Valid in all three parks for five (not necessarily consecutive) days; includes use of WDW transportation; allows admission to Typhoon Lagoon, Blizzard Beach, River Country, Discovery Island, and Pleasure Island for up to seven days from the first use of the pass. Any unused park admissions may be used on a future visit.

LENGTH OF STAY PASS: Available to WDW resort guests only. Valid for the duration of a guest's stay for admission to all three parks, as well as Typhoon Lagoon,

The Pass Word

Admission passes may be purchased at the theme park entrances, at any WDW resort, at any Disney Village Hotel Plaza property, and at the Transportation and Ticket Center (a bus and monorail hub located near the Magic Kingdom that's commonly known as the TTC). WDW resort guests may charge admission passes to their room if they wish. Cash, traveler's checks, personal checks (with presentation of driver's license and major credit card), Visa, MasterCard, American Express, and The Disney Credit Card are accepted.

Those who prefer to buy passes in advance may do so at The Disney Store or via mail order. To receive passes by mail, send a check or money order (for the exact amount plus $2 for handling) payable to Walt Disney World Company to: Walt Disney World; Box 10,030; Lake Buena Vista, FL 32830; Attention: Ticket Mail Order. Allow at least four weeks for processing.

Note: When you purchase a Four-Day Park Hopper Pass, a Five-Day World Hopper Pass, or a Length of Stay Pass, you must have your photo mounted on the pass to validate it. These photos may be taken at the theme park entrances and at the TTC.

Blizzard Beach, River Country, Discovery Island, and Pleasure Island; includes use of WDW transportation. Prices are $166.42 for 4 days; $193.98 for 5 days; $217.30 for 6 days; $241.68 for 7 days; $259.70 for 8 days; $277.72 for 9 days; and $288.32 for 10 days.

THEME PARK ANNUAL PASS ($242.74): Valid for unlimited admission to the three parks for one year; includes use of WDW transportation and free parking.

PREMIUM ANNUAL PASS ($338.14): Valid for unlimited admission to the three theme parks, the water parks, Discovery Island, and Pleasure Island for one year; includes use of WDW transportation.

MEDICAL MATTERS

Although quality medical care is readily available at Walt Disney World, travelers with chronic health problems are advised to carry copies of all prescriptions and to ask their physicians to provide names of local doctors. Diabetics should note that WDW resorts will provide refrigeration for insulin. More generally:

■ Emergencies can be reported to 911 operators or the nearby Sandlake Hospital (351-8550).

■ Each theme park offers a First Aid Center staffed by a registered nurse. In the Magic Kingdom, it's located next to the Crystal Palace; at Epcot, it's housed in the Odyssey Center, between the Mexico and World of Motion pavilions; and at the Disney-MGM Studios, it's in the Guest Relations building near the park entrance.

■ For nonemergency medical care, physicians employed by the HouseMed health service (396-1195) make house calls 24 hours a day. HouseMed also operates the MediClinic (same phone number), located just east of Interstate 4 on U.S. 192, and open daily from 8 A.M. to 9 P.M. Transportation to MediClinic is offered from WDW resorts, area hotels, and First Aid Centers. The Buena Vista Walk-In Medical Center, on S.R. 535 (828-3434), is open from 8 A.M. to 8 P.M. daily, and shuttles are provided from WDW resorts and First Aid Centers.

■ Turner Drugs, in the Buena Vista Walk-In Medical Center (828-8125), fills prescriptions from 8 A.M. to 8 P.M. daily. Delivery to any WDW resort can be arranged. The Gooding's supermarket at the Crossroads of Lake Buena Vista shopping center also has a pharmacy.

Keep in Mind

■ All admission passes are nontransferable.

■ When we say that any unused days on a Four-Day Value Pass, Four-Day Park Hopper Pass, and Five-Day World Hopper Pass may be used on a future visit, we mean that these days don't expire until you do.

■ As long as you have at least one day remaining on your Four-Day Value Pass or Four-Day Park Hopper Pass, you can upgrade to a Five-Day World Hopper Pass by paying the difference.

■ If you want to do things like spend the afternoon in the Magic Kingdom and then head to Epcot for dinner and IllumiNations viewing, you need a Four-Day Park Hopper Pass, a Five-Day World Hopper Pass, or a Length of Stay Pass.

GETTING AROUND

Before you can find your way around Walt Disney World, you must first have a sense of where you are (and where you are not). While Walt Disney World is closely associated with Orlando, it is actually located about 22 miles southwest of Orlando proper in a much smaller community called Lake Buena Vista.

The most important highway in the Orlando area is I-4, which runs southwest to northeast, cutting through the southern half of Walt Disney World before bisecting Orlando and winding up just shy of Daytona Beach at I-95 (a major coastal artery). All the area's other major highways intersect I-4. Among the more frequently traveled is Route 435 (a.k.a. Kirkman Road), a north-south route that links I-4 to the major hotel-and-business thoroughfare called International Drive, known locally as I-Drive.

Will you need a car during your stay? Only if you plan to spend time touring and exploring outside the World. Most area hotels offer buses to and from Walt Disney World. And Disney's own resorts and parks are serviced by a legion of buses, monorails, and boats, which provide efficient means of getting from point to point within WDW borders. This

Tips for Drivers

■ State law requires use of headlights in the rain.

■ Running near empty? The Exxon Tiger Mart, located on Floridian Way near the Magic Kingdom Auto Plaza, has a self-service gas station that is open daily from 7 A.M. until 1½ hours after the Magic Kingdom closes. A second Exxon Tiger Mart opened recently on Buena Vista Drive right across from Pleasure Island.

■ Expect unexpected showers, and don't leave windows down when you park your car.

■ Be alert to slippery road conditions when it rains here, as the fine layer of oil (a.k.a. Florida ice) that accumulates when it hasn't rained in a while combines with the rainwater to create very slick road surfaces.

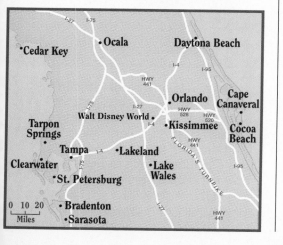

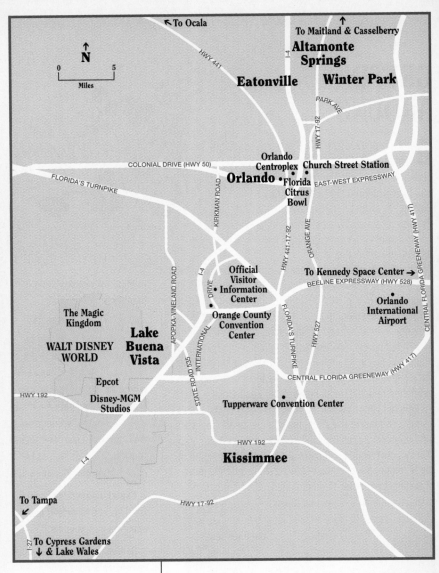

transportation is free to visitors staying at WDW resorts and to those with a multi-day park pass (guests with a one-day ticket to the Magic Kingdom, Epcot, the Disney-MGM Studios, River Country, or Discovery Island have limited access). If you think reliance on mass transit will cramp your style, by all means, rent a car. Disney's transportation is convenient (departing from most areas every 15 to 20 minutes) and comfortable (buses and monorails are air conditioned), but it can accommodate only limited spontaneity. If you decide to get around by car, note that parking at the Magic Kingdom, Epcot, and the Disney-MGM Studios costs $5 per day (free for WDW resort guests).

Transportation options available at WDW resorts are described in each hotel entry of the *Checking In* chapter. Details on accessibility and special parking privileges for guests with disabilities are provided in the "Special Needs" section of this chapter. The following listing—a compilation of WDW transportation to key destinations—will prove useful as a quick reference when you simply need to know how to get somewhere in the World. Schedules coordinate with park operating hours (service begins one hour before park opening, even on special early-entry days, and continues until 1½ hours after park closing), so there's little chance of being stranded. Call 824-4321 to confirm available routes. We also have included transportation options for guests at the Disney Village Hotel Plaza, which has separate bus service to WDW parks.

MAGIC KINGDOM: From the *Grand Floridian, Contemporary,* and *Polynesian:* monorail (the *Contemporary* also has a walkway). From Epcot: monorail to the TTC, then transfer to the TTC–Magic Kingdom monorail or ferry. From the Disney-MGM Studios, the Disney Village Marketplace, and the Disney Village Hotel Plaza: buses to the TTC, then transfer to ferry or monorail. From *Fort Wilderness* and the *Wilderness Lodge:* boats. From all other WDW resorts: buses.

EPCOT: From the *Dolphin, Swan, Yacht Club, Beach Club,* and the *BoardWalk:* walkway or boats to the International Gateway entrance. From the *Grand Floridian, Contemporary,* and *Polynesian:* local hotel monorail to the TTC, then switch for the TTC-Epcot monorail. From the Magic Kingdom: express monorail to the TTC, then switch for the TTC-Epcot monorail. From *Fort Wilderness* and the Disney Village Marketplace: buses to the TTC, then change for the TTC-Epcot monorail. From the Disney-MGM Studios, all other WDW resorts, and the Disney Village Hotel Plaza: buses.

DISNEY-MGM STUDIOS: From the *Dolphin, Swan, Yacht Club,* and *Beach Club:* water launches. From the *BoardWalk:* boat or walkway. From *Fort Wilderness* and

Meet the TTC

Think of the Transportation and Ticket Center (TTC) as the friendly neighborhood hub. Easily the most "connected" place in the World, the TTC is equipped to shuttle guests to any WDW location. It is most important as a traffic-free link between Epcot and the Magic Kingdom; WDW's two monorail loops merge here, making for efficient commutes to these parks (see map on inside back cover). The TTC also provides connections for day visitors and guests whose resorts do not offer direct transport to certain parts of the World. Parking is available and costs $5 per day. Park admission passes may be purchased at the TTC.

Directions from the Orlando Airport

The distance is about 22 miles. If you're driving, take the Central Florida Greeneway (Route 417) to State Road 536, which leads directly to WDW; tolls total $2. You can also take Route 528 (a.k.a. the Beeline Expressway) west to I-4 west, and turn off at the appropriate WDW exit; tolls total $1.25.

Get off at Exit 27 for Pleasure Island, the Disney Village Marketplace, the Disney Village Hotel Plaza, or *The Villas at The Disney Institute.*

Take Exit 26B for Epcot, Typhoon Lagoon, *Disney's BoardWalk, Disney Vacation Club, Caribbean Beach, Swan, Dolphin, Yacht Club, Beach Club, Port Orleans,* or *Dixie Landings.*

Stay on until Exit 25 for the Magic Kingdom, Disney-MGM Studios, River Country, Blizzard Beach, *Fort Wilderness, Grand Floridian, Contemporary, Polynesian, Wilderness Lodge, All-Star Sports,* or *All-Star Music.*

For those without wheels, Mears Motor Shuttles offer an economical alternative to the airport taxi (a $35 or so proposition), at about $13 one way or $23 round-trip. The shuttles, which serve all area hotels, make the trip every 10 to 25 minutes around the clock. Call 423-5566 for reservations.

the Disney Village Marketplace: bus to the TTC, then transfer to the Disney–MGM Studios bus. From the Magic Kingdom, Epcot, all other WDW resorts, and the Disney Village Hotel Plaza: buses.

PLEASURE ISLAND/DISNEY VILLAGE MARKETPLACE: From *The Villas at The Disney Institute:* walkway or bus. From *Port Orleans, Dixie Landings,* and the *Disney Vacation Club:* boats or buses. From the Magic Kingdom, Epcot, the *Grand Floridian, Contemporary,* and *Polynesian:* monorail to the TTC, then transfer to Disney Village bus. From the Disney-MGM Studios, the *Wilderness Lodge,* and *Fort Wilderness:* bus to the TTC, then switch for Disney Village bus. From all other WDW resorts: buses.

FORT WILDERNESS/RIVER COUNTRY: From the *Wilderness Lodge:* bus or bike path. From the Magic Kingdom and the *Contemporary:* boats. From Epcot, the *Grand Floridian, Contemporary,* and *Polynesian:* monorail to the TTC, then transfer to bus to *Fort Wilderness.* From the Disney-MGM Studios, the Disney Village Marketplace, and the Disney Village Hotel Plaza: buses to the TTC, then change for *Fort Wilderness* bus. For all other WDW resorts: bus to the Disney Village Marketplace, switch for bus to the TTC, then take *Fort Wilderness* bus. Note: Visitors planning to arrive by car must park in the *Fort Wilderness* parking lot, then take internal buses to River Country, Pioneer Hall, and all other *Fort Wilderness* destinations.

TYPHOON LAGOON: From *Fort Wilderness:* bus to the TTC, then change for Typhoon Lagoon bus. From the TTC, the Disney Village Marketplace, all other WDW resorts, and Disney Village Hotel Plaza properties: buses.

BLIZZARD BEACH: From *Fort Wilderness:* bus to the TTC, then switch for Blizzard Beach bus. From the TTC, the Disney Village Marketplace, all other WDW resorts, and Disney Village Hotel Plaza locations: buses.

DISCOVERY ISLAND: From the Magic Kingdom, the *Grand Floridian, Contemporary, Polynesian, Wilderness Lodge, Fort Wilderness,* and River Country: boats. Discovery Island admission ticket or WDW resort ID necessary to ride.

MIX & MATCH SAMPLE SCHEDULES

The task of deciding how your days at Walt Disney World will be spent only seems daunting. Yes, there is a lot of ground to cover. Beyond the obvious (the Magic Kingdom, Epcot, and the Disney-MGM Studios) there's a splashy trio of water parks, a quintet of fine golf courses, an armada of pleasure boats, a zoological park, a nightlife metropolis, and tons of shopping opportunities. It all sounds quite unwieldy, but you'd be surprised how much fits neatly into a week's vacation. Banish all thoughts of a step-by-step itinerary that provides a pathway so narrowly defined it might as well be a mass-transit tightrope. We have assumed you are capable of using a map and would prefer not to be told when to tie your shoelaces.

Rather than provide cues that require cue cards, we've taken the liberty of simplifying matters. To that end, we have carved Walt Disney World's most compelling recreational options for adults into concise activity and touring modules whose contents can generally be accomplished in a day or half day (as allotted). To complement these daytime schedules, we've included evening and rainy day supplements. Fully intended to be mixed and matched (and expanded or compressed) at your whim, the schedules offer our best guidance and tips to each individual park or diversion; we leave it to you to decide if, when, and how fast. The plans work in tandem with the detailed descriptions provided in the *Theme Parks, Diversions,* and *Dining & Entertainment* chapters. We refer you to these chapters for more information, and encourage cross-referencing during the planning stages. Gauging your enjoyment of various experiences in advance will inevitably serve to enhance your visit overall. For a sense of location, turn to the Walt Disney World map on the inside back cover or the detailed park maps provided in the *Theme Parks* chapter.

Before we set you loose on the schedules, a few general touring guidelines are in order.

First, we have allotted four self-contained days to the theme parks—including one day each at the Magic

Did you know...

Walt Disney World encompasses 45 square miles, an area about twice the size of Manhattan.

Be Prepared

■ **If you want to see one of WDW's dinner shows—particularly the Hoop-Dee-Doo Musical Revue, the World's toughest ticket—reserve a table in the same breath that you book your accommodations. Reservations are taken up to two years in advance; call WDW-DINE (939-3463).**

■ **If you or one of your traveling companions has a disability, request a copy of the *Walt Disney World Guidebook for Guests with Disabilities* (see "Special Needs" in this chapter for details) well ahead of time and study it closely. While Walt Disney World is very wheelchair accessible, you don't want to take the monorail to the *Contemporary* resort only to find that this is the one monorail station that cannot accommodate guests in wheelchairs.**

■ **Call 824-4321 to confirm park hours in effect during your visit, and plan an itinerary using the flexible schedules provided in this chapter.**

■ **Make reservations for WDW restaurants (up to 60 days in advance) by calling WDW-DINE.**

■ **If you're a golfer, reserve tee times as far in advance as possible—30 days ahead if you're staying at a WDW resort or a Disney Village Hotel Plaza property,**

Kingdom and the Disney-MGM Studios, and two days at Epcot—because this is the minimum amount of time necessary to cover the adult essentials at an unharried pace. As for order, we suggest spending the first day at Epcot, and devoting successive days to touring the Disney-MGM Studios, the Magic Kingdom, and Epcot. If four days swallow your entire visit, we recommend a day exploring each park with a flexible day to revisit your favorite attractions or take advantage of another pursuit that's caught your eye. These schedules are ideally used at times when extended evening hours are in effect at the parks, but smaller crowds during the off-season can help you cover the same territory. WDW resort guests participating in the early-entry program at the Magic Kingdom, Epcot, or the Disney-MGM Studios should take advantage of attractions open during this time, and slip into the schedule after the park's official opening.

A DAY AT EPCOT

■ Note that guests are frequently permitted to enter the park a half hour before Future World's scheduled opening.

■ If you were unable to obtain lunch or dinner reservations prior to arrival, head for Guest Relations straightaway to book a table at one of the international restaurants of World Showcase. Pick up a map and entertainment schedule while there.

■ If you haven't had breakfast or could use a jolt of java, stop in at *Fountain View Espresso & Bakery.*

■ Visit Wonders of Life (your priorities here: Cranium Command and Body Wars) and The Land.

■ This should take you up to 11 A.M., when World Showcase opens. Consider grabbing an early bite at The Land's *Sunshine Season Food Fair* before crossing over from Future World into World Showcase.

■ View *O Canada!* at the Canada pavilion and *Impressions de France* at the France pavilion. Backtrack to take in the shops, gardens, and pub at the United Kingdom pavilion before fully exploring France.

■ Aiming to reach The American Adventure and see the next show there before dinner (check your entertainment schedule for showtimes), pause en route to take in the street entertainment, shops, gardens, and art galleries in Morocco and Japan.

■ After dinner, return to Future World and visit Spaceship Earth (if you have time, pop into Innoventions for a peek).

■ Keep an eye on the time so that you can secure a good spot around World Showcase Lagoon (we recommend the little island between Italy and The American Adventure) to watch the evening's performance of IllumiNations.

A DAY AT THE DISNEY-MGM STUDIOS

■ Note that doors frequently open a half hour early, and plan to arrive 45 minutes to an hour before the official opening time.

■ Pick up a map and an entertainment schedule at Guest Relations; note that many attractions have set showtimes and some attractions don't open until later in the morning.

■ Haven't had breakfast yet? Consider stopping by the *Starring Rolls Bakery.*

■ If you were unable to book a table for dinner before leaving home, stop at the kiosk at the corner of Hollywood and Sunset boulevards and make reservations for the *50's Prime Time Café* or the *Hollywood Brown Derby.* Note: This plan assumes a quick lunch taken whenever your personal lunch bell rings (good bets are *Hollywood & Vine, Commissary,* and *Backlot Express*).

■ If you're up for a 13-story plunge, head directly for The Twilight Zone Tower of Terror on Sunset Boulevard (but do so before you eat). For something much tamer, you might try to get a jump on the notoriously long line at Voyage of the Little Mermaid.

■ Afterward, head across the park to take in Star Tours, Jim Henson's Muppet*Vision 3-D, and The Spirit of Pocahontas Stage Show. Stroll down New York Street. Next, see The Magic of Disney Animation, The Great Movie Ride, and SuperStar Television.

■ Having taken care of your highest touring priorities, check your entertainment schedule and slot in times before or after dinner to see what you can of the Monster Sound Show, Indiana Jones Epic Stunt Spectacular, Backstage Studio Tour, and the Special Effects and Production Tour.

4 days ahead if you're not—to secure your preferred time(s) and venue(s). For visits during WDW's peak links season (see "Sports" in the *Diversions* chapter for details), consider a golf package, which allows you to reserve tee times up to 90 days in advance. Lessons may be reserved up to a year ahead. Call 824-2270.

■ Note that tennis lessons may be booked up to a year in advance (call 824-3578), and guided fishing trips may be reserved up to two weeks ahead (call 828-2621).

■ A few days before you leave home, make a quick round of calls to confirm all travel arrangements, including flight, rental car, airport transfer, and lodging.

Photographic Details

Whether you need a roll of film, a battery, or a camcorder loaner, Disney's theme parks are prepared to provide. Camcorders ($25 per day with a $300 deposit) may be rented at the Camera Center in the Magic Kingdom, at Cameras and Film and the Camera Center in Epcot, and at The Darkroom in the Disney-MGM Studios. Deposits are refundable and may be charged to American Express, MasterCard, or Visa. Two-hour film processing is available (wherever you see a Photo Express sign) at the theme parks, WDW resorts, and the Disney Village Marketplace.

■ Make note of the last performance of the Beauty and the Beast Stage Show, and make a point of seeing it then.

■ Between attractions, check out the interesting shops and the *Sunset Ranch Market*. For a relaxing breather, slip into the *Catwalk Bar* or the *Tune-In Lounge*.

A DAY AT THE MAGIC KINGDOM

■ Plan to be in the parking lot at least 45 minutes before the park is scheduled to open, so as to be at the Central Plaza end of Main Street at the opening time.

■ Send a member of your party to City Hall to pick up a park map and an entertainment schedule, and to make any desired lunch or dinner reservations (we recommend *Liberty Tree Tavern* or *Tony's Town Square,* preferably for an early lunch). Regroup.

■ If you haven't had breakfast, grab a bite at the *Main Street Bake Shop.*

■ When the park opens, see what you can of the top priorities, at your own pace. It's good to begin with Space Mountain and Alien Encounter, then move on to Splash Mountain, Big Thunder Mountain Railroad, Pirates of the Caribbean, Haunted Mansion, The Hall of Presidents, and The Timekeeper.

■ Pausing for lunch when your reservation comes due or hunger calls, begin a second sweep of the park, targeting such attractions as the Walt Disney World Railroad, Carousel of Progress, Cinderella Castle, Liberty Square Riverboat, Country Bear Jamboree, and Diamond Horseshoe Saloon Revue. Stop to check out any shops and entertainment en route that catch your eye.

■ About 20 minutes before the afternoon parade: Stop everything and head for Fantasyland to see as many key attractions—Peter Pan's Flight, Legend of The Lion King, and It's A Small World—as possible before the crowds swell back to normal.

■ Spend the remainder of the day tying up loose ends on your touring checklist and perusing the shops on Main Street (while there, check out the Main Street Cinema).

■ If your visit falls during a time when the park is open late, consider making dinner reservations at a restaurant accessible via monorail (perhaps the *California Grill* at the *Contemporary* resort) and returning to the park in time to snare a spot on Main Street to watch the SpectroMagic parade. If there are two runnings of SpectroMagic, see the later one.

ANOTHER DAY AT EPCOT

■ Follow the initial guidelines provided in the first Epcot touring schedule.

■ Visit Journey Into Imagination (your priorities here: Honey, I Shrunk the Audience and Image Works) and The Living Seas, then check out the Walt Disney Imagineering Laboratory at Innoventions.

■ Once World Showcase has opened, cross over into this area of the park, beginning this time with Mexico. Be sure to wander into the pyramid (and don't miss the artifacts exhibit and the handicraft market). For lunch, we recommend watermelon juice from Mexico's *Cantina de San Angel* and a sandwich from Norway's *Kringla Bakeri og Kafe,* followed by a soft pretzel at Germany's *Sommerfest.*

■ Moving along into Norway, ride Maelstrom, pop into the Stave Church Gallery, and then head for China to take in the featured film and gardens. Stroll through Germany and Italy, as well as any World Showcase pavilions you didn't get enough of on your first day (France and its pastries are not far).

■ Return to Future World, and make your way through Innoventions, being sure to check out the fiber-optic sidewalks and the Eclectronics exhibits.

■ If you have dinner reservations at a World Showcase restaurant, consider prefacing the meal with a drink at the United Kingdom's *Rose & Crown Pub,* Japan's *Matsu No Ma Lounge,* or the *Cantina de San Angel* in Mexico.

WATER PARKS (HALF DAY)

■ Choose from River Country, an old-fashioned swimming hole nestled into a cove of Bay Lake; Typhoon Lagoon, seven times the size of River Country, with the world's largest wave pool; and Blizzard Beach, WDW's newest and biggest water park, themed as a ski resort.

■ Whichever you visit, be at the entrance gate when the park opens, as these places frequently fill up before noon during the warmer months. When River Country has reached capacity, only guests with tickets in hand will be admitted until crowds thin out, which usually happens between 2 P.M. and 3 P.M. When parking lots fill at Typhoon Lagoon and Blizzard Beach, only guests staying

HOT TIP

America Online subscribers can receive an interactive preview or update on WDW's offerings by using the keyword "disney." Internet users can simply enter *http://www.disneyworld.com/ vacation.html* to access Walt Disney World updates.

In the Evening Hours

Here's a good week's worth of evening activities for your consideration. For a complete guide to after-dark amusements, see our "Nightlife Guide" in the *Dining & Entertainment* chapter.

■ Attend a dinner show (all require advance reservations, and our favorite, the Hoop-Dee-Doo Musical Revue, requires more forethought than any).

■ For a cheap thrill (just $5 per person) and an early night, go for a hayride at *Fort Wilderness*.

■ Grab a partner and play the coolest tennis at Walt Disney World. There are a couple dozen WDW courts lighted for night play. The courts at the *Dolphin* and *Swan* are open 24 hours.

at WDW resorts using WDW buses will be admitted until crowds subside. Last ones in the door get the lounge chairs near the kiddie pool or farthest from the snack bars!

■ Due to the novelty of Blizzard Beach (it opened in spring of 1995), it is the water park of the moment; guests should come prepared for lots of company and seek lounge chairs off the beaten water-slide track. Ask an attendant to point out any quiet zones.

■ Note that you may bring a picnic lunch and non-alcoholic beverages into any of the water parks, and while fast food is available, it's fun to b.y.o.

■ Typhoon Lagoon and Blizzard Beach each features a lazy waterway (grab one of the inner tubes and settle in) perfect for a cool respite from the water-slide traffic.

■ River Country offers a brief, but pretty and extremely peaceful nature trail that winds through egret territory on the lake's edge; peer through a trailside telescope for a close-up of Discovery Island, across the lake.

GOLF (HALF DAY)

■ Essential for anyone who has even a minor passion for the game, Disney's five outstanding 18-hole courses challenge golfers of all abilities. Demand requires that you reserve space as far in advance as possible—30 days for WDW resort and Disney Village Hotel Plaza guests—to secure your preferred venue and time.

■ Morning tee times, the toughest to come by, provide the most comfortable temperatures; but consider, too, the significant savings afforded by twilight rates, in effect from April through December.

■ Beginners might want to start with the Lake Buena Vista course which, while no pushover, offers a forgiving layout. Experienced golfers should not miss Osprey Ridge or Eagle Pines. Skill clinics, some geared for beginners, others honing different aspects of the game, are held at the Palm and Magnolia. The nine-hole Oak Trail practice course is another great skill sharpener.

BOATING (HALF DAY)

■ When you add up all the Water Sprites, sailboats, pedal boats, canoes, pontoons, and such, WDW's marinas have the country's largest fleet of

pleasure boats. All provide a great intermission from the theme parks' hubbub.

■ The sailing's best on Bay Lake and Seven Seas Lagoon; for Water Sprites, we like the running room of Buena Vista Lagoon at the Disney Village Marketplace. Canoeing the canals of *Fort Wilderness* is a particulary peaceful way to spend the morning.

■ If you're up for trying something new—and brave enough to hover 200 feet over Bay Lake—check out the parasailing operation at the *Contemporary* marina.

DISNEY VILLAGE MARKETPLACE (HALF DAY)

■ A great afternoon or evening outing on the last day of your visit, this pleasant waterside shopping enclave has the biggest stash of Disney merchandise anywhere. And it's open until 11 P.M.

■ Be sure to poke into Mickey's Character Shop, The Art of Disney, 2R's Reading and Riting, Christmas Chalet, Gourmet Pantry, Team Mickey's Athletic Club, and *Planet Hollywood's* gift shop.

■ Additional temptations include the food (especially at *Portobello Yacht Club* and *Planet Hollywood*), the delicious strawberry margaritas at *Cap'n Jack's Oyster Bar,* and the opportunity to take a boat for a spin on Buena Vista Lagoon. The Gourmet Pantry's got plenty of inspiration for a pontoon-bound picnic, and an array of waterfront umbrella tables form a do-it-yourself sidewalk café.

DISCOVERY ISLAND (HALF DAY)

■ The perfect antidote to theme park overdose, this lushly landscaped island wildlife sanctuary is a terrific late morning/early afternoon retreat. And it's totally covered with shade.

■ Check out the entertainment schedule upon arrival, and try to catch the next Feathered Friends show. Keep an eye on the time, as this is the sort of place where distraction comes easily.

■ Make an extravaganza of your evening meal (securing reservations in advance). Our recommendations for dining as event: *Victoria & Albert's, Sum Chows, Artist Point, Bistro de Paris, California Grill, Yachtsman Steakhouse,* and *Ariel's.*

■ For a relaxing night out, catch a movie at Pleasure Island's high-tech AMC Theatres.

■ If ready-made nightlife appeals, go club-hopping at Pleasure Island, where all kinds of live music, dancing opportunities, and a terrific comedy club attract locals and weary-footed visitors alike. One stop, seven different venues, plus a New Year's Eve street party every night.

■ Take a wine tour. *Martha's Vineyard Lounge* at the *Beach Club* resort takes crushed grapes seriously, and pours wines both by the glass and by the "flight" (two-ounce samples that follow a theme).

■ Prefer the grain to the grape? Beer lovers' hangouts include Pleasure Island's *Fireworks Factory* restaurant, the *Crew's Cup Lounge* at the *Yacht Club* resort; downtown Orlando's *Hubb's Pub;* and *Laughing Kookaburra* at the *Buena Vista Palace.*

Rainy Day Inserts

The sun will come out tomorrow (maybe in a few hours). In the meantime, here are some great ways to pass the time.

■ Take afternoon tea at the *Rose & Crown Dining Room* in Epcot's World Showcase or at the *Grand Floridian's Garden View Lounge*. Reservations are necessary for tea at the *Rose & Crown*; at the *Garden View Lounge*, it's first-come seating.

■ See a movie with all the comforts in the state-of-the-art AMC Theatres at Pleasure Island.

■ Get a massage. Several of the World's health clubs have licensed massage therapists on hand, and they too need something to do on a rainy day. Of course, the clubs' personal trainers also may be able to spare an hour or so.

■ Sink into a sofa in the lobby of the *Grand Floridian*, and simply listen to the graceful music.

■ Shop your way through the Disney Village Marketplace, and out beyond Walt Disney World, where outlets and antiques centers will keep you dry.

■ Before and after showtime, follow the path on a clockwise tour of the island. Don't rush, as the enjoyment's in the leisurely observation of the 100-some species. Be sure to notice the Galápagos tortoises, crocodiles, scarlet ibis, flamingos, Indian fishing cat, and South American primates (look for puffball-size newborns).

■ Bring your own picnic lunch, or pick up a salad or sandwich at the *Thirsty Perch;* bypass the main picnic area for tables tucked into a pleasantly removed alcove back by the toucan exhibit.

FORT WILDERNESS (HALF DAY)

■ When the mood strikes for outdoor activity that's decidedly low-key, this campground and recreation area set on a forested, canal-crossed expanse alongside Walt Disney World's largest lake stands by with plenty of options.

■ In the morning, canoeing is the preferred mode of exploration, as the canals are misty and serene; it's fun to bring some fishing gear along (both watercraft and fishing poles are available for rent). In the afternoon, we like to rent bikes and pedal the shady trails. But there's a lot more on the activity roster, including trail rides, nature hikes, swimming, boating, and waterskiing.

■ If hunger strikes, your best bet is to grab a quick bite at *Trail's End Buffet.*

FISHING (HALF DAY)

■ The two-hour guided fishing trips that ply the World's waters several times daily rank among the most relaxing interludes available to WDW visitors.

■ As for timing, consider the appeal of being out on Seven Seas Lagoon bonding with friends and the (rather large) largemouth bass that reside there, while the rest of the World is gulping down breakfast and running for the theme parks.

■ While WDW's various guided catch-and-release trips offer similar experiences, we recommend outings on Bay Lake and Seven Seas Lagoon for the biggest catches; *Dixie Landings'* early-morning gig is great for singles and twosomes, who can save money by paying by the seat (rather than by the boat).

SPECIAL NEEDS

GUESTS WITH DISABILITIES

Walt Disney World has long earned kudos from guests with disabilities because of the attention paid to their needs. Still, familiarization with the World as it relates to one's personal requirements is essential, and to this end, the comprehensive *Walt Disney World Guidebook for Guests with Disabilities* is required reading. The guide is available at all wheelchair rental locations (as well as City Hall in the Magic Kingdom and Guest Relations at Epcot and the Disney-MGM Studios). However, we strongly recommend getting hold of this publication well before you leave home to become familiar with procedures and accessibility. To do this, send a written request to Walt Disney World Guest Letters; Box 10,000; Lake Buena Vista, FL 32830.

Those interested in guided tours should note: The Society for the Advancement of Travel for the Handicapped (347 Fifth Ave., Suite 610; New York, NY 10016; 212-447-7284) can provide a list of travel agents who are knowledgeable about tours for travelers with disabilities and experienced in arranging individual and group tours. To receive the listing, send a self-addressed stamped envelope and a check or money order for $3. If you prefer to connect directly with a tour operator, consider Flying Wheels Travel (800-535-6790), which also can arrange trips for individuals.

While we defer to the *Walt Disney World Guidebook for Guests with Disabilities* for its comprehensiveness, we offer the following advice as an indication of existing facilities and services:

■ Special parking is available at the major theme parks (inquire at Auto Plazas upon entering).

■ All monorail stations are accessible to guests in wheelchairs *except* the one at the *Contemporary* resort, which can be reached only by escalator. WDW buses are frequently, but not always, equipped with wheelchair lifts.

■ Most theme park attractions are accessible to guests who can be lifted to and from their wheelchairs with the assistance of a member of their party, and many can

Keeping the Faith

Among the religious services most convenient for Walt Disney World guests are those held at the *Polynesian* resort. Every Sunday at the *Polynesian's* Luau Cove, a Protestant service is offered at 9 A.M., and Catholic masses are held at 8 A.M. and 10:15 A.M.

For information on nearby Protestant and Catholic parishes, call the Christian Service Center at 425-2523. The closest Catholic church is Mary, Queen of the Universe Shrine, about 2½ miles north of Lake Buena Vista on the I-4 service road; call 239-6600 for mass times.

Jewish visitors may attend conservative services at Temple Ohalei Rivka (11,200 Apopka Vineland Rd.; 239-5444) or reform services at the Congregation of Liberal Judaism (928 Malone Dr.; 645-0444).

Muslim services are held at Jama Masijid (11,543 Ruby Lake Rd.; 238-2700).

For Woofers and Meowers

No pets other than service dogs are permitted in the theme parks. Travelers may lodge Fluffy or Fido in one of WDW's four air-conditioned Pet Care Kennels, opt for a designated pet site at the *Fort Wilderness* resort and campground, or call the Orlando/Orange County Convention and Visitors Bureau (363-5871) to locate one of the number of area hotels that allow pets. WDW's kennels are available for day or overnight stays, and may be found near the TTC, at the entrances to Epcot and the Disney-MGM Studios, and at *Fort Wilderness*, where the facility is next to an open field. WDW resort guests pay $9 for overnight pet stays, including food; others pay $11. Day rates are $6 and include one feeding. For kennel hours and other information, call 824-6568.

accommodate guests who must remain in their wheelchairs at all times. Also, guests traveling in wheelchairs and members of their party need only check in with the attendant to bypass the line at those attractions requiring ramp access.

■ Note that all hotels listed in this book's *Checking In* chapter offer rooms for guests with disabilities. All WDW resorts are easily explored by wheelchair. While room and bathroom configurations vary among hotels, lending themselves better to guests with different needs, all but the *Polynesian* resort offer roll-in showers. For assistance in selecting a WDW hotel whose public areas and barrier-free rooms best serve your specific requirements, ask to speak to someone in the Special Requests Department when you call Central Reservations (934-7639). The representatives are extremely informed and helpful.

■ Wheelchairs are available for rent at each of the theme parks, as are Electronic Convenience Vehicles (ECVs). At the Magic Kingdom, the rental area is just inside the main entrance on the right; at Epcot, rentals are available inside the entrance plaza on the left, at the gift shop to the right of the ticket booths, and at the International Gateway; and at the Disney-MGM Studios, rentals are handled at Oscar's Super Service, just inside the entrance. Wheelchair rentals cost $5 per day, and require a $1 refundable deposit. Guests planning to visit more than one park on the same day may obtain a replacement wheelchair at the next park with no additional charge or deposit (just be sure to save your receipt). Due to the limited number of ECVs, they usually sell out within the first couple of hours that the parks are open. The cost to rent an ECV is $30 (plus a $20 refundable deposit) per park per day.

■ Special vans, with motorized platforms that lift wheelchairs inside, are available (allow about 20 minutes for pickup). Day guests should inquire at the Guest Relations counter at the TTC, Epcot, or the Disney-MGM Studios, or at City Hall in the Magic Kingdom. WDW resort guests should contact Guest Services in their hotel.

■ For guests who are sight impaired, the theme parks offer cassettes designed to accentuate their enjoyment of each park through description. A $25 refundable deposit is required for use of a tape recorder.

■ Listening devices that assist in amplifying attraction sound tracks for the benefit of guests who are hearing impaired are available (with a $25 refundable deposit) at City Hall in the Magic Kingdom and at Guest Relations in Epcot and the Disney-MGM Studios. Scripts also are available at each show and attraction for hearing-impaired guests.

■ Guests who use telecommunications devices for the deaf (TDDs) can call 827-4141 for WDW Information. Complimentary TDDs are available for guest use at City Hall in the Magic Kingdom; at Guest Relations in Epcot and the Disney-MGM Studios; and at Guest Services at the Disney Village Marketplace.

OLDER TRAVELERS

W alt Disney World is a friendly and welcoming place, but its sheer enormity and energy level, and its mere heat, particularly during the summer, have the potential to overwhelm. While knowing what to expect is half the battle, knowing how to plan accordingly is even more important. The keys to an enjoyable, relaxed visit for older visitors apply to everyone (although the stubborn younger crowd will likely resist). Our suggestions:

■ Familiarize yourself with the areas you plan to visit by reading Walt Disney World literature before you arrive.

■ Schedule your visit for the least crowded times of the year (see "When to Go" earlier in this chapter).

■ Don't be shy about asking Disney employees for directions or advice. They are always happy to help out.

■ Consider enlisting the services of a private guide to usher you through the theme parks. There are two Orlando firms that we've recommended over the years. Eventures Unlimited Inc. (826-0055 or 800-356-7891) charges $20 per hour (with a four-hour minimum, plus admission for the guide). Suncoast Destination Management (859-0027 or 800-827-0028) offers its guide services for the same hourly rate (with four-hour minimum, plus guide admission) or $200 for the entire day (including the guide's admission).

■ In the parks, eat early or late to avoid mealtime crowds, and snack on the fresh fruit and vegetables sold at stands. Touring takes energy.

■ Protect yourself from the sun by wearing a hat and a good sunscreen. Be sure to cover your legs (as sunlight reflecting off the pavement leaves them vulnerable to sunburn) and the back of your neck.

Important Phone Numbers

Central Reservations:
W-DISNEY (934-7639)

Dining Reservations:
WDW-DINE (939-3463)

Donald Duck: Unlisted

Lost and Found: 824-4245

Time and Weather:
646-3131

WDW Information:
824-4321

• • •

AMC Theatres: 827-1300

Disney Village Marketplace:
828-3800

Disney's Racquet Club:
824-3578

Epcot Learning Seminars:
560-6150

Golf Reservations/Lessons:
824-2270

HouseMed Physician
Services: 396-1195

Pleasure Island: 934-6374

Sandlake Hospital:
351-8550

Lions, Tigers, and Dragons, Oh My!

Disney's Wild Animal Kingdom— a live-action adventure park slated to open here in spring 1998—is nothing short of the biggest gig in Disney history. Five hundred acres on the western edge of WDW property have been earmarked for the new park, which will be five times the size of the Magic Kingdom. The central icon for *this* Kingdom will be not a castle, but a 14-story structure called the Tree of Life. The enormous tree will feature intricate animal carvings done by Disney artists, and inside its 50-foot-wide trunk there will be a show.

The park will offer encounters with animals in three different contexts. In one section, you will go on safari and observe great herds of wild animals living on landscapes that replicate the creatures' natural habitats. A second section invites you to come to grips with unicorns, dragons, and other creatures of legend. The third (and final) section of the park will lure you into a primeval forest and revive mammoth creatures of the Cretaceous period in a thrill attraction that raises the curtain on Disney's most sophisticated Audio-Animatronics figures yet.

■ Drink lots of liquids, and take frequent rest stops in the shade (for the best locales in each park, see the "Quiet Nooks" lists in the margins of the *Theme Parks* chapter).

■ Don't underestimate the distances to be covered at Epcot; the park is bigger than the Magic Kingdom and the Disney-MGM Studios combined, and visitors often log a few miles in a full day of touring. However you're getting around, take it slowly. Broken into small increments with plenty of air-conditioned or tree-shaded breaks, it's not so tiring. Both the buses that round World Showcase Lagoon and the launches that cross it provide a nice break for weary feet, but only when there are no long queues. Lots of older travelers who enjoy walking around the other parks choose to treat themselves to a wheelchair here. As in the other parks, wheelchairs and snappy Electric Convenience Vehicles are easily rented at the park entrance.

SINGLE TRAVELERS

While Walt Disney World may not exactly be the last word for singles in search of romance (single rates aren't even available at WDW hotels), the fact is, singles can have an absolute blast exploring Walt Disney World.

The novelty of being a solo traveler in a sea of groups invites friendly conversation from WDW employees and fellow visitors alike. The freedom to set one's own course—pausing to chat with the young World Showcase employees born and educated in the country their pavilion represents, for example—truly enhances the WDW experience. And there is no shortage of places and situations for meeting people. Some ideas:

■ Pleasure Island's nightclubs typically attract lots of locals on weekends.

■ The *Biergarten* restaurant and *Teppanyaki Dining Rooms* at Epcot, where smaller parties are seated together, offer especially convivial atmospheres.

■ Lounges in the theme parks (specifically Epcot's *Rose & Crown Pub* and *Matsu No Ma Lounge*, and the *Catwalk Bar* at the Disney-MGM Studios) are exceptionally welcoming and relaxed, as are those located in the WDW resorts (see our "Nightlife Guide" in the *Dining & Entertainment* chapter for additional cues).

■ River Country, Typhoon Lagoon, Blizzard Beach, and hotel swimming pools are all great spots for friendly encounters, provided you don't mind meeting people in your bathing suit.

■ At WDW's five 18-hole golf courses, companionship is inevitable; golfers are grouped into foursomes when tee times are allotted.

■ If you're a tennis player sans partner, consider the "Tennis Anyone?" program at Disney's Racquet Club, which matches up players.

■ Tour programs such as Gardens of the World and Hidden Treasures of World Showcase are engaging—and enlightening—alternatives to exploring Epcot's World Showcase independently (see "Class Acts" in the *Diversions* chapter).

COUPLES

There is a place for lovebirds at Walt Disney World. Actually, there are many spots in the World perfectly suited for those with romantic intentions. The Magic Kingdom's nostalgic carousel-and-castle combo invokes enchantment in the truest fairy-tale tradition. Epcot's World Showcase has the aura of a whirlwind tour (and inspiration for a future trip?), with 11 countries as exotic and far-reaching as Japan and Morocco (and it has even bottled France). The Disney-MGM Studios recaptures an era of starry-eyed elegance. By day, there is romance in the theme parks for those already inclined to hold hands; by night, the parks sparkle with an intensity that inspires sudden mushiness in those who never considered themselves the type, and that's *before* the fireworks displays.

As the themed resorts of Walt Disney World go about transporting guests to various times and places, they make quite a few passes through settings straight out of the vacation fantasy textbook. From the endearing Victorian charms of the *Grand Floridian* to the exotic island getaway that is the *Polynesian,* it's safe to say that Disney has romantic notions that go way beyond heart-shaped tubs. You won't find a more picture-perfect setting than the wondrously rustic *Wilderness Lodge*, marked by geysers, waterfalls, steamy hot springs, and the grandest stone fireplace you've ever seen.

And there's more. Consider a restaurant that starts with candlelight, then takes things a step farther by setting the dining room inside a Maya pyramid fitted out with such decorative flourishes as a moonlit river and a smoking

WDW Resort Phone Numbers

All-Star Music: 939-6000

All-Star Sports: 939-5000

Beach Club: 934-8000

Caribbean Beach: 934-3400

Contemporary: 824-1000

Disney's BoardWalk: 939-5100

Disney Vacation Club: 827-7700

Dixie Landings: 934-6000

Dolphin: 934-4000

Fort Wilderness: 824-2900

Grand Floridian: 824-3000

Polynesian: 824-2000

Port Orleans: 934-5000

Swan: 934-3000

The Villas at The Disney Institute: 827-1100

Wilderness Lodge: 824-3200

Yacht Club: 934-7000

The Most Romantic Places in the World

RESORTS
Wilderness Lodge
Grand Floridian
Polynesian
Port Orleans
Dixie Landings
Yacht Club

RESTAURANTS
Victoria & Albert's
Bistro de Paris
Yachtsman Steakhouse
Artist Point
Ariel's
California Grill
Liberty Tree Tavern
Portobello Yacht Club
King Stefan's Banquet Hall
San Angel Inn

LOUNGES
Martha's Vineyard
Matsu No Ma Lounge
Garden View Lounge
Tambu Lounge
Pleasure Island Jazz
   Company

volcano. (See the left margin and the *Dining & Entertainment* chapter for more of our romantic picks.)

Those couples with bigger things in mind, like tying the knot, might consider "I do"–ing it here. While no one yet has likened Mickey Mouse to Eros, newlyweds have beaten such a path to Mickey's doorstep over the years that Walt Disney World rates as the most popular honeymoon destination in the country. In fact, more than 1,000 couples flock to Walt Disney World each year to exchange vows. Why this place, you ask? For some couples it's a matter of mutual Disney adoration, a sense of getting things off to a magical start; for others it's a convenient answer to the dilemma posed by the bride being from one area of the country and the groom, quite another (they figure if everybody's going to be traveling for the wedding, they might as well get a vacation out of it). Still others see it as an opportunity to, for example, have a semblance of a Polynesian-style honeymoon without the hassle of actually *going* there.

WEDDINGS: In these parts, the sky is truly the limit. Intimate weddings for up to 15 guests start at $2,300; for larger affairs, figure $17,000 minimum. WDW coordinators work with couples from six months to a year in advance to create a wedding tailored to their specifications—from elegant affairs without a hint of Disneyana to the sort in which the bride arrives in Cinderella's coach and Goofy serves as ring bearer. These wedding gurus are equipped to handle most any imaginable detail and, indeed, a litany of unimaginables.

The possibilities are infinite and growing, with evening nuptials in the theme parks the most dramatic addition to the World's wedding circuit. Theme park weddings (which hover in the $32,000 range) take place after park closing, and allow couples to take their vows in front of Cinderella Castle in the Magic Kingdom or in a traditional English courtyard in Epcot's World Showcase, among other places. For an extra $15,000, a free-spending couple can get a sprinkling of pixie dust and a personal exhibition of Fantasy in the Sky fireworks. Indoor and outdoor settings for wedding celebrations also are available at the *Grand Floridian, Yacht Club, Beach Club, Wilderness Lodge, Contemporary,* and *Polynesian* resorts. The garden-bound wedding gazebo at the *Yacht Club,* and Sunset Point at the *Polynesian* have long been popular spots to tie the knot. With the 1995 addition of the Wedding Pavilion—a dainty structure reminiscent of a Victorian summerhouse that sits on a lushly landscaped man-made island between the *Grand Floridian* and *Polynesian* resorts—couples also have a new indoor setting to consider. The glass-enclosed pavilion, which offers a vista of Cinderella Castle, seats 250, and features a covered driveway and stained-glass windows on either side of the altar. It also has a wedding salon that, despite its lack of gowns (this is accessory-ville), reads like a three-dimensional bridal magazine. Wedding packages vary broadly depending upon the type of ceremony and reception desired, and include discounted rates at certain WDW resorts for family and friends attending the wedding. For additional information about weddings at Walt Disney World, call 363-6333.

HONEYMOONS: Most WDW resorts have designated honeymoon suites. You needn't buy a honeymoon package to get special treatment; just let the staff know that you're newlyweds. For information on honeymoon package options, call W-DISNEY (934-7639).

A Match Made in Heaven?

Couples tying the knot at Walt Disney World have incorporated Disneyana in some rather interesting ways. Take the bride who wore Mickey Mouse ears with her veil. Or the couple who chose to walk back up the aisle to "Zip-A-Dee-Doo-Dah." Certainly, the bride and groom who exchanged Donald and Daisy caps instead of wedding rings set a precedent.

Checking In

Like a photograph whose mood changes depending upon the frame in which it is displayed, a Walt Disney World vacation is colored by the context in which it is experienced. Guests have quite a variety of frames—rather, resorts—from which to choose, and each yields a unique perspective on the World. Some hotels imbue the mousedom with surprising elegance; others render it especially whimsical, homey, or romantic. Looking for grand seaside digs or a home base straight out of New Orleans? It's here. Something Polynesian? No problem. From campsites and economy-priced rooms to villas and suites, there are accommodations in Cinderella's neighborhood to suit most every taste and billfold.

If you're the sort who favors a gilded frame for your vacation, you'll find the chandelier quotient you're looking for—and a rich Victorian aura—at Disney's turreted *Grand Floridian* resort. Here, the WDW experience is defined by private verandas, a whirlpool surrounded by roses, and room service that delivers the likes of chocolate-covered strawberries "dressed" in tuxedos.

If rustic romance is more your style, your ultimate WDW roost is the *Wilderness Lodge*, which patterns its grandeur after National Park Service lodges of the early 1900s. The resort's soaring totem poles and tepee chandeliers, bubbling hot spring, and roaring waterfall have forever altered our conception of a log cabin.

If you simply must make every dollar count, the *All-Star Sports* and *All-Star Music* resorts come through with perfectly comfortable accommodations starting at $69 a night. The brightest dwellings you'll ever want to call home, augmented by three-story sports and music icons, ensure you'll not

---

At Walt Disney World, there's a hotel to suit every taste, budget, and mood.

forget for a moment that you're staying on WDW turf.

If you're not quite sure what you want, that's fine, too. This chapter provides descriptions of every WDW resort, from the overall atmosphere to the rooms, facilities, and amenities. In addition to the basic rate information, you'll find summaries of each hotel's big draws, plus tips that will help you make a choice that's in line with your budget, interests, and touring priorities. While we've covered all of the Disney-owned resorts plus their favored siblings, the *Dolphin* and *Swan*, careful readers will easily discern those we recommend most highly for adults (hint: look for clues in the "Big Draws" category). Be aware, too, that within each entry the information provided is selective, encompassing details most relevant to the adult visitor. When it comes to the Disney Village Hotel Plaza—seven properties that are within Disney's borders but independently managed—we've included our three top choices for adults. Finally, for those willing to give up the convenience of staying on property, we've also listed some hotels worth considering outside the World's boundaries. So think about what's important to you in a resort and in this trip to Walt Disney World. Then read on for all the information you need to choose the perfect frame.

Calling Cue

Unless otherwise noted, all telephone numbers are in area code 407.

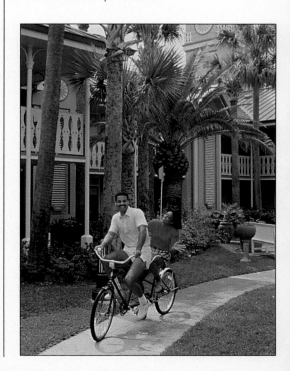

WALT DISNEY WORLD RESORTS

As an example of the meticulous theming that is a hall-mark of the Disney hotels, consider *Port Orleans*, a moderately priced resort designed to evoke New Orleans' French Quarter. As you check in, you might catch the aroma of fresh beignets wafting over from the resort's food court, decorated as a Mardi Gras warehouse. The lobby has French horns for light fixtures and restrooms with such great jazz coming over the speakers they could almost impose a cover charge.

In addition to compelling theming, Disney's resorts are marked by staffs trained to bend over backward to ensure guests' happiness, and well-kept, comfortably furnished accommodations comparable in size to those found outside WDW borders. There are also practical advantages to staying on property. Chief among these benefits are convenience and easy access to Disney services. Other privileges enjoyed by WDW resort guests include guaranteed admission even when parks are full; free use of WDW transportation; early admission to the major theme parks on designated days; discounted golf fees; and the ability to reserve tee times on Disney golf courses up to 30 days in advance. At all WDW resorts except the *Dolphin* and *Swan*, amenities also include free package delivery and guests' ability to charge meals and merchandise back to their rooms.

This resort listing is organized according to price tiers—Deluxe, Moderate, and Value—with the exception of the Home Away From Home category, used to distinguish all-suite and villa-type accommodations. These categories are consistent with Disney's new rating system for its resorts (explained on the next page). But consider location as well as price, particularly if you know you'll be spending a lot of time touring a particular theme park. The "Vital Statistics" section of each entry will help you place the resorts on the World map. You'll notice in this listing that certain twosomes are earmarked as "sister resorts"; these are adjacent properties that feature complementary designs and shared facilities. With the exception of *Port*

Getting Around

Use of WDW transportation is free to visitors staying at WDW resorts and those with a multi-day park pass; guests with a one-day ticket to the Magic Kingdom, River Country, or Discovery Island have limited transportation privileges.

The Last Word On...

RATES

Figures listed were correct at press time, but prices are subject to change. Season rates refer to: December 17, 1995 through December 31, 1995; February 11, 1996 through April 20, 1996; and June 9, 1996 through August 7, 1996, except at *Caribbean Beach*, *Port Orleans*, and *Dixie Landings*, where season dates are December 17, 1995 through December 31, 1995, and February 11, 1996 through August 17, 1996. All other dates are considered off-season. At the *Swan* and the *Dolphin*, the summer months of June, July, and August also are considered off-season.

Orleans and *Dixie Landings*, whose greater separation and distinct identities we feel merit individual attention, sister resorts' descriptions are combined.

We've packed in as much detail as possible about the offerings at each resort, but to learn more about restaurants and lounges, see our recommendations in the *Dining & Entertainment* chapter. For further details about WDW transportation, including a description of options at the Transportation and Ticket Center (TTC), consult *Planning Ahead*. For additional information on recreational opportunities available at the resorts, turn to the "Sports" section of the *Diversions* chapter.

Mickey Rates the Resorts

After years of effort, the Disney folks recently established a ranking system for their resorts. Categories reflect not only price, but the style of the accommodation and the level of service. The hotels fall into Deluxe, Moderate, and Value classifications. Home Away From Home encompasses villa-type lodgings (and the trailer homes at *Fort Wilderness*), while Disney's Campground category is occupied solely by the *Fort Wilderness* campground.

For the sake of clarity and comparison, we have used these same categories in this chapter, with a few exceptions for *Fort Wilderness* and other properties with two types of accommodations.

In general, here's what to expect in our categories:

- Deluxe properties (rates for double rooms range from $159 to $265) are defined by large, graciously appointed rooms, several restaurants, and such amenities as 24-hour room service.
- Home Away From Home (rates from $35 to $250) applies to villas, vacation homes, all-suite hotels, trailer homes, and campsites.
- Moderate properties (rates from $95 to $150) represent comfortably sized rooms, full-service restaurants paired with food courts, and bellman luggage service.
- Value properties (rates from $49 to $90) offer fewer frills and smaller yet adequate quarters. Meals are provided at food courts or lobby lounges only. Recreation options are usually limited to swimming pools.

DELUXE
Contemporary

First impressions might suggest that the enormous A-frame tower of this imposing resort is simply a 15-story concrete tent that's been pitched here, a stone's throw from Space Mountain, for the benefit of the monorail trains regularly schussing through it. And the *Contemporary* is certainly defined by a sort of Future World ambience. But there's more to the *Contemporary*, namely bold decor, from the lobby to the sleek guestroom furnishings; a fine new restaurant; and, for those who bypass the three-story Garden Wings for a room in the Tower (the higher, the better), terrific views of the Magic Kingdom or Bay Lake.

BIG DRAWS: Location. Monorail service. Extensive water sports options. Plus, this is the one resort a serious tennis player should not miss.

WORTH NOTING: Guestrooms here are, on average, larger than at any other WDW resort hotel; most feature two queen-size beds plus a daybed (king-size beds may be requested). Amenities at the 1,041-room resort include spacious bathrooms and 24-hour room service. Concierge services are available for guests staying in the hotel's 14th-floor suites. On the basis of its top-notch tennis facility alone, the *Contemporary* would be a recreational hub; but it also boasts parasailing, a bustling marina, and a health club. Waterskiing and fishing excursions may be arranged. A convention center offers business services. The *Contemporary's* theming doesn't elicit the cozy ambience that comes so easily to some of the World's other resorts and rarely comes off as romantic.

    Where to eat: *California Grill* (features West Coast cooking and a 15th-floor vista of the Magic Kingdom); *Concourse Steak House* (casual for its genre); *Contemporary Café* (breakfast and dinner buffets); and *Food and Fun Center* (snacks).

    Where to drink: *California Grill Lounge* (emphasis on wine and panoramic views) and *Outer Rim Cocktail Lounge* (comfy alcove overlooking Bay Lake).

RESERVATIONS

Rooms at WDW resorts are generally easy to obtain, since there are nearly 20,000 available; but to get your first choice, it's a good idea to book accommodations in advance. If you plan to visit during summer and holiday periods (see *Planning Ahead*), you should make arrangements well ahead of time. Note that while the hotels can often accommodate special requests, they cannot guarantee a specific room location. Call W-DISNEY (934-7639) to make reservations for all but the independently owned *Dolphin* and *Swan* resorts (numbers provided in listing).

CHECKING IN

The check-in time for WDW resorts is 3 P.M., except at *The Villas at the Disney Institute* and the *Disney Vacation Club*, where it is 4 P.M., and *Fort Wilderness*, where campsite check-in is 1 P.M. Check-out time is 11 A.M.

Contemporary Tips

■ The wine program at the *California Grill* is among the very best in the World.

■ The resort's Garden Wings generally do not yield notable views, which is why their rates are lower than in the Tower.

■ Tennis players will do well to stay in the Garden Wing North because of its proximity to the resort's six lighted courts.

■ The marina here is full of choices for sailors, from Water Sprites to sailboats. It's also parasailing central.

■ Unless you're dying to have coffee with Goofy, think twice about eating breakfast at the *Contemporary Café*, which has a character affair every day.

■ Tower guests have especially convenient access to business services at the convention center.

VITAL STATISTICS: The *Contemporary* occupies a prime location, with the Magic Kingdom virtually in its front yard and Bay Lake right out back; the only hotel with a walkway to the Magic Kingdom and one of just three on the monorail line to that park, it is also one of the few with direct transportation to Discovery Island. Monorail links extend the resort's neighborhood to the *Polynesian* and the *Grand Floridian*, and provide for convenient commutes to Epcot. *Contemporary;* 4600 N. World Dr.; Lake Buena Vista, FL 32830; 824-1000; fax 824-3539.

Transportation: A monorail resort (platform is located just above the Grand Canyon Concourse inside the atrium area of the Tower, and is not wheelchair accessible). Walkway or monorail to the Magic Kingdom. Monorail to the TTC; from there, monorail or bus to Epcot and buses to the Disney-MGM Studios, Typhoon Lagoon, Blizzard Beach, Pleasure Island, and the Disney Village Marketplace. Water launches to Discovery Island, *Fort Wilderness*, and River Country.

Rates: Standard rooms are $215 to $290 (or $195 to $270 during off-season); suites start at $845 year-round. A $15 per-diem charge applies for each extra adult (beyond two) sharing a room.

Disney's BoardWalk

This resort and entertainment complex, slated to open during the summer of 1996, recaptures an ephemeral (if not fictional) period in eastern seaboard history. Along *Disney's BoardWalk* you'll find a lively piano bar and a dance club for the Big Band set, not to mention an ESPN sports bar and a microbrewery. When hunger calls, you can sit down to a seafood dinner, people-watch while having a Mediterranean meal alfresco, or slurp up an egg cream at an old-time soda fountain. Located on the shore of Crescent Lake immediately opposite the *Yacht Club* and *Beach Club*, *Disney's BoardWalk* is noteworthy not just as an entertainment district; it also adds two new lodging options to the World. The first, the *BoardWalk Inn*, is a 378-room deluxe hotel patterned after a bed-and-breakfast. The second is the *BoardWalk Villas*, 532 units styled in the tradition of family vacation cottages.

BIG DRAWS: Disney's newest accommodations. An entertainment zone right outside your door. Walkways to both Epcot and the Disney-MGM Studios.

WORTH NOTING: Guestrooms at the *BoardWalk Inn* are comparable in size to those at Disney's other deluxe properties, and offer two queen-size beds plus a daybed. Elegant touches include mahogany furnishings and French doors that open to private balconies. Two-story suites feature a master bedroom loft (with king-size bed and adjoining bath with whirlpool tub) that overlooks a living room with a wet bar; they come complete with a private garden enclosed in a white picket fence. Single-story concierge rooms are similarly appointed (no gardens, alas).

Units at the *BoardWalk Villas* are equipped with either kitchenettes or full kitchens, and thus fall into Disney's Home Away From Home category. All *Villas* accommodations have balconies. Studios feature a large bedroom with a queen-size bed and a double sleeper sofa; a kitchenette with microwave, coffeemaker, sink, and small refrigerator; and a spacious bathroom. Larger units (one-, two-, and three-bedroom cottages) feature a dining room, a fully equipped kitchen, laundry facilities, a master bath complete with whirlpool tub, and a VCR. They also include a king-size bed in the master bedroom, a spacious living room with a queen sleeper sofa, and two queen-size beds or a queen-size bed and double sleeper sofa in any additional bedrooms. A private lounge accessible only to guests staying at the *BoardWalk Villas* has a rooftop veranda with an exceptional vantage on Epcot's nightly IllumiNations show.

The two accommodations share a lobby, which works the theme with antique miniatures of early boardwalk amusement rides. As for amenities and recreational offerings, both properties offer 24-hour room service. Guests at the *Inn* and the *Villas* have exclusive use of the *BoardWalk's* amusement park–themed pool with "dunk tank," as well as whirlpools and smaller, more isolated pools. Other *BoardWalk* recreation facilities include two soft-surface tennis courts, a health club, and a manicured croquet lawn. A convention center offers access to business services.

Where to eat: Options include a fine seafood restaurant; a Mediterranean eatery with outdoor seating; a bakery; and an old-fashioned soda fountain.

Where to drink: There's a lounge at the *Inn* for cocktails, and a poolside bar for refreshments. A microbrewery, a Big Band ballroom, an ESPN sports club, and a piano bar offer limited menus as well as drinks.

Disney's BoardWalk Tips

■ Anticipate high demand for reservations at the World's newest properties, and book rooms at the *Inn* or the *Villas* well in advance.

■ *Villas* guests should take advantage of the exceptional view of IllumiNations from the rooftop veranda in the *Villas'* private lounge.

Dolphin and Swan Tips

■ Both the *Dolphin* and *Swan* feature large convention centers, with the *Dolphin's* being the larger by far. If you're visiting for pleasure, check the name-badge quotient *before* you book.

■ *Sum Chows*, the *Dolphin's* Asian restaurant, is a great place to discover how well Champagne goes with everything from sushi to Szechuan.

■ The eight tennis courts at the *Dolphin* are kept lighted all night.

VITAL STATISTICS: Guests at the *Inn* and the *Villas* have enviable access (walkways and water launches) to Epcot and the Disney-MGM Studios. Blizzard Beach also is quite close at hand. *Disney's BoardWalk*; 2101 N. Epcot Resorts Blvd.; Lake Buena Vista, FL 32830; 939-5100.

Transportation: Water launches and walkways to Epcot's International Gateway entrance (near the France pavilion) and to the Disney-MGM Studios. Buses to the Magic Kingdom, Typhoon Lagoon, Blizzard Beach, Pleasure Island, the Disney Village Marketplace, and other WDW resorts.

Rates: At the *Inn*, standard rooms are $240 to $304 (or $225 to $285 during the off-season); concierge rooms are $400 to $480 (or $380 to $460); and suites begin at $450. At the *Villas*, studios are $225 to $250 (or $210 to $235 during the off-season); one-bedroom units are $310 (or $285); two-bedroom units are $406 (or $385); and three-bedroom units are $780 year-round.

Dolphin and Swan

The motto for these whimsical yet sophisticated resorts might be "expect the unexpected." Certainly, noted architect Michael Graves designed these postmodern bookends with entertainment in mind.

At the *Dolphin*, a 27-story turquoise triangular tower is flanked by coral-colored buildings that are not only topped by 56-foot-tall dolphin statues but also covered in a mural of banana leaves. The lobby resembles a circus tent. One restaurant is the epitome of understated elegance; another features chandeliers hung with monkeys. In short, guestrooms with such decorative touches as cabana-like doors do not preclude access to a top-notch fitness center, business facilities, or a showroom with Cartier gems.

It's more of the same—playful luxury—next door at the *Swan*, which carves its own distinctive silhouette with 46-foot namesake statues perched atop its (12-story) arched central building and coral facades accented with turquoise waves. The *Swan* has 758 rooms, about half as many as the *Dolphin*. Rooms tend toward bird lamps and pineapple-stenciled headboards.

BIG DRAWS: Serious luxury in a lighthearted wrapper, plus top-notch service and exceptional facilities including a fine fitness center add up to a unique combination. And oh yes, you can walk to Epcot.

WORTH NOTING: The *Dolphin* (operated by ITT Shera-ton) and the *Swan* (managed by Westin) are the only two WDW hotels whose value season extends through the summer months. Guests staying at either of the two hotels have access to the restaurants and recreational activities at the other, and may charge meals and activities enjoyed at the sister resort to their room tab. Such charging privi-leges do not extend to the theme parks or other WDW resorts. Standard guestrooms at both the *Dolphin* and the *Swan* are comparable to those at Disney's other deluxe resorts. Whereas standard rooms at the *Dolphin* feature two double beds, queen-size beds are the rule at the *Swan* (king-size beds available on request at both). Room amenities at both hotels include mini-bars, newspaper delivery, and 24-hour room service, plus nightly turndown at the *Swan* and coffeemakers, hair dryers, and ironing boards and irons at the *Dolphin*. Concierge rooms at the *Dolphin* are located in the hotel's triangular tower; at the *Swan* they are found on the upper two floors of the resort's main building. The *Swan's* health center is complimentary; the *Dolphin's* Body By Jake Health Studio is among the most complete fitness facilities on property. In addition to a white-sand beach where boats may be rented, the resorts share a water recreation area. Here, you'll find a pool ideal for lap swimming, a themed pool filled with waterfalls and alcoves, a small flock of whirlpools between the hotels, and a smaller rectangular pool. The fireworks displays of IllumiNations may be enjoyed from both resorts.

Where to eat: At the *Dolphin*: *Coral Café* (casual dining); *Dolphin Fountain* (ice cream parlor); *Harry's Safari Bar and Grille* (grilled steaks and seafood); *Juan & Only's Cantina* (Mexican fare); *Sum Chows* (sophisticated Asian cuisine); and *Tubbi's Buffeteria* (cheery cafeteria with 24-hour convenience store). At the *Swan*: *Garden Grove Café* (dining in a greenhouse setting); *Kimono's* (sushi bar); and *Palio* (Italian bistro).

Where to drink: At the *Dolphin*: *Cabana Bar & Grill* (poolside refreshments); *Copa Banana* (tropical setting with dancing); *Harry's Safari Bar* (for cocktails, beer by the yard); and *Only's Bar* (for rare tequilas, homemade sangria, specialty margaritas). At the *Swan*: *Lobby Court Lounge* (classy cocktail setting) and *Splash Grill* (pool-side refreshments).

F.Y.I.

All WDW resorts offer rooms equipped for guests with disabilities and nonsmoking rooms. For more detailed information, inquire with Central Reservations (934-7639). Also, see the "Special Needs" section of the *Planning Ahead* chapter.

Grand Floridian Tips

■ For optimum quiet and a striking panorama, request a lagoon-view room.

■ Rooms on upper floors afford the greatest privacy.

■ You can sit on the beach or grass and watch the nightly fireworks over Cinderella Castle with little or no company.

■ Consider a honeymoon room for your second (or third) honeymoon.

■ The pair of tennis courts here have clay surfaces and a resident pro.

■ Book dinner at *Victoria & Albert's* way in advance—that is, before you leave home.

■ The resort is surprisingly popular with families, considering the posh surroundings.

VITAL STATISTICS: The *Dolphin* and *Swan* offer exceptionally easy access to Epcot and the Disney-MGM Studios. Located side by side on the shore of Crescent Lake, a virtual stone's throw from World Showcase, the hotels are flanked by the *Yacht Club* and *Beach Club* resorts and *Disney's BoardWalk,* slated to open in mid-1996. *Walt Disney World Dolphin;* 1500 Epcot Resorts Blvd.; Lake Buena Vista, FL 32830; 934-4000; fax 934-4099. *Walt Disney World Swan;* 1200 Epcot Resorts Blvd.; Lake Buena Vista, FL 32830; 934-3000; fax 934-4499.

Transportation: Boat launch or walkway to Epcot's International Gateway entrance. Boat launches to the Disney-MGM Studios. Buses to the Magic Kingdom, the TTC, Typhoon Lagoon, Blizzard Beach, Pleasure Island, and the Disney Village Marketplace.

Rates: At the *Dolphin*, standard rooms start at $285 (or $245 during the off-season), concierge rooms start at $380 (or $350), and suites start at $550 (or $475). A $15 per-diem charge applies for each extra adult (beyond two) sharing a room. Reservations can be made by calling 800-227-1500. At the *Swan*, standard rooms are $275 to $305 (or $245 to $270 during off-season), concierge rooms are $350 (or $335), and suites start at $350 (or $325). A $25 per-diem charge applies for each extra adult (beyond two) sharing a room. For reservations call 800-248-7926.

Grand Floridian

This romantic slice of Victorian confectionary, a quick hop (and a world apart) from the Magic Kingdom, eloquently recalls the opulent hotels that beckoned high society to Florida at the turn of the century. The *Grand Floridian's* main building and five guest buildings—snow-white structures laced with verandas and turrets, and topped with gabled roofs of red shingles—sprawl over 40 manicured acres of Seven Seas Lagoon shorefront. On these grounds, not an eyeful lacks for towering palms, stunning lake views, or exquisite rose gardens. The resort's magnificent Grand Lobby—Victoriana in excelsis—features immense chandeliers, stained-glass skylights, and live piano and band music that often inspires spontaneous dancing. Guestrooms exude bygone elegance, with old-fashioned armoires, marble-topped sinks, and room service graciously delivered on lace-covered tablecloths.

BIG DRAWS: The *Grand Floridian* offers the height of luxury with a view of Cinderella Castle. It's the spot for a romantic honeymoon or an escape to a kinder, gentler era. All this, and the monorail stops here, too.

WORTH NOTING: Standard accommodations at this 900-room resort are larger than those at most deluxe hotels in the World and include two queen-size beds, plus a daybed. Many of the rooms have terraces, with those in top-floor rooms affording the greatest privacy. Amenities include special toiletries, bathrobes, hair dryers, mini-bar, nightly turndown, 24-hour room service, and newspaper delivery. Concierge rooms and suites are located on the upper floors of the main building, and access to these floors is restricted to the guests staying in these accommodations.

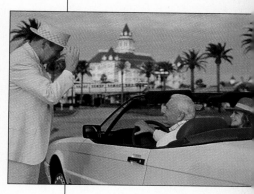

The resort offers some of the best dining rooms on property, including *Victoria & Albert's*. Traditional afternoon tea is served with considerable style in the *Garden View Lounge*. The Electrical Water Pageant and the Magic Kingdom fireworks can be watched from most lagoon-view rooms. The resort is such a popular spot for weddings that an adjacent waterside wedding pavilion was added in 1995. A convention center offers access to business services. Boats may be rented, and waterskiing and fishing excursions may be arranged. Volleyball and croquet equipment is available. A small but savvy health club offers massages by appointment. The resort's vast swimming pool and large rosebush-ringed whirlpool are open 24 hours with quiet hours in effect at night. A white-sand beach generally provides quiet respite from the pool din.

Where to eat: *Flagler's* (festive Italian dinners); *Gasparilla Grill and Games* (24-hour snacks); *Grand Floridian Café* (all-day casual Floridian fare); *Narcoossee's* (steak and seafood on the waterfront); *1900 Park Fare* (buffet breakfast and dinner); and *Victoria & Albert's* (sophisticated six-course dinners).

Where to drink: *Garden View Lounge* (scenic afternoon tea and cocktails); *Mizner's Lounge* (classic cocktails); *Narcoossee's* (yards of beer); and *Summerhouse* (poolside refreshments).

Bygone Era

At the *Grand Floridian*, it's not uncommon to see housekeepers twirling peach-colored parasols as they walk along the footpaths in their Victorian dress.

Get the Message?

All WDW resort guestrooms have telephones with voice mail.

It's a Jungle in There

At the *Polynesian*, waterfalls cascading over volcanic rock in the lobby complement the gorgeous tangle of greenery, which establishes an immediate sense of place with coconut palms, banana trees, orchids, even parrots.

VITAL STATISTICS: The *Grand Floridian's* prime Seven Seas Lagoon location allows for exceptionally easy access to (and extraordinary views of) the Magic Kingdom. Close proximity to the Palm and Magnolia links is a boon for golfers. Monorail connections stretch the hotel's neighborhood beyond the adjacent *Polynesian* resort to include the *Contemporary* resort and provide for convenient commutes to Epcot. *Grand Floridian;* 4401 Floridian Way; Lake Buena Vista, FL 32830; 824-3000; fax 824-3186.

Transportation: A monorail resort (platform is situated under an awning on the hotel's second floor). Monorail or water launch to Magic Kingdom. Monorail to the TTC to connect with monorail to Epcot and buses to all other theme parks. Direct buses to the Disney-MGM Studios, Pleasure Island, and the Disney Village Marketplace. Boat launch to *Polynesian* resort.

Rates: Standard rooms are $290 to $365 (or $265 to $340 during off-season), concierge rooms are $470 to $490 (or $450 to $470), and suites start at $620. A $15 per-diem charge applies for each adult beyond two sharing a room.

Polynesian

This resort echoes the romance and beauty of the South Pacific with enchanting realism. Hawaiian music is piped throughout the lushly landscaped grounds, which feature white-sand beaches, tiki torches that burn nightly, and sufficient flowers to perfume the air. Sprawled amid tropical gardens are 11 two- and three-story "longhouses," all named for Pacific islands, where 853 guestrooms are located. But the *Polynesian's* centerpiece and primary mood setter is unquestionably the Great Ceremonial House, which (in addition to the usual front desk, shops, and restaurants) contains a huge, three-story-high garden that all but consumes the atrium lobby.

BIG DRAWS: A breathtaking, you-are-there South Seas ambience makes the *Polynesian* exceptionally romantic and helps to explain the resort's busy wedding calendar. Monorail service makes it especially convenient.

WORTH NOTING: Standard guestrooms, comparable in size to those at the *Contemporary*, are roomy, and feature two queen-size beds plus a daybed. Those in the newer buildings—Oahu, Moorea, and Pago Pago—are slightly larger and feature a bedside vanity area as well. Decor features ti-leaf-shaped mirrors, bamboo accents, and batik cloth draped over and behind the beds. All third-floor rooms (and second-floor rooms in the Bali Hai, Oahu, Moorea, and Pago Pago longhouses) have balconies. Room service is offered until midnight. A new concierge lounge with a choice view of the Magic Kingdom provides a comfortable retreat for guests staying in the Bali Hai (all suites) and Tonga longhouses, the resort's most luxurious accommodations. The resort attracts both honeymooners and a lot of families with small children. In addition to the themed swimming pool there is a second, more removed pool where the soothing Hawaiian music isn't drowned out by splashing children. A grassy knoll known for good reason as Sunset Point juts out into the lagoon near the Oahu longhouse, and offers a hammock. The resort boasts three white-sand beaches and many great vantage points for viewing Magic Kingdom fireworks and the Electrical Water Pageant. Boats may be rented, waterskiing and fishing excursions may be arranged, and a 1¼-mile jogging trail winds around the tropical grounds.

Where to eat: *Captain Cook's Snack and Ice Cream Company* (for 24-hour grazing); *Coral Isle Café* (all-day dining with hints of Polynesian influence); *'Ohana* (family-style Pacific Rim dinners featuring grilled meats); and *Tangaroa Terrace* (gardenlike setting with breakfast buffets).

Where to drink: *Barefoot Bar* (poolside refreshments) and *Tambu Lounge* (tropical emphasis, showy bartenders).

VITAL STATISTICS: The *Polynesian* is located on the shore of Seven Seas Lagoon directly opposite the Magic Kingdom, and offers both an enviable view and fast access to the park. Monorail links extend the resort's neighborhood beyond the adjacent *Grand Floridian* to include the *Contemporary* and provide for convenient commutes to Epcot. Golfers appreciate the *Polynesian's* proximity to the Palm and Magnolia golf courses. *Polynesian;* 1600 South Seas Dr.; Lake Buena Vista, FL 32830; 824-2000; fax 824-3174.

Transportation: A monorail resort (platform on second floor of Great Ceremonial House). Boat launches to the Magic Kingdom and the *Grand Floridian*. Monorail to the Magic Kingdom and the TTC. Monorail or bus from TTC to Epcot. Buses from TTC to Disney-MGM Studios,

Polynesian Tips

■ **The Tahiti and Fiji longhouses tend to be calmer than other guest buildings because they are generally reserved for adult guests, but there's a catch: their location near Luau Cove, where the lively Polynesian Luau dinner show is held nightly.**

■ **Moorea is a good choice for its relative seclusion and Magic Kingdom views (request a lagoonside room).**

■ **Rooms on upper floors afford the most privacy.**

■ **Tucked down below Sunset Point in front of Moorea is a beach that many guests don't realize is there.**

■ **Couples celebrating their honeymoon or anniversary should alert their reservation agent to the special occasion (they'll receive a complimentary bottle of Champagne).**

Wilderness Lodge Tips

■ Request a higher floor for optimal view and privacy.

■ Courtyard and lake-view rooms are especially romantic, with audio accompaniment that includes waterfall gushing, brook babbling, and geyser eruptions.

■ Junior suites are an especially good value here, given their spaciousness. Honeymooners should request room number 7084, for its fireworks views and big whirlpool tub.

■ Some rooms come with a queen-size bed and a bunk instead of two queen-size beds. Be sure to make your preference known.

■ Seek, and you will find countless cozy alcoves with armchairs, sofas, and sometimes fireplaces, in the corridors overlooking the resort's main lobby.

Typhoon Lagoon, Blizzard Beach, Pleasure Island, and the Disney Village Marketplace. (Note: The TTC is within walking distance of the *Polynesian* for guests inclined to get a little exercise instead of changing vehicles.)

Rates: Standard rooms are $215 to $305 (or $200 to $285 during off-season); concierge rooms are $325 to $380 (or $305 to $360); suites start at $545 year-round. A $15 per-diem charge applies to each extra adult (beyond two) sharing a room.

Wilderness Lodge

Rustic romance infuses every inspired detail of this resort, patterned after the grand National Park Service lodges of the early 1900s. Hidden away on an isolated shore of Bay Lake, the *Wilderness Lodge* is surrounded by towering pine forests that provide a drum roll of sorts along the winding road leading to the dramatic timbered hotel. The soaring atrium lobby kindles the spirit of the great American West with handpainted tepee chandeliers, a pair of totem poles, a bubbling hot spring, and an 82-foot-tall fireplace whose layered stones replicate the Grand Canyon's strata. Huge bundled log columns ascend to roof dormers that swathe the intricately patterned floor in sunlight. As if Bay Lake weren't a sufficiently beautiful backdrop, the resort's natural landscape is supplemented by a roaring waterfall, a swimming area surrounded by boulders and wildflowers, hot and cold mineral pools, and a steaming geothermic meadow complete with geyser. Guestrooms are located in two wings that extend back from the lobby to the lakefront forming a U-shaped frame around the inner courtyard. In other words, the *Wilderness Lodge* is no mere log cabin in the woods.

BIG DRAWS: Luxury. Romance. Considerable value. Extraordinary setting.

WORTH NOTING: The 728 guestrooms, all of which have balconies, are slightly more compact than those at Disney's other deluxe resorts, and feature two queen-size beds. Colorful quilted bedspreads, buffalo lamps, and armoires etched with mountain scenes maintain the theme. Room service is available until midnight, and includes selections from the resort's excellent Pacific Northwest restaurant, *Artist Point*. The four corridors ringing the lobby offer more than an extraordinary view of the lobby itself; they also provide access to porches overlooking the main courtyard and contain some great undiscovered nooks with comfortable sofas and tucked-away fireplaces. Fire Rock Geyser faithfully spouts off 120-foot water plumes at the top of every hour from 8 A.M. until 10 P.M. A white-sand beach fronts the lake. Boats and bicycles may be rented. A ¾-mile path ideal for biking and jogging leads from the resort to *Fort Wilderness*. The resort is so laden with Hidden Mickeys (images of Mickey Mouse placed out of context, for example, in a fireplace screen) that scavenger hunts are held to locate them. The Wilderness Lodge Mercantile is a stand-out among Disney's resort shops. The resort affords a great view of Magic Kingdom fireworks and the Electrical Water Pageant.

Where to eat: *Artist Point* (sophisticated Pacific Northwest cuisine); *Roaring Forks* (round-the-clock snacks); and *Whispering Canyon Café* (hearty family-style dining).

Where to drink: *Territory Lounge* (western-style watering hole) and *Trout Pass* (poolside refreshments).

VITAL STATISTICS: The *Wilderness Lodge* is located on a secluded shore of Bay Lake with the *Contemporary* resort and *Fort Wilderness* as its nearest neighbors. Close proximity makes it the quickest commute to the Magic Kingdom among non-monorail resorts. The *Wilderness Lodge* also has unrivaled access to *Fort Wilderness* and is centrally located for golfers who plan to play on a few different WDW venues. *Wilderness Lodge;* 901 Timberline Dr.; Lake Buena Vista, FL 32830; 824-3200; fax 824-3232.

Transportation: Boat launch to the Magic Kingdom. Direct buses to Epcot, the Disney-MGM Studios, the TTC, Typhoon Lagoon, Blizzard Beach, Pleasure Island, and the Disney Village Marketplace. Pathway makes it possible to walk or ride a bicycle to *Fort Wilderness* and River Country.

Rates: Standard rooms are $174 to $290 (or $159 to $270 during off-season); suites start at $215 (or $200 during off-season). A $15 per-diem charge applies for each extra adult (beyond two) sharing a room.

Yacht Club and Beach Club

This inspired duo conjure such a heady vision of turn-of-the-century Nantucket and Martha's Vineyard you'd swear you smell salt in the air. Certainly, the resorts (architect Robert A. M. Stern's two-part evocation of the grand old seaside hotels) have the gulls fooled. The *Yacht Club* and *Beach Club* stretch along a picturesque shoreline complete with white-sand beach, swimming lagoon, lighthouse, marina, and boardwalk. As the five-story gray clapboard structure of the *Yacht Club* gives way to the sky-blue *Beach Club* (the two are connected), the interior motif shifts from seriously nautical to seashore whimsical. The *Yacht Club* has a rich, exclusive feel to it—there's a wooden bridge leading to the entrance, a stunning globe anchoring the lobby, and polished brass and hardwood floors abound. Next door at the *Beach Club*, things are much more casual. Bright beach umbrellas act as pillars, clambakes are a nightly occurrence, and fanciful fish mobiles make their way into the resort's fine seafood restaurant.

BIG DRAWS: Gracious service and accommodations. Compelling theming. Exceptional swimming area. Some of the World's finest restaurants and lounges. Enviable access to Epcot and the Disney-MGM Studios.

WORTH NOTING: There are 630 guestrooms at the *Yacht Club* and 583 rooms at the *Beach Club*. All are comparable in size to those at Disney's other deluxe resorts; as a rule, they feature two queen-size beds and a daybed (king-size beds are available). At the *Yacht Club*, rooms maintain the nautical theme with such subtle touches as ocean-blue carpeting and brass-trimmed bathroom mirrors patterned after portholes; most rooms have good-size balconies. The *Yacht Club* also offers concierge rooms. At the *Beach Club*, guestrooms keep the seashore motif with the likes of cabana-style striped curtains and seashell-patterned headboards. Amenities at both resorts include mini-bars, newspaper delivery, and 24-hour room service.

A three-acre mini water park called Stormalong Bay earns the *Yacht Club* and *Beach Club* bragging rights to the best resort swimming area in the World; the sprawling lakefront pool, open only to hotel guests, includes sections with jets and sandy bottoms, swirling current loops, and slides (traditional whirlpools also stand by). Stormalong Bay is anchored on one side by a white-sand beach, and on

Gullible Gulls

At the *Yacht Club* and *Beach Club*, the gulls perch on posts along the resorts' pier, perhaps thinking themselves pretty slick indeed for having crossed the Atlantic so quickly (France and the rest of Epcot's World Showcase is just around the bend).

the other by a marina, where boats may be rented. Each resort also has a smaller satellite pool and whirlpool, so removed you have to know about them to find them. The resorts' Ship Shape Health Club is among the most complete fitness centers at a WDW property. Two tennis courts are offered. Volleyball and croquet equipment is available. Joggers may choose from several pleasant, well-mapped courses. The *Yacht Club* features a wedding gazebo.

Where to eat: At the *Beach Club: Ariel's* (stylish seafood) and *Cape May Café* (character breakfasts and clambake buffets). At the *Yacht Club:* the *Yacht Club Galley* (all-day casual dining) and the *Yachtsman Steakhouse* (a New York–style chophouse). Shared by both hotels is the *Beaches & Cream Soda Shop* (a classic soda fountain).

Where to drink: At the *Beach Club: Martha's Vineyard Lounge* (cloud nine for wine lovers) and the *Rip Tide Lounge* (small lobby niche). At the *Yacht Club:* the *Ale and Compass Lounge* (cozy lobby nook) and the *Crew's Cup Lounge* (well-heeled beer emporium). For poolside refreshments, there's *Hurricane Hanna's Grill*.

VITAL STATISTICS: The *Yacht Club* and *Beach Club* enjoy extraordinary proximity and enviable access to Epcot and the Disney-MGM Studios. Located side by side on a shore of Crescent Lake that offers a footpath to Epcot's International Gateway entrance, these sister resorts are joined lakeside by the *Dolphin*, the *Swan*, and *Disney's BoardWalk*, slated to open in mid-1996. Blizzard Beach is also close at hand. *Yacht Club;* 1700 Epcot Resorts Blvd.; Lake Buena Vista, FL 32830; 934-7000; fax 934-3450. *Beach Club;* 1800 Epcot Resorts Blvd.; Lake Buena Vista, FL 32830; 934-8000; fax 934-3850.

Transportation: Boats or walkway to Epcot's International Gateway entrance near the France pavilion. Boat launches to the Disney-MGM Studios. Buses to the Magic Kingdom, Typhoon Lagoon, Blizzard Beach, Pleasure Island, and the Disney Village Marketplace.

Rates: Standard rooms at both resorts are $240 to $305 (or $225 to $285 during the off-season); concierge rooms, available only at the *Yacht Club*, are $390 to $405 (or $370 to $385); suites at both resorts start at $520 year-round. A $15 per-diem charge applies to each extra adult (beyond two) sharing a room.

Yacht Club and Beach Club Tips

■ Rooms on the upper floors afford the greatest privacy.

■ At both the *Yacht Club* and the *Beach Club*, it's a lengthy walk to the lobby from the outermost reaches of guest wings.

■ The stunning views at both properties belong strictly to those with lake-view rooms.

■ At the *Beach Club*, second- and fourth-floor rooms have balconies; rooms on the fourth floor are slightly larger.

■ Balconies at the *Yacht Club* are bigger than those at the *Beach Club*, which are standing room only.

■ The *Beaches & Cream Soda Shop* (conveniently sandwiched between the two hotels) may serve the single best burgers in the World.

■ There's a great hideaway table for two (with love seat) tucked into the *Ale and Compass Lounge* at the *Yacht Club*.

HOME AWAY FROM HOME
Disney Vacation Club

Pastel-hued clapboard guesthouses with tin roofs and white picket fences set the cheerful tone of this Key West–themed retreat. Here, unassuming luxury dovetails with an intimate, laid-back atmosphere to create the look and feel of a friendly resort community. A sprawling village, it is bounded by the wooded fairways of the Lake Buena Vista links, and anchored at its center by a lighthouse that overlooks the main swimming area and moonlights as a sauna. A picturesque waterway called the Trumbo Canal flows from the heart of the resort, eventually uniting with the Buena Vista Lagoon. Spacious accommodations equipped with kitchens may set the *Disney Vacation Club* apart, but what gives the place cachet is its incredible warmth and homeyness. Every doorstep in every one of its two- and three-story guest buildings is fronted with a mat that reads WELCOME HOME.

BIG DRAWS: Exceptionally spacious accommodations, ideal for longer stays. Homey and soothing environs. Great value for groups. Convenience of kitchens. Well located for golfers.

WORTH NOTING: *Disney Vacation Club* also is a vacation ownership property. For a one-time purchase price and annual dues, members receive an allotment of vacation points to use for stays at the resort, plus a host of other benefits. Those studio accommodations and one-, two-, and three-bedroom units not occupied by members are available for nightly rental. The vacation homes have a Key West feel, and are decorated in light woods, ceiling fans, and color schemes of seafoam green and mauve. Studios feature a large bedroom with two queen-size beds; a kitchenette with microwave, coffeemaker, sink, and small refrigerator; and a spacious bathroom. Larger units offer a dining room, a fully equipped kitchen, laundry facilities, a master bath complete with whirlpool bathtub, and a VCR. They also feature a king-size bed in the master bedroom, two queen-size beds in each additional bedroom, and a spacious living room with queen-size sofa bed. All accommodations have balconies. As for recreation, boats and bicycles are available for rent. Volleyball, basketball, and shuffleboard courts and equipment are on hand. The three

Disney Vacation Club Tips

■ For a waterfront setting that's pleasantly removed from the hubbub of the main recreation area, request accommodations in the Turtle Shack vicinity. Numbers 43 and 44 are particularly good calls, given their water views and close proximity to swimming pool, snack bar, tennis court, and bus stop alike.

■ Try the conch fritters. They're available at the snack bars.

■ It's possible to have a whole Key lime pie from *Olivia's* delivered to your room.

■ All but the smallest accommodations (studios) feature whirlpool bathtubs.

■ One-bedroom units yield more than twice the space for a relatively small jump in cost.

tennis courts tend to be quiet and accessible. In addition to the main swimming area, which features a huge whirlpool and sauna, there are three pleasantly removed pools. A small fitness center is provided, and the resort's winding streets lend themselves well to jogging or cycling. The Conch Flats Community Hall offers table tennis, board games, complimentary video rentals, and nightly movies.

Where to eat: *Good's Food to Go* (poolside snacks) and *Olivia's* (casual all-day dining with Key West flourishes). Grills and picnic tables are available. Pizza delivery from *Dixie Landings* is offered until midnight. Conch Flats General Store stocks groceries.

Where to drink: *Gurgling Suitcase* (tiny spirited pub) and *Turtle Shack* (poolside refreshments).

VITAL STATISTICS: *Disney Vacation Club* is well located for golfers, as the Lake Buena Vista course is just next door and Osprey Ridge and Eagle Pines are close at hand. The resort also enjoys especially easy access to the Disney Village Marketplace and Pleasure Island, and good proximity to Epcot and the Disney-MGM Studios. *Disney Vacation Club;* 1510 N. Cove Rd.; Lake Buena Vista, FL 32830; 827-7700; fax 827-7710.

Transportation: Buses to the Magic Kingdom, Epcot, the Disney-MGM Studios, Typhoon Lagoon, Blizzard Beach, Pleasure Island, and the Disney Village Marketplace. Water launches to Pleasure Island and the Disney Village Marketplace.

Rates: Studios are $215 (or $195 during off-season); one-bedroom units are $290 (or $265); two-bedrooms are $385 (or $365); and three-bedrooms are $780 year-round.

Fort Wilderness Resort and Campground

No fewer than 700 acres of woodland just hopping with rabbits combine with WDW's largest lake to provide the foundation for *Fort Wilderness*, a relaxing retreat that relies wholly on the great outdoors for atmosphere. A glorious breath of fresh air that's as much about recreation as low-key accommodations, it is riddled with inspiration for nature walks, fishing, and canoeing. Nicely

Fort Wilderness Campground Tips

■ Bikes and electrical carts are, sudden rains aside, the preferable means for getting around *Fort Wilderness*.

■ Tent campers should request loop 1500 or 2000 to avoid RV gridlock.

■ RV campers will find greater privacy and quiet on loops 1600 through 1900.

■ Although you won't read about it in any brochure, an adorable, tiny log cabin designed strictly for sleeping is available as part of a pilot program (it has beds, a ceiling fan, electric outlets, lights, and a porch with chair swing) for about $60 a night. Ask about it when you call to reserve your spot.

■ Good views of Magic Kingdom fireworks and the Electrical Water Pageant are readily available.

shaded campsites are arranged on 28 loops that branch off from main throughways. While some of the 1,192 sites are designated for tents, most are devoted to RV camping; 408 spots are set up with air-conditioned Wilderness Homes (a.k.a. trailer homes).

BIG DRAWS: Natural setting. Value. Recreation galore.

WORTH NOTING: All loops have at least one air-conditioned comfort station equipped with restrooms, showers, laundry facilities, telephones, and an ice machine. Campsites range in length from 25 to 65 feet. All sites offer a 110/220-volt electric outlet, a barbecue grill, and a picnic table. Most include sanitary-disposal connections, and close to half have cable television hookups. Wilderness Homes are separated from the other campsites in eight different loops. Each air-conditioned trailer home features rustic decor in a comfortable setup that includes a fully equipped kitchen, a living room complete with color TV, and a full bathroom. While most offer both a double bed and bunk bed in the bedroom and a pull-down bed in the living room, some models skip the bunk. Pets are welcome at designated campsites for an extra $3 per day. Recreation opportunities (described fully in the *Diversions* chapter) include nature trails, swimming, boating, fishing, horseback riding, and waterskiing. The popular Hoop-Dee-Doo Musical Revue dinner show is presented here nightly (for details, consult the *Dining & Entertainment* chapter).

Where to eat: Most guests cook their own meals (supplies are available at the Meadow Trading Post and the Settlement Trading Post), but there's also *Crockett's Tavern* (for chicken, steak, and rib dinners) and *Trail's End Buffet* (home-style dining).

Where to drink: *Crockett's Tavern* (cocktails) and *Trail's End Buffet* (beer and sangria).

VITAL STATISTICS: *Fort Wilderness* occupies a large expanse of land stretching southward from Bay Lake; while convenient primarily to its own vast recreational opportunities (including River Country and the Hoop-Dee-Doo Musical Revue), it also offers ready access to the Magic Kingdom and Discovery Island, and closely borders the Osprey Ridge and Eagle Pines golf courses. *Fort Wilderness*; 4510 N. Fort Wilderness Trail; Lake Buena Vista, FL 32830; 824-2900; fax 824-3508.

Transportation: Electric golf carts and bikes can be rented to supplement the internal bus system that links all campsites and recreation areas (buses circulate at 20-minute intervals). Water launches to the Magic Kingdom, Discovery Island, and the *Contemporary* resort. Buses depart from the *Fort Wilderness* guest parking lot for the TTC. From the TTC, monorails service the Magic Kingdom, Epcot, and the *Contemporary, Polynesian,* and *Grand Floridian* resorts; buses cover all other bases.

Rates: Preferred sites with full hookups including water, electricity, sewage, and cable TV go for $58 (or $49 during the off-season); other sites with full hookups minus the cable TV are $52 (or $43); sites without hookups are $44 (or $35). There is a maximum of ten persons per campsite. Wilderness Homes are $215 (or $185). A $5 per-diem charge applies to each extra adult (beyond two) sharing a Wilderness Home, with a maximum occupancy of six.

The Villas at The Disney Institute

This community of villas stretching from the fairways of the Lake Buena Vista Golf Course to the shores of the Buena Vista Lagoon meshes rustic charm with homey comforts for a relaxed atmosphere. Spread over a lightly wooded and canal-crossed expanse, the exceptionally peaceful resort offers few hints of its Disney parentage and theme park proximity. Among the five types of accommodations are a cluster of high-rise treehouses set back in the woods, a collection of skylight-blessed fairway villas, and a stock of cedar-sided all-suite buildings that ring a small lake.

BIG DRAWS: Rustic and relaxing environs. Golf close at hand. Efficiency kitchens. Convenient access to the programs and facilities of The Disney Institute. A good value for groups.

WORTH NOTING: The most modest of the accommodations—the only ones without full kitchens—are the Bungalows, which feature a living area, a bedroom with two queen-size beds and a balcony, and a wet bar with a microwave and a small refrigerator.

The Villas at The Disney Institute Tips

■ Unless you're a night owl, the resort's Town Houses are too close to Pleasure Island for comfort.

■ Paved pathways leading to Pleasure Island and the Disney Village Marketplace allow guests to reach these destinations by electric golf cart and, in the case of the nearest villas, by foot.

■ If it's space you're after, the two-bedroom Town Houses have about 50 percent more footage than the Treehouse Villas—*and* they cost less.

■ The resort is crisscrossed with trails ideal for jogging.

Town Houses are either one-bedroom (with a king-size bed in the bedroom and a sleeper sofa in the living room) or two-bedroom (with a king-size bed in the loft bedroom, a king- or queen-size bed in the second bedroom, and a double sleeper sofa in the living room). The roomy Fairway Villas have cathedral ceilings, and offer a queen-size bed in one bedroom, two double beds in the other, and a sleeper sofa in the living room. The Treehouse Villas offer three bedrooms, two bathrooms, and a utility room in two-story octagonal houses-on-stilts that are among the World's truly unique and secluded accommodations. Grand Vista Homes are luxurious villas whose amenities include stocked refrigerators and nightly turndown. Lodging for guests with disabilities is available solely in the Fairway Villas.

The resort is headquarters for The Disney Institute (slated to open in February 1996), and Bungalows, Town Houses, and certain facilities are reserved for guests participating in the Institute's programs. (See the *Diversions* chapter for details about the Institute.) Recreational options available to all guests include the nearby golf course, swimming pools, two clay tennis courts, and bike rentals.

Where to eat: Most guests cook their own meals (groceries may be ordered by phone from the Village Resort Mart and from the Gourmet Pantry at the Disney Village Marketplace). Gooding's supermarket is located at the nearby Crossroads of Lake Buena Vista shopping center.

Where to drink: Nearest options are Pleasure Island and the lounges of the Disney Village Marketplace.

VITAL STATISTICS: *The Villas at The Disney Institute* is on the northern shore of Buena Vista Lagoon, and has unsurpassed proximity to the Lake Buena Vista links, Pleasure Island, and the Disney Village Marketplace. Epcot, Typhoon Lagoon, and the Disney-MGM Studios also are nearby. *The Villas at The Disney Institute;* 1901 Buena Vista Dr.; Lake Buena Vista, FL 32830; 827-1100; fax 934-2741.

Transportation: Buses to the Magic Kingdom, Epcot, the Disney-MGM Studios, Typhoon Lagoon, Blizzard Beach, Pleasure Island, and the Disney Village Marketplace. Paved pathways lead to Pleasure Island and the Disney Village Marketplace.

Rates: Bungalows are $215 (or $195 during the off-season); one-bedroom Town Houses are $305 (or $285); two-bedroom Town Houses are $340 (or $320); Treehouse Villas are $375 (or $355); Fairway Villas are $400 (or $375); and Grand Vista Homes are $975 to $1,150 year-round.

MODERATE
Caribbean Beach

In this colorful evocation of the Caribbean, the spirit of the islands is rendered via an immense lake ringed by white-sand beaches and villages representing Barbados, Martinique, Trinidad, Jamaica, and Aruba. Each village is marked by clusters of two-story guest buildings that transport you to the Caribbean with cool pastel facades, white railings, and vivid metallic roofs. The separate Custom House reception building resembles one you might encounter at a tropical resort. Lush landscaping adds to the ambience. And Old Port Royale, which houses the resort's food court and opens out to its main recreation area and themed pool, takes cues from an island market.

BIG DRAWS: Excellent value. Cheery environs with a convincingly Caribbean feel.

WORTH NOTING: The resort has a total of 2,112 rooms. Slightly larger than those at Disney's other moderately priced resorts, they feature two double beds (king-size beds are available) and soft-hued decor. Amenities include a mini-bar and a coffeemaker. Room service, which ventures just a touch beyond pizza, is offered until midnight. The resort's 45-acre centerpiece, Barefoot Bay, is larger than World Showcase Lagoon. Villages are sprawled around it in a way that can make travel between some guest areas cumbersome despite footbridges and "local" buses. The resort's sole whirlpool is nestled into its bustling themed pool. Each village offers its own beach, quiet pool, and array of courtyards.
  Where to eat: *Captain's Tavern* (for hearty American fare with limited Caribbean influence) and *Old Port Royale* food court (featuring six counter-service restaurants).
  Where to drink: *Banana Cabana* (poolside refreshments) and *Captain's Tavern* (beer, wine, cocktails).

VITAL STATISTICS: *Caribbean Beach* is located off on its own but is geographically well situated for any pursuits other than the Magic Kingdom, with Epcot, the

Caribbean Beach Tips

■ For optimum privacy, request a room on the second floor.

■ Aruba, linked by bridge to Old Port Royale, is a good choice for both proximity and seclusion.

■ For honeymoon-style isolation, request a room in Trinidad South. The village is located just off the main loop and its buildings and beach are especially secluded.

■ Note that Martinique tends to be the liveliest village.

■ The 1.4-mile promenade circling Barefoot Bay is ideal for jogging, biking, and skating. Bikes and boats may be rented. There is a special length-of-stay option available for boat renters.

Disney-MGM Studios, and Blizzard Beach close at hand on one side and Typhoon Lagoon, Pleasure Island, and the Disney Village Marketplace nearby on the other. *Caribbean Beach;* 900 Cayman Way; Lake Buena Vista, FL 32830; 934-3400; fax 934-3288.

Transportation: Buses stop at each village en route to the Magic Kingdom, Epcot, the Disney-MGM Studios, Typhoon Lagoon, Blizzard Beach, Pleasure Island, and the Disney Village Marketplace.

Rates: Rooms are $99 to $129 (or $95 to $124 during off-season). A $12 per-diem charge applies for each extra adult (beyond two) sharing a room.

Dixie Landings

Southern hospitality takes two forms at this 2,048-room resort: pillared mansions with groomed lawns and *Gone With the Wind* elegance and, farther upriver, rustic homes with tin roofs and rough-hewn bayou charm that are tucked among trees and bushes. Guestrooms located in the three-story Magnolia Bend Mansions and the two-story Alligator Bayou Lodges are similarly appointed. The man-made Sassagoula River winds through the heart of the resort, curling around its main recreation area like a moat. Bridges link guest areas with this area and the steamship-style building that houses the resort's eateries, shop, and check-in facilities.

BIG DRAWS: An excellent value. An exceedingly lovely natural setting.

WORTH NOTING: Rooms are smaller than those at Disney's more expensive hotels, but comfortable and inviting. Each features two double beds (some king-size beds are available). This is a large, sprawling resort with twice as many rooms as its sister resort, *Port Orleans;* and some accommodations are a bit removed from the central building or the nearest bus stop. Room service is limited to pizza. Bikes and boats may be rented. The resort's extensive pathways are well suited for joggers, and a carriage path leads to *Port Orleans.* Five quiet pools (open 24 hours, provided they stay quiet) are sprinkled through the Bayou and Mansion guest areas. A whirlpool is located near the main pool. Fishing excursions are offered, as is a stocked, secluded fishing hole (cane poles provided). Guests may use the themed pool at *Port*

Dixie Landings Tip

■ For both atmosphere and minimal walking, request a room in the Magnolia Bend's Oak Manor or lodge number 18 or 27 in the resort's Alligator Bayou section.

Orleans in addition to the one here. The Sassagoula River Cruise is a pleasant outing in addition to being a convenient means of transportation.

Where to eat: *Boatwright's Dining Hall* (casual restaurant specializing in Cajun and southern cuisine) and *Colonel's Cotton Mill* food court (stands with inexpensive eats galore, including picnic offerings).

Where to drink: *Cotton Co-Op* (featuring fireplace and evening entertainment) and *Muddy Rivers* (poolside refreshments).

VITAL STATISTICS: *Dixie Landings* is located on the shores of a waterway called the Sassagoula River that allows for quick conveyance to Pleasure Island and the Disney Village Marketplace, not to mention its sister resort, *Port Orleans* (also reachable via a carriage path). Epcot and the Disney-MGM Studios are close at hand, as are three of WDW's five 18-hole golf courses. *Dixie Landings;* 1251 Dixie Dr.; Lake Buena Vista, FL 32830; 934-6000; fax 934-5777.

Transportation: Buses to the Magic Kingdom, Epcot, the Disney-MGM Studios, Typhoon Lagoon, Blizzard Beach, Pleasure Island, and the Disney Village Marketplace. Sassagoula River Cruise travels to *Port Orleans*, Pleasure Island, and the Disney Village Marketplace.

Rates: Rooms are $99 to $129 (or $95 to $124 during off-season). A $12 per-diem charge applies for each extra adult (beyond two) sharing a room.

Port Orleans

New Orleans' historic French Quarter is evoked in this resort's prim row house–style guest buildings, which are wrapped in ornate wrought-iron railings and set amid romantic gardens, quiet courtyards, and tree-lined city blocks. Old-fashioned lampposts add to the ambience, as do signs denoting such streets as Rue D'Baga and Café Au Lait Way. The resort is entered via Port Orleans Square, an airy atrium with adjoining one-story buildings that house the hotel's front desk, shop, and arcade on one side, and its restaurant, lounge, and food court on the other. (Follow the French horn chandeliers to the Mardi Gras mural to check in.) Guestrooms are located in seven 3-story buildings,

Port Orleans Tips

■ This is too pretty a place to wake up to a view of the parking lot, so reserve a room overlooking the gardens or splurge on riverscape digs.

■ Of the buildings with riverfront rooms, number 1 is nicely isolated.

■ Note that pool views can spoil the ambience.

■ Request a top-floor room for optimum quiet.

■ Experience *Port Orleans'* romantic atmosphere via a tandem bicycle alongside the river.

■ Don't miss the fresh beignets (a true taste of the Big Easy), whose aroma regularly wafts through the food court.

which are set on either side of the central thoroughfare that begins just beyond Port Orleans Square and ends at the resort's large themed pool. The whole enclave is set alongside a stand-in Mississippi known as the Sassagoula River.

BIG DRAWS: A terrific bang for the buck. The truly charming environs rank among Disney's most memorable. Easily the least sprawling and most manageable of the moderately priced resorts.

WORTH NOTING: The pretty, homey rooms are a bit smaller than those at Disney's more expensive hotels, but are perfectly comfortable. Each of the 1,008 rooms features two double beds (some king-size beds are available). Room service is limited to pizza, but the vast food court and the hearty fare at *Bonfamille's Café* earn repeat guests. A Dixieland band often entertains in the main courtyard. A street artist is available for portraits. Lobby restrooms, fitted with tall, old-fashioned toilets, have piped-in jazz worthy of a sound track. A carriage path—ideal for jogging, strolling, and biking—wends alongside the river to *Port Orleans'* sister resort, *Dixie Landings,* less than a mile upriver. Bikes and boats may be rented. Croquet equipment is available for play on the resort's lawns. A large whirlpool is centrally located. In addition to the fantasy swimming pool here, *Port Orleans* guests are permitted use of *Dixie Landings'* themed pool; they also may take advantage of its stocked, secluded fishing hole. The Sassagoula River Cruise is a pleasant outing in addition to being a convenient mode of transportation.

   Where to eat: *Bonfamille's Café* (a dining room with French Quarter style and Creole cooking) and *Sassagoula Floatworks & Food Factory* (food court with Mardi Gras ambience and inexpensive fare).

   Where to drink: *Mardi Grogs* (poolside refreshments) and *Scat Cat's Club* (for specialty drinks and evening entertainment).

VITAL STATISTICS: *Port Orleans* enjoys special access to Pleasure Island and the Disney Village Marketplace via the Sassagoula River Cruise, which also links *Port Orleans* with its sister resort upriver, *Dixie Landings*. It's close to Epcot, the Disney-MGM Studios, and three 18-hole golf courses, as well. *Port Orleans;* 2201 Orleans Dr.; Lake Buena Vista, FL 32830; 934-5000; fax 934-5353.

Coming Attraction

The themed resort at the top of Disney's "To Do" list is *Coronado Springs*, a moderately priced convention hotel with Spanish-style roofs, adobe walls, and a romantic Southwest aura. Scheduled to open in fall 1997, the resort will be located on the west side of World Drive, near the Disney-MGM Studios.

Transportation: Buses to the Magic Kingdom, Epcot, the Disney-MGM Studios, Typhoon Lagoon, Blizzard Beach, Pleasure Island, and the Disney Village Marketplace. Water launches to *Dixie Landings*, Pleasure Island, and the Disney Village Marketplace.

Rates: Rooms are $99 to $129 (or $95 to $124 during off-season). A $12 per-diem charge applies for each extra adult (beyond two) sharing a room.

VALUE
All-Star Sports and All-Star Music Resorts

Bright in a manner normally reserved for toy packaging, these fun-loving resorts exist at the intersection of entertainment architecture and pop art. Picture a landscape in which three-story football helmets, surfboards, cowboy boots, and maracas are the norm, and you have an idea of the oversize sense of whimsy that governs the *All-Star Sports* and *All-Star Music* resorts. Identical in all but their telltale preoccupations, the adjacent properties are separate entities. Each has its own utterly felicitous central check-in building complete with food court, and its own signature swimming pools. Each features ten improbable-looking guest buildings that are divided into five distinct (sports or music) themes and 1,920 thematically correct rooms. Sports fans have a larger–than–Shaquille O'Neal raison d'être in the *All-Star Sports* resort's homages to basketball,

All-Star Sports and All-Star Music Resorts Tips

■ These resorts attract families with small children in droves, though *All-Star Music* tends to have a higher ratio of adults to children than its sportive compatriot.

■ For maximum quiet, request a third-floor room in a building away from the food court or main pool action (at *All-Star Music*, that's Broadway or country music; at *All-Star Sports*, tennis or basketball).

■ Reservations are required for luggage assistance upon check-out; call the night before.

■ The budget-conscious will note that the only difference between the $69 room and the $79 room is the view.

■ Unless you plan to drive everywhere, request a room near the lobby (i.e., bus stop).

All-Star Stats

The sports and music icons at the *All-Star* resorts are *sooo* big that...

- The juke boxes at the rock guest building could hold 4,000 compact discs, enough music for 135 straight days.
- It would take more than nine million tennis balls to fill one of the tennis cans at *All-Star Sports*.
- The boots doing the two-step at *All-Star Music* measure a whopping size 270.

baseball, football, tennis, and surfing. The *All-Star Music* resort makes equally exaggerated overtures to calypso, jazz, Broadway, rock, and country music.

BIG DRAW: All the advantages of staying on WDW turf at a fraction of the cost of its other resorts.

WORTH NOTING: Requests for specific sport or music genres cannot be guaranteed, but are likely to be met considering the enormous capacity (384 rooms per theme, five themes per resort) of *All-Star Sports* and *All-Star Music*. Rooms are, not surprisingly, the smallest of those at any WDW resort hotel. While spare, they're still perfectly adequate; what they lack in drawer space they nearly make up in a mini-bar. Sports and music themes are maintained with a great deal more subtlety—bedspreads, curtains, light fixtures—in guestrooms than on the startling grounds. Rooms with king-size beds are available on request, as are additional amenities such as down pillows and hair dryers. On-site recreation is limited to arcades and swimming. Each resort has two whimsically designed pools that are open 24 hours, with quiet hours ostensibly in effect from 10 P.M. until 8 A.M. Pizza delivery is available until midnight. *All-Star* guests have special marina privileges at the *Caribbean Beach*, where one fee provides unlimited boat rentals. There's an ATM at Stadium Hall.

Where to eat: At *All-Star Sports:* the *End Zone* (a vast sports-themed food court). At *All-Star Music:* *Intermission* (same food stands, different theme).

Where to drink: At *All-Star Sports:* the *Team Spirits Pool Bar*. At *All-Star Music:* the *Singing Spirits Pool Bar*.

VITAL STATISTICS: *All-Star Sports* and *All-Star Music* enjoy exceptional proximity to the Disney-MGM Studios and Blizzard Beach, with Epcot close at hand as well. *All-Star Sports* resort; 1701 W. Buena Vista Dr.; Lake Buena Vista, FL 32830; 939-5000; fax 939-7333. *All-Star Music* resort; 1801 W. Buena Vista Dr.; Lake Buena Vista, FL 32830; 939-6000; fax 939-7222.

Transportation: Buses to the Magic Kingdom, Epcot, the Disney-MGM Studios, Typhoon Lagoon, Blizzard Beach, Pleasure Island, and the Disney Village Marketplace.

Rates: Rooms are $69 to $79 year-round. A $8 per-diem charge applies to each extra adult (beyond two) sharing a room.

DISNEY VILLAGE HOTEL PLAZA

The three properties described below occupy a unique position among non-Disney-owned accommodations because they, along with four other hotels, are located inside the boundaries of Walt Disney World, within walking distance of the Disney Village Marketplace and Pleasure Island.

While convenient location is the chief advantage of staying at one of these properties, Hotel Plaza guests have other privileges: the ability to book tee times on Disney golf courses 30 days in advance and preferred admission to *Planet Hollywood* (you get to go to the head of the line before 5 P.M.). The latter benefit is unique to Hotel Plaza guests—and no small perk given the mind-boggling waits. Rooms can be booked through WDW Central Reservations (934-7639) or through each individual hotel. While Hotel Plaza properties are not on the Disney transportation system, they provide their own free bus service to the Magic Kingdom, Epcot, and the Disney-MGM Studios.

Buena Vista Palace

The largest of the Disney Village Hotel Plaza properties, it is actually a cluster of towers (one of them 27 stories). Its all-suites building with a peach-and-green Art Deco facade is easy to spot. Many of the 1,028 rooms and suites have a private patio or balcony, along with a view of Epcot's Spaceship Earth.

BIG DRAWS: Popular night spots, ranging from romantic to raucous, and first-rate dining rooms.

WORTH NOTING: All rooms have ceiling fans, remote-control TV, and two telephones (one with voice mail). Four of the Crown Level concierge rooms have private whirlpools. There are one- and two-bedroom suites. Guests also have access to two pools, a health club, three lighted tennis courts, a large arcade, 24-hour room service, and Disney-run gift and sundry shops.

Where to eat: *Arthur's 27* (rooftop restaurant with a creative international menu); the *Outback* (for fresh seafood and Black Angus beef); and *Watercress Café & Bake Shop* (for counter-service baked goods and deli items).

Buena Vista Palace Tips

■ The *Top of the Palace* lounge serves wine by the glass along with music and a great view of IllumiNations, and is one of the most romantic spots in the Orlando area.

■ *Arthur's Wine Cellar in the Sky,* a private dining room in *Arthur's 27* restaurant, stocks 800 bottles and seats up to 12 people (reservations are essential).

65

Where to drink: *Laughing Kookaburra* (live entertainment and 99 beer labels) and *Top of the Palace* (a lounge with quite a view).

VITAL STATISTICS: The hotel is just across the road from the Disney Village Marketplace and Pleasure Island. *Buena Vista Palace;* 1900 Buena Vista Dr.; Lake Buena Vista, FL 32830; 827-2727 or 800-327-2990; fax 827-6034.
Transportation: Regularly scheduled complimentary bus transport to the WDW theme parks is provided.
Rates: Rooms range from $145 to $250; suites are $240 to $455.

Hilton

Set on 23 acres, the Hilton has a laid-back ambience, a lobby filled with comfy chairs and couches, and 814 rooms and suites decorated in mauve, peach, and earth tones.

BIG DRAWS: Directly across the road from the Disney Village Marketplace and Pleasure Island (it has the closest proximity of all the Hotel Plaza properties). Spacious pool area with adult appeal. Free transportation to all WDW golf courses.

WORTH NOTING: All the rooms have mini-bars and feature voice mail and computer hookups. There are two lighted tennis courts and two heated swimming pools. Two whirlpools are tucked away under palms and pines.
Where to eat: *Finn's Grill* (seafood or steak dinners and an oyster bar in a Key West atmosphere); *Benihana* Japanese steak house; *County Fair* (breakfast, lunch, or dinner); *County Fair Terrace* (outdoor dining); and the *Old-Fashioned Soda Shoppe and Arcade* (everything from ice cream to pizza).
Where to drink: *Rum Largo Pool Bar & Café* (for tropical concoctions) and *John T.'s Plantation Bar* (an Old South–inspired lobby lounge).

VITAL STATISTICS: Located right across the road from the Disney Village Marketplace and Pleasure Island. *Hilton* at Walt Disney World Village; 1751 Hotel Plaza Blvd.; Lake Buena Vista, FL 32830; 827-4000 or 800-782-4414; fax 827-6369.

Hilton Tip

■ Rooms with the best views overlook the pools or the fountain at the hotel's entrance.

Transportation: Regularly scheduled complimentary bus transport to the WDW theme parks.

Rates: Rooms are $190 to $250, and suites are $459 to $759, depending on the season.

Courtyard by Marriott

A recent $4.5 million refurbishment transformed this 323-room hotel from a *Howard Johnson* into the country's second-largest *Courtyard*. Recreational facilities include three heated pools, a whirlpool, an arcade, and a fitness center with Nautilus equipment.

BIG DRAW: Beautifully redecorated rooms are some of the most spacious in the Hotel Plaza.

WORTH NOTING: Guestrooms are divided between a 14-story tower and a 6-story annex. Each includes a sitting area, computer-data ports, clock radios, marble vanities, and coffeemakers. Cheerful umbrella-shaped tables decorate the Florida-casual atrium lobby.

Where to eat: The *Courtyard Café and Grille* (a full-service restaurant with breakfast buffet); the *Village Deli* (for snacks and sandwiches); *TCBY Yogurt;* and *Pizza Hut.*

Where to drink: There is a lobby bar; a pool bar is open during the warmer months.

VITAL STATISTICS: Located just two blocks from the Disney Village Marketplace and Pleasure Island. *Courtyard by Marriott;* Box 22,204; 1805 Hotel Plaza Blvd.; Lake Buena Vista, FL 32830; 828-8888 or 800-223-9930; fax 827-4623.

Transportation: Regularly scheduled complimentary bus transport to the WDW theme parks.

Rates: Rooms are $79 to $149 year-round.

Courtyard by Marriott Tip

■ This is a high-rise hotel, unlike many of the national chain's properties, so if you want a picturesque view rather than one of nearby Interstate 4, specifically request a courtyard view when making reservations.

No Room at the Inn?

■ For more information about other Orlando area accommodations, including rental condominiums, apartments, single-family houses, and the local hostels, contact the Orlando/Orange County Convention & Visitors Bureau (363-5871 or 800-551-0181).

■ The Kissimmee–St. Cloud Convention & Visitors Bureau operates a reservations system covering most of the properties along U.S. 192 (for information call 800-327-9159; for reservations, 800-333-5477).

■ If you arrive in Orlando without a hotel reservation, rather than driving around looking for the right place to suit your needs and your pocketbook, head for the Official Visitor Information Center (which is operated by the Orlando/Orange County Convention & Visitors Bureau), in the Mercado Mediterranean Shopping Village, at 8445 International Drive, Suite 152. Reservationists there can check their "black book" for the day's room availability and (reduced) prices. This is an in-person service only.

BEYOND THE WORLD

When visitors to Walt Disney World consider staying somewhere other than at the on-property resorts, it's normally for one of two reasons. First, many people simply don't realize that Mickey is in the hotel business at all, or that he's so great at it. And second is the notion that Disney accommodations are too expensive. Since the new *All-Star Sports* and *All-Star Music* resorts have opened, the latter objection is less persuasive. But no matter what your style or budget calls for, when it comes to deciphering the options beyond WDW's hotels, the difficulty lies in sorting out the best from all the rest.

Not to worry: We've simplified matters by highlighting our top choices—from luxury to economy. For ease of comparison, this listing places the off-site properties into Disney resort categories consistent with their rate scales and accommodation type. There's Deluxe, Moderate, and Value, plus the Home Away From Home category, used to distinguish all-suite and villa-type lodging options. For details on notable restaurants and lounges located in off-property hotels, see the *Dining & Entertainment* chapter.

DELUXE
Grand Cypress

When this outstanding resort opened in 1984, it garnered acclaim for its eye-catching 18-story design. The upscale 750-room *Hyatt Regency Grand Cypress* is this destination resort's centerpiece, while its secluded villas largely remain a well-kept secret. The resort's recreation roster includes a health club, golf courses, tennis courts, water sports, a nature preserve, fitness and jogging trails, croquet, and horseback riding.

BIG DRAWS: This resort would merit a visit even if Walt Disney World weren't just down the road. It's got style, service, and great golf. And the lobby's a knockout.

WORTH NOTING: The Mediterranean-style *Villas of Grand Cypress* dot this resort's fairways. The smaller club suites consist of a spacious bedroom with separate dressing area, large bath, and either a patio or a veranda. Many of the one- to four-bedroom villas have fireplaces and whirlpools. The villa enclave has its own pool. Hotel guestroom decor is Florida casual. A million-dollar art collection graces the public areas and landscaped grounds. There's a free-form swimming pool with waterfalls, water slides, grottoes, and whirlpools. The highly regarded Grand Cypress Academy of Golf provides instruction. An equestrian center offers lessons and trail rides. Grand Cypress Racquet Club has 12 tennis courts (five are lighted).

Where to eat: At the *Villas:* Three dining choices include the casual *Fairways* restaurant and *Black Swan* (a sophisticated dining room at the golf clubhouse). At the hotel: Five dining options include *La Coquina* (nouvelle cuisine) and *Hemingway's* (seafood, steaks, and game).

Where to drink: *Trellises* (atrium piano bar); *Hurricane Bar* (Key West style); *On the Rocks* (poolside refreshments); and *Papillon* (floating bar).

VITAL STATISTICS: The resort is located adjacent to Disney Village Hotel Plaza. *Villas of Grand Cypress;* One N. Jacaranda Blvd.; Orlando, FL 32836; 239-4700 or 800-835-7377; fax 239-7219. *Hyatt Regency Grand Cypress;* One Grand Cypress Blvd.; Orlando, FL 32836; 239-1234 or 800-233-1234; fax 239-3800.

Transportation: The *Hyatt Regency* provides shuttle service to the Disney theme parks for $5 round-trip; free transport between the villas and the hotel is offered as well.

Rates: At the *Villas of Grand Cypress*, club suites are $180 to $325; one-bedroom villas are $255 to $400; two-bedroom units are $360 to $650; three-bedroom units are $540 to $975; and four-bedroom units are $720 to $1,300. At the *Hyatt Regency Grand Cypress*, guestrooms range from $185 to $420, and suites start at $600.

Peabody Orlando

The only sister property to the famed *Peabody* in Memphis, this imposing 891-room luxury tower is one of the top properties in the area. Recreational facilities include a vast heated pool, four lighted tennis courts, a pro shop, a health club with personal trainers, and an arcade.

BIG DRAWS: A modern, well-run resort hotel known for its graciousness and service. Plus those ducks.

Grand Cypress Tips

■ *La Coquina's* kitchen is transformed into a "French Market" with a fine Champagne brunch on Sundays.

■ Don't miss the resort's New Course, which conjures visions of the Old Course at Scotland's venerable St. Andrews.

■ And don't overlook the nine-hole "pitch and putt" course designed by Nicklaus.

■ Another unique offering is the 45-acre nature area.

Peabody Orlando Tips

■ *Capriccio* restaurant offers a Champagne brunch on Sundays.

■ *Club Capriccio* makes the most of the *Peabody's* exceptional wine cellar with monthly themed wine tastings and seminars, especially popular with local residents.

■ The famous *Peabody* ducks ceremoniously parade from a private elevator into the three-story atrium lobby, down a red carpet, and into a marble water fountain daily at 11 A.M., then reverse the pomp and circumstance at 5 P.M.

Best Western Buena Vista Suites Tip

■ The location at S.R. 535 and the relatively new International Drive extension is convenient for those who plan to take in a number of Orlando-area attractions in addition to Walt Disney World.

WORTH NOTING: Nicely appointed guestrooms feature a small television set in the bathroom, nightly turndown service, and daily newspaper delivery. Afternoon tea is served Mondays through Fridays in the *Dux* restaurant. The lobby is the site of two daily duck marches.

Where to eat: *Dux* (the elegant signature restaurant, where the menu is creative but no duck is served); *Capriccio* (Northern Italian cuisine and mesquite grilled specialties in an exhibition kitchen); and *B-Line Diner* (a 1950s-style diner that's open 24 hours).

Where to drink: *The Lobby Bar*, the place to be for daily duck marches and nightly live entertainment.

VITAL STATISTICS: The *Peabody's* location directly across the street from Orlando's convention center makes it a popular group hotel. *Peabody Orlando;* 9801 International Dr.; Orlando, FL 32819; 352-4000 or 800-732-2639; fax 351-9177.

Transportation: The hotel's whimsical "Double-Ducker" bus provides regular shuttle service to the three Disney theme parks for $6 round-trip.

Rates: Rooms run $210 to $270; suites are $395 to $1,300.

HOME AWAY FROM HOME

Best Western Buena Vista Suites

This 280-suite hotel, which opened in mid-1993, has been such a success that its owners are proceeding with a separate 1,250-unit luxury version on an adjacent lot. Facilities include a fitness center, a heated pool, a whirlpool, an arcade, and a mini-market.

BIG DRAW: An all-suite property with a full breakfast (even grits) included in the room rate.

WORTH NOTING: Standard two-room suites have a separate bedroom and a living room with a queen-size sleeper sofa. Each unit has a coffeemaker, a refrigerator, two televisions, a VCR (movie rentals are available), two telephones, a safe, and a microwave. The phones are equipped with voice mail and data ports. Deluxe suites have a king-size bed and a whirlpool tub.

Where to eat: *Patio Grille* for made-to-order sandwiches and snacks.

Where to drink: The *Citrus Lounge* provides poolside lunch and evening cocktails.

VITAL STATISTICS: The property is situated about 1½ miles from Walt Disney World and close to the central tourist strip along International Drive. *Best Western Buena Vista Suites;* 14,450 International Dr.; Orlando, FL 32830; 239-8588 or 800-537-7737; fax 239-1401.

Transportation: Complimentary shuttle service is provided to and from the three Disney theme parks four times a day.

Rates: Standard suites range from $99 to $149; deluxe suites are $109 to $169.

Summerfield Suites

This 146-unit property is a variation on the all-suite theme; the twist here is a 24-hour convenience store with microwave entrées and movie rentals. Other amenities include a fitness center, a heated pool, and a whirlpool. A breakfast buffet and a cocktail hour are complimentary.

BIG DRAWS: Bedrooms are completely removed from the living room area in most units. The suites are roomy enough for two couples traveling together.

WORTH NOTING: Both one- and two-bedroom suites are unusually spacious. In addition to a fully outfitted kitchen, each unit features a VCR, an iron and ironing board, a desk in each bedroom, computer hookups, and telephones equipped with voice mail messaging service. There are no restaurants or lounges on property.

VITAL STATISTICS: It's at the south end of International Drive, convenient to the Disney theme parks. *Summerfield Suites International;* 8480 International Dr.; Orlando, FL 32819; 352-2400 or 800-833-4353; fax 352-4631.

Transportation: No shuttle service to the Disney theme parks is provided.

Rates: One-bedroom units (sleeping four) are $149 to $189; two-bedroom units (sleeping six) are $169; and two-bedroom trio units (sleeping eight) are $189 to $229.

Summerfield Suites Tips

■ Reservations require plenty of advance notice during peak periods because the inn is frequently sold out.

■ A sister property in Lake Buena Vista does offer shuttle service to Walt Disney World, but it's also more kid-oriented (hence our pick of the International Drive location).

■ To have groceries delivered to your room by 6:30 P.M., leave a completed form with the front desk early in the morning.

MODERATE

Clarion Plaza

This 810-unit hotel, which opened in 1991, last year was named "Inn of the Year" by Choice Hotels International, its franchisor. In addition to a heated outdoor pool and whirlpool, facilities include a coin laundry on every other floor and an arcade.

BIG DRAWS: A business hotel by design, the property's reasonable room rates make it popular with leisure travelers.

WORTH NOTING: The spacious guestrooms have in-room safes, separate vanity areas, and in-room check-out. There are 32 suites.

Where to eat: *Jack's Place* (complete with caricature sketches à la Manhattan's legendary *Sardi's*, for seafood, steaks, and formidable desserts) and *Café Matisse* (all-you-can-eat buffets for breakfast, lunch, and dinner).

Where to drink: *Backstage at the Clarion*, where live bands and top local deejays play nightly until 2 A.M.

VITAL STATISTICS: Located on International Drive adjacent to the convention center. *Clarion Plaza;* 9700 International Dr.; Orlando, FL 32819-8144; 352-9700 or 800-627-8258; fax 354-5774.

Transportation: Shuttle service from the hotel to the three Disney theme parks costs $11 round-trip.

Rates: Standard rooms are $125 to $145; suites are $200 to $660.

VALUE

Country Hearth Inn

Formerly the *Heritage Inn*, this two-story, gingerbread-style property has rocking chairs on the porch and is about the closest you'll come to finding a quaint inn on International Drive. The landscaped grounds include a pool and tropical courtyard.

BIG DRAWS: Charming ambience, reasonable prices.

WORTH NOTING: The hotel's 150 guestrooms have polished cherry furniture, and homey touches such as dust

Clarion Plaza Tip

■ Discounted rates as low as $79 are usually available in the spring and fall.

ruffles on the beds and French doors. Most have two double beds (some king-size beds are available). All rooms have balconies. Hardwood floors, a patterned tin ceiling, and a chandelier grace the lobby.

Where to eat: *Plantation Room* serves buffet or à la carte breakfast and à la carte dinner. There also is a Sunday Champagne brunch.

Where to drink: The hotel's *Front Porch Lounge.*

VITAL STATISTICS: It's across from the Orange County Convention Center. *Country Hearth Inn;* 9861 International Dr.; Orlando, FL 32819; 352-0008 or 800-447-1890; fax 352-5449.

Transportation: Hotel shuttles run to and from the three Disney theme parks daily, and cost $9 round-trip.

Rates: Prices range from $49 to $109.

Holiday Inn Express

This former *Rodeway Inn* has been revamped into an attractive property, with 217 rooms, a large heated pool, and a gameroom.

BIG DRAWS: Value. National chain affiliation. Convenient location near numerous restaurants.

WORTH NOTING: The guestrooms are a comfortable size and were recently redecorated in bright colors. Each room has two double beds, a seating area, a VCR (a variety of movie rentals are available in the lobby), and a safe (with a nominal fee).

Where to eat: *Expressions Pool Café*, open seasonally from mid-morning to midnight for sandwiches.

Where to drink: Ditto.

VITAL STATISTICS: It's about 20 minutes' drive from Walt Disney World. *Holiday Inn Express;* 6323 International Dr.; Orlando, FL 32819; 351-4430 or 800-365-6935; fax 345-0742.

Transportation: There is free scheduled transportation for guests to all the WDW theme parks.

Rates: Standard rooms range from $49 to $84; prices include breakfast.

Country Hearth Inn Tip

■ Popular with conventioneers, the inn also attracts a loyal following among locals who congregate in its lounge for happy hours.

Holiday Inn Express Tip

■ To avoid traffic on this busy stretch of International Drive, opt to walk to neighborhood restaurants instead of driving.

Theme Parks: The Big Three

To experience Walt Disney World's trio of major theme parks without children is tantamount to celebrating a major holiday without the complication of travel or in-laws. It's positively liberating.

Let the Magic Kingdom runneth over with strollers and too-tired toddlers. Let cumbersome families try to fend off five-headed-monster syndrome. As adults free to roam the Magic Kingdom, Epcot, and Disney-MGM Studios on our own terms, we need not be concerned with such things. We are a distinct minority (read: non-teenaged individuals having no obligation whatsoever to facilitate the entertainment of any young person within 45 square miles) in one of those rare settings in which the minority has all the advantages.

If we sometimes feel a bit conspicuous touring the parks as unaccompanied adults, it's because we're flaunting the inherent freedom. We're taking advantage of the fact that we're among friends who readily agree that a shaded bench, a nap in a hammock, or a soak in the whirlpool back at the resort really would hit the spot right now. We are free to buzz through the Magic Kingdom at a clip no character-conscious family could maintain or meander through Epcot's World Showcase pavilions at what might be called escargot pace.

When we see people consumed by a self-imposed game of tag that obliges them to touch each and every attraction, we wish we could somehow interrupt the game and remind them that they are on vacation. The immense collection of experiences that comprises Walt Disney World has a way of inspiring a desire to "collect them all." This is only natural. But by

---

Spectacular fireworks come with the territory at Walt Disney World.

Not a Thing to Wear

Try this on for wardrobe inequity: Mickey Mouse has 101 different costumes whereas Minnie owns about 50 outfits.

being more selective and pausing to say, "You know, Mickey, as much as I appreciate all the entertainment you've lined up, I just don't have the time to do everything," you wind up with a much more enjoyable and satisfying experience.

Each park has stuff on its shelves that we want in our shopping cart. It's easy to rationalize visiting all three; they're specialty stores, after all, and the Magic Kingdom may have such essentials as Splash Mountain and Pirates of the Caribbean, but it just doesn't sell that new 3-D movie we like so much, Honey, I Shrunk the Audience. For that, we have to go to Epcot. And although we can find a lot of our favorites here, we can't get The Twilight Zone Tower of Terror; it's available exclusively at the Disney-MGM Studios.

That's okay. We like to immerse ourselves in the inspiring atmospheres that make these parks so distinct. When we're at the Magic Kingdom, we take one look at Cinderella Castle and simply cease to function as adults. Suddenly we are in the amusement business, with only ourselves to please. It's funny, a lot of the adults we've met there are similarly engaged. In any case, we've never had even the slightest problem entertaining ourselves in the Magic Kingdom.

In Epcot, Disney's "experimental prototype community of tomorrow," it's easy to retain our adult sensibilities, since the point of Epcot is not to be an amusement park in the first place (although there's certainly plenty of funny business going on in, say, Cranium Command). The highly conceptual, experiential environs of Future World nudge our curiosity, engage our interest, and heighten our awareness. But when we need a change of pace, we move on to the Magic Snackdom, otherwise known as World Showcase. Granted, there is much more to this part of Epcot than compelling snacks from 11 different countries. One day, we got so caught up watching drummers in Japan we almost let seagulls get away with our soft pretzels from Germany.

When we're at the Disney-MGM Studios, savoring the relaxed atmosphere of this starry-eyed tribute to 1930s Hollywood, we're inclined to become a bit starry-eyed ourselves. The place has such a sophisticated air, a cozy nostalgia, a plucky sense of fun.

We believe the parks are best explored in a certain order, especially your first time out. Starting with the least character-intensive theme parks lets you ease into Disneyana gradually, so that by the time Mickey Mouse appears in butter form at your dinner table, you've been conditioned to expect it. By visiting Epcot first, you're able to appreciate it for its own merit. For a good one-two combination, follow your first day at Epcot (it takes at least two to effectively cover both Future World and World Showcase) with a day at the Disney-MGM Studios. This works well for two reasons: Enchantment is a great chaser for enlightenment, and the Disney-MGM Studios ups the character presence a bit without overwhelming. If you're raring to meet Mickey or eager for a closer look at Cinderella Castle, spend your third day exploring the Magic Kingdom and your fourth finishing up at Epcot. (In this chapter, the parks are presented in the order they were created at Walt Disney World: the Magic Kingdom, 1971; Epcot, 1982; and the Disney-MGM Studios, 1989.) After you've toured each park, spend any remaining days exploring other compelling corners of the World and revisiting favorite attractions—preferably between soaks in a soothing whirlpool.

Loose Change

Keep some pennies handy, or you'll be toting home a small mountain of change every night, as snacks and sundries in the parks have a peculiar way of skirting round figures for prices along the lines of $3.01.

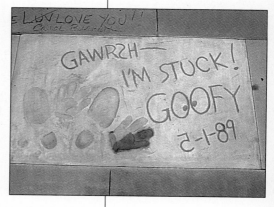

MAGIC KINGDOM

As once upon a timish and happily ever afteresque a place as exists, the Magic Kingdom is sure proof that you can judge a park by its largest icon (in this case, Cinderella Castle). While it is the the most character-intensive, and certainly the strongest kid magnet of all the parks, flying pink elephants couldn't keep us away.

What puts the Magic Kingdom on the adult map? For starters, it's manageable. Unlike in the far larger Epcot, the essentials here are easily traversed in a leisurely day. High on the list of imperatives is a threesome of rides—Space Mountain, Splash Mountain, and Big Thunder Mountain Railroad—that make the Magic Kingdom the thrill seeker's park of choice. What it lacks in culture, fine cuisine, and opportunities to imbibe, it more than makes up for in magic. Disney has made a real art of coaxing folks into a state of wonderment that seldom occurs in adulthood, and this park represents that art taken to its highest level. Even if the singsongy tune of Fantasyland's It's A Small World drives you crazy, odds are good that your brand of enchantment lies around the corner. It's a rare adult who doesn't fall under the spell of the Magic Kingdom's ballroom of waltzing apparitions, its convincing den of leering pirates, or its heavy-breathing ode to an alien encounter. For bouts of nostalgic whimsy, there are kiddie rides such as Peter Pan's Flight that don't aspire to recapture the magic of childhood so much as momentarily revive it.

Of course, a gazillion children can have a way of getting on one's nerves after a while, so some strategies are in order. First, master the art of noticing children only when they are being cute. We've gotten so good at this that during a recent visit to the park we recall seeing but one child: a girl about four years old whose eyes nearly doubled in size at the sight of Cinderella. To keep the "magic barometer" from falling, either make quick work of the park or weave in and out of major traffic zones (Fantasyland and Frontierland are generally the most crowded areas). Seek refuge in the quiet nooks described in the margins of this chapter and in such havens as The Hall of Presidents and the Liberty Square Riverboat; for a bigger break, indulge in a leisurely lunch at the *Grand Floridian* or another of the resorts that are easily accessible via a quick trip on the monorail.

The Magic Kingdom is usually open from 9 A.M. to 6 P.M.; park hours are extended during holiday periods and the summer months. Call 824-4321 for up-to-the-minute details. One-day park admission is $39.27 for adults (see *Planning Ahead* for ticket options). Prices are subject to change.

GUIDING PRINCIPLES: Know thy touring priorities. Know thy path of least resistance. These commandments are the basis of any enjoyable theme park visit—but they take on even greater importance for adults venturing through the Magic Kingdom.

Of course, you can't exactly determine your priorities or your route without first knowing your turf. The section that follows is therefore designed to offer a telling preview for first-time visitors and a timely review for returnees. Structured as a counterclockwise walking tour through the seven themed lands that comprise the park, it provides a geographical orientation to the Magic Kingdom while also taking a critical inventory of the attractions as they relate to adults. Land by land, it highlights the adult essentials, points out redeeming and unfortunate characteristics of the nonessentials, and flags the newest additions. For the sake of easy reference, we've also included a Touring Priorities list ranking the park's best adult bets. To learn the most efficient touring strategies, consult Hot Tips in the margins of this section and the flexible tour plan provided in the *Planning Ahead* chapter.

For information on how to get to the Magic Kingdom, via Walt Disney World transportation system or by car, see the "Getting Around" section of the *Planning Ahead* chapter. For the goods on Magic Kingdom shops worth

For the Birds?

A forest of nearly 33,000 trees forms a Hidden Mickey about 40 acres west of the Magic Kingdom.

exploring, see the "Shopping" section of the *Diversions* chapter. To find out about the best bets for dining, see the book's evaluative "Restaurant Guide" in the *Dining & Entertainment* chapter.

GETTING ORIENTED: No matter what your mode of transportation, you'll arrive at the same set of gates. Go through the turnstiles, past an area with coin-operated lockers, and you're in Town Square, a cul-de-sac at the foot of Main Street that looks straight out to the park's best landmark, Cinderella Castle. At the opposite end of Main Street is an area known as the Central Plaza, or the Hub. It is here that you'll find the **Magic Kingdom Tip Board**, a blackboard listing the current waiting times for popular attractions.

It's helpful to think of the layout of the Magic Kingdom as a tree. Main Street is the trunk; the other six themed areas—Adventureland, Frontierland, Liberty Square, Fantasyland, Mickey's Starland, and Tomorrowland—dangle at the ends of the tree's gnarled boughs (actually bridges). The first bridge on your left leads to Adventureland; the second, to Liberty Square and Frontierland; the pathway straight ahead passes through Cinderella Castle on its way to the heart of Fantasyland; another bridge passes to the right of the castle to enter Fantasyland nearest Mickey's Starland and Tomorrowland; and the bridge on your immediate right leads directly to Tomorrowland. The lands are also linked via a broad footpath that wends its way behind the castle.

A WALKING TOUR

Let's begin our tour in **Town Square**, which is important as the site of Sun Bank, one of two full-service banks on WDW property (yes, it has an ATM), and as the location of **City Hall**, where a person can make all manner of reservations and arrangements (no, you can't get married here). It's a good idea to stop in at City Hall for a listing of the day's scheduled street and stage entertainment.

A few suggestions: Make a decision on the 3 P.M. Mickey Mania parade based on your tolerance for rap and hip-hop music; and don't miss the nightly SpectroMagic parade (the best thing since fireworks) if it's happening during your visit.

Looking back toward the park's entrance from Town Square, you can see that the building we walked through

HOT TIPS

■ On Mondays, Thursdays, and Saturdays, guests staying at WDW resorts may enter the Magic Kingdom 1½ hours prior to the official opening time and get an early crack at Space Mountain and all Fantasyland attractions. Early-entry days and attractions are subject to change.

■ Not coincidentally, Mondays, Thursdays, and Saturdays now tend to be the most crowded days at the Magic Kingdom.

■ The afternoon parade is a golden opportunity to take advantage of shorter lines at the most popular attractions.

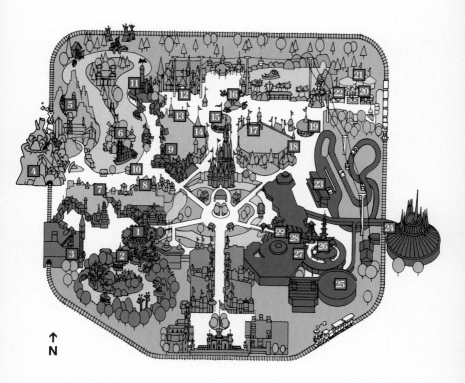

↑
N

ADVENTURELAND
1 Swiss Family Treehouse
2 Jungle Cruise
3 Pirates of the Caribbean

FRONTIERLAND
4 Splash Mountain
5 Big Thunder Mountain Railroad
6 Tom Sawyer Island
7 Country Bear Jamboree
8 Diamond Horseshoe Saloon Revue

LIBERTY SQUARE
9 The Hall of Presidents
10 Liberty Square Riverboat
11 The Haunted Mansion

FANTASYLAND
12 It's A Small World
13 Peter Pan's Flight
14 Legend of The Lion King

15 Cinderella's Golden Carrousel
16 Dumbo, the Flying Elephant
17 Snow White's Adventures
18 Mr. Toad's Wild Ride
19 Mad Tea Party

MICKEY'S STARLAND
20 Mickey's House
21 Mickey's Starland Show
22 Mickey's Hollywood Theatre

TOMORROWLAND
23 Grand Prix Raceway
24 Space Mountain
25 Walt Disney's Carousel of Progress
26 Astro Orbiter
27 Dreamflight
28 The Timekeeper
29 Alien Encounter

Touring Priorities

DON'T MISS

Splash Mountain*

Space Mountain*

Big Thunder Mountain
   Railroad*

Haunted Mansion

Pirates of the Caribbean*

The Timekeeper

The Hall of Presidents

Peter Pan's Flight*

Alien Encounter*

DON'T OVERLOOK

Walt Disney World Railroad

Legend of The Lion King*

Liberty Square Riverboat

Carousel of Progress

Main Street Cinema

It's A Small World*

Swiss Family Treehouse

Mad Tea Party*

Tomorrowland Transit
   Authority

Country Bear Jamboree

Diamond Horseshoe Saloon
   Revue**

to get here is actually the **Walt Disney World Railroad** depot. A 1928 steam engine that once carted sugarcane across the Yucatán now hauls freight (largely first-time visitors, train buffs, and homesick commuters) on a 21-minute loop around the Magic Kingdom. We recommend the ride for anyone interested in a great overview and a pleasant respite. It's also a fine way (albeit not always the fastest way) to get to Frontierland and Mickey's Starland if you don't want to walk.

Onward.

Main Street, U.S.A.

Main Street is notable as the tidy strip of storefronts where adults first gawk at, then feel compelled to photograph Cinderella Castle. Understand, this will probably happen to you. While there's no shame in it, don't be so distracted you overlook the street's turn-of-the-century charm. Amusements here are decidedly low-key. **Main Street Cinema's** ten-minute film clip about how Mickey hit the Big Time is cute; if it's a real hot day, it's even cuter. For grooming as entertainment, there's the old-fashioned Harmony Barber Shop (tucked behind the Emporium), where the Dapper Dans sometimes accompany a haircut. By all means, check out their sweet four-part harmonies.

Main Street stays open a good half hour after the rest of the park has closed, although the shops (see "Shopping" in the *Diversions* chapter for tips) tend to be less crowded during the afternoon. If you're not in the mood to dally or to fight foot traffic, the horse-pulled trolley cars are a fun way to travel from Town Square to the Hub.

Tomorrowland

Futuristic in a way that would likely go right over Buck Rogers' head, Tomorrowland is a city of the future that never was. Because it's home base for two of the park's most popular attractions—perennial favorite Space Mountain and Alien Encounter, the biggest hit to come out of the land's 1994–95 overhaul—Tomorrowland is best visited first thing after the gates open.

Space Mountain, a must-do for all but those who categorically avoid the fast stuff, is one to head for straightaway. Once the lines reach outside this white structure at the far side of Tomorrowland, they generally don't ease up until the evening during periods when the park is open late. To gauge whether Space Mountain is for you, consider how you feel about roller coasters. This one rockets at speeds of up to 28 miles per hour through a space-age sheath of darkness, shooting stars, and flashing lights. It's a fast and furious 2 minutes 38 seconds of spectacular special effects—an absolute must for the adventurous, and an unforgettable adventure for the suddenly courageous. Space Mountain is also a pretty turbulent ride, however, so riders need be in good health and free from heart conditions, back and neck problems, and other physical limitations (such as pregnancy), as the posted signs warn. If you've just eaten, wait a while. At the exit, you can play video games or the resident ATM.

If you decide you'd rather observe the rockets' red glare from the vantage point of a train that's doing more like ten miles per hour, the **Tomorrowland Transit Authority** offers a preview to Space Mountain and other Tomorrowland attractions on a track that's strictly horizontal. The train, powered by an innovative linear induction motor, is boarded in the heart of Tomorrowland near **Astro Orbiter** (an elevated ride with rockets that's primarily for kids but good fun; it seems to go faster the lower you fly in your Buck Rogersmobile).

The scariest thing ever to hit the Magic Kingdom, **Alien Encounter** even has scary lines. It's not a motion ride, but rather an intense 20-minute experience born of an interplanetary-travel demo gone awry. The story: A company on Planet X has developed something called a teleporter that's capable of beaming people between planets, and is treating you to

a demonstration via live broadcast. You are seated in a dimly lit room with one of these teleporters occupying center stage when unsettling events begin to occur. A restraint is lowered over your shoulders. Lights scan the crowd looking for a good subject for teleportation. The chairman of the Planet X corporation volunteers to come to

Earth, but an alien arrives in his place. There is an explosion. Suddenly, it is completely dark and you hear screams and groans, feel panting on the nape of your neck, and are sprayed with what in this context seems to be alien slime. The verdict: Special effects *are* the experience. Although this attraction is more suspenseful and unsettling than terrifying, if you're the type who scares easily or are simply good at playing along, you'll get some nice chills up your spine.

Just opposite Alien Encounter is **The Timekeeper**, another newcomer to Tomorrowland that warrants your attention, only this one's a hoot, not a holler. A good bet for early in the day because it's a standing engagement, The Timekeeper is an arresting 20-minute Circle-Vision 360 film amusingly hosted by Audio-Animatronics characters. Basically, a wacky robot who could leave the attraction and *be* Robin Williams sends his buddy, a flying robot camera named 9-Eye, back in time on assignment to transmit photos of all she sees for our enjoyment. At the 1900 Paris Exposition, she bumps into H. G. Wells and Jules Verne, one of whom hitches a ride to the future. If you're a "Cheers" fan, you'll probably recognize 9-Eye's voice as that of Rhea Perlman (the robot isn't such a ringer for the actress as Timekeeper is for Williams). As for old-fashioned actors, the sort with no Audio-Animatronics stand-ins, you'll see Jeremy Irons playing the role of H. G. Wells and Michel Piccoli as Jules Verne. The bottom line: Pass only if you've been there (to Innsbruck, Austria, say) and done that (bobsledded down a 1,200-meter run at 60 miles per hour).

Right next to The Timekeeper is **Dreamflight**, a fanciful 4½-minute journey through the history of flight complete with giant pop-up books. Carry-on luggage must be smaller than the entranceway. Around the bend at **Walt Disney's Carousel of Progress**, the stage stays put and you rotate around it during the 20-minute show. The attraction fulfills its promise as a warm and fuzzy portrayal of how electricity has altered our lives. It's made better by a new scene that offers a lighthearted glimpse of life in the year 2000. Don't be dismayed by crowds; this place swallows them whole. Next door to the Carousel of Progress is **Skyway to Fantasyland**, an airlift that provides a wonderful scenic overlook, but isn't much of a time-saver. Heading north toward Fantasyland, you pass Space Mountain and come upon the rather low-octane **Grand Prix Raceway**.

Quiet Nooks

- Rose garden on the right as you face Cinderella Castle
- *Crystal Palace*
- Walt Disney World Railroad
- Main Street Cinema
- Harmony Barber Shop
- Shaded tables behind the shops in Liberty Square
- Liberty Square Riverboat
- Rocking chairs on the front porches of Frontierland and Liberty Square shops
- Anywhere but Fantasyland

Mickey's Starland

This tiny blip between Tomorrowland and its northern neighbor, Fantasyland, is relevant only as the site of **Mickey's Starland**, a 20-minute live musical featuring Disney characters that's primarily for kids but still a lot of fun. The best way to get here is a one-way ticket to Duckburg, U.S.A., on the Walt Disney World Railroad. (Board the train in Town Square.) Once in Mickey's Starland, head for Mickey's house, the biggest one in town. Don't knock. Just wander through the house and out the back door to reach an air-conditioned tent, where Mickey Mouse cartoons will entertain you until showtime.

Fantasyland

The danger to the adult entering this, the cheeriest, most magical, and most nostalgic corner of the Magic Kingdom, is that there's a very fine line between rubbing elbows with Cinderella, Peter Pan, and Snow White and being caught in a child thicket. The optimum way to take in Fantasyland's whimsy is to visit just before and during the daily 3 P.M. parade. Because there is nothing adult about Fantasyland, whimsy is the name of the game.

The Mouse Is Spoken For

Walt Disney himself supplied the voice for Mickey Mouse from 1929 to 1946.

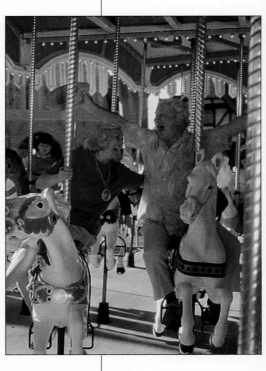

That said, certain attractions are so artfully executed that they transcend the kiddie genre. Of these, **It's A Small World**—a boat ride through the happiest, busiest, and most diversely populated dollhouse on the planet—is surely the most elaborate. A special treat if you've got a sweet tooth, a safe bet if you could use a mood boost. Ride it once and, like it or not, the song is your sound track for the rest of the day. Much more subtle is **Peter Pan's Flight**, an alluring sprinkle of pixie dust in which you can—and do—fly for three minutes above absolutely delightful scenes of Captain Hook and nighttime London

Entertainment

Performance times vary, so pick up a schedule at City Hall to be assured of catching specific entertainers. The Walt Disney World Band performs every morning in Town Square. The Dapper Dans barbershop quartet harmonizes periodically on Main Street, either a cappella or with bamboo organ chimes. The Mickey Mania Parade—a Mickeyfied romp set to rambunctious rap music—takes over Main Street every day at 3 P.M. And the Diamond Horseshoe Saloon Revue, a musical affair complete with can-can dancing, hits the boards seven times daily in Frontierland's dance-hall saloon.

During busy seasons when the park is open until 10 P.M. or later, a spectacular fireworks show (200 shells released in five minutes) called Fantasy in the Sky is presented nightly. And the dazzling Spectro-Magic light parade wends its luminous fiber-optic way down Main Street twice every night (the best vantage point is the platform of the Walt Disney World Railroad depot; the later performance is always less crowded).

in a pirate ship built for two. **Legend of The Lion King**, a 25-minute stage show based on the animated film *The Lion King*, is a knockout mix of puppetry, film clips, and special effects that kids adore but fail to appreciate. It's a rare adult who doesn't savor the sharp sarcasm and wit of Timon the meerkat.

Then there are the purely nostalgic attractions, worth your time only if you're hankering to relive a certain story or amusement ride from your past. Have a thing for carousels in general or **Cinderella's Golden Carrousel** in particular? Go for it. Think you'd get a huge kick out of squeezing your group into an oversize teacup and spinning yourselves silly? Get to the **Mad Tea Party**. Don't skip **Dumbo, the Flying Elephant** if you'll regret it later; but at the same time, don't expect to be wowed by a straightforward kiddie attraction such as **Mr. Toad's Wild Ride**. And **Snow White's Adventures** has more moments than it used to, with the happy addition of Audio-Animatronics dwarfs and Snow White herself. Be sure not to miss the gorgeous mosaic murals beneath the open archway of **Cinderella Castle**. No less than a million well-placed pieces of Italian glass tell the whole tale, ugly stepsisters, glass slipper, and all.

Liberty Square

Tucked between Fantasyland and Frontierland, this comparatively small area tends to be relatively peaceful. Brick and clapboard buildings carry the theme—Colonial America—as does the Liberty Tree, a 130-something oak hung with 13 lanterns to recall the original colonies.

Though Liberty Square has just a few attractions, it still takes more than an hour to take them all in. **The Hall of Presidents** merits attention not just as a well-delivered 20-minute dose of patriotism in which Abraham Lincoln and Bill Clinton speak, but as a chance to observe all 42 chief executives of our country in action. The shifting, swaying, and nodding begins the moment the curtain rises on the amazingly faithful and impeccably dressed group of Audio-Animatronics figures. The pace is slow, but just right for an air-conditioned theater with comfy seats. Don't be intimidated by a big line—this is a *big* theater. The **Liberty Square Riverboat**—a large, paddle wheel–driven steamboat that makes 15-minute loops around Tom Sawyer Island—is a pleasant distraction, especially on a steamy afternoon. The multi-tiered riverboat offers a great vantage of the park (for the best view, sit right up front or in the very back), and its resounding horn ensures that passengers never lack for landlubbers' attention. Don't ask what the **Haunted Mansion** is doing in Liberty Square. Just note that it's a not-to-be-missed, eight-minute experience so overrun with clever special effects and ghoulish delights (your typical ballroom of waltzing ghosts, door knockers that knock by themselves, and spirited graveyards), you'll be thankful it's here.

Frontierland

This land conjures something of the Old West, with a little country charm thrown in for good measure. Although there's more to Frontierland than mountains, it is most notable as the home to two of the Magic Kingdom's biggest (and most addictive) adult thrills—Splash Mountain and Big Thunder Mountain Railroad.

The first thing to know about **Splash Mountain** is that it's okay to feel anxious just watching the log boats plunge down this ride's big drop—you're looking at the steepest flume in the world (although it appears to be a straight drop, it's actually 52 feet down at a 45-degree angle). Even so, this water-bound ride themed to Disney's *Song of the South* is tamer than it looks from the ground. Steep plunge aside, there are just three small dips during

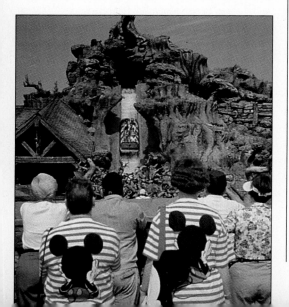

Did you know...

■ The Magic Kingdom opened on October 1, 1971, with 23 attractions. Among the major additions to the park since opening day: Pirates of the Caribbean (1973), Space Mountain (1975), Big Thunder Mountain Railroad (1980), Splash Mountain (1992), and Alien Encounter (1995).

■ The facade of Cinderella Castle is not stone, but fiberglass supported by steel beams. In the upper reaches of the castle there are security rooms and an apartment originally intended for members of the Disney family (but never occupied).

■ While the Magic Kingdom is the park people most often equate with Walt Disney World, it's actually the smallest of the three major theme parks. In fact, at 107 acres, it's a mere speck on the 27,800-acre World map (only 7,000 acres have been developed).

Snacker's Guide

For a healthy bite, visit the *Liberty Square Market* in Liberty Square for fresh fruit, carrot sticks, and baked potatoes; *Sleepy Hollow* (also in Liberty Square) for the likes of veggie sandwiches, vegetarian chili, and bagel chips; *Auntie Gravity's Galactic Goodies* in Tomorrowland for fruit, juices, and frozen yogurt; or *Aloha Isle* in Adventureland for pineapple spears and refreshments.

For a sweet treat, seek out old-fashioned lollipops at the Market House on Main Street; fudge, peanut brittle, marshmallow crispies, and Mint Chocolate Cookie Gems at the Confectionery on Main Street; or the humongous fresh-baked cookies, including Snickerdoodles, at the *Main Street Bake Shop*.

For a frozen refresher, try the ice cream and strawberry bars from a vendor cart or choose a flavor at the *Plaza Ice Cream Parlor* on Main Street.

For a savory pick-me-up, head for the *Egg Roll Wagon* in Adventureland, the *Turkey Leg Wagon* in Frontierland, or the cappuccino cart right outside *Tony's Town Square* at the foot of Main Street.

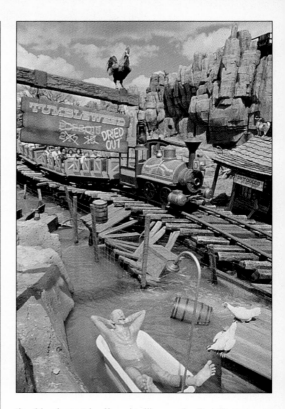

the 11-minute trip. If you're like us, the first time around you'll be way too nervous about when "it" is going to happen to fully appreciate the delightful humor, enormously appealing characters, and uplifting "Zip-A-Dee-Doo-Dah" ambience of Splash Mountain. But coax yourself into riding once, and you'll be hooked. If you prefer to get splashed, not drenched, sit in the back of the log. A note on timing: Both Splash Mountain and Big Thunder Mountain Railroad tend to draw big crowds all day long; your best bet is to aim for early evening.

Think of **Big Thunder Mountain Railroad** as a thrilling ride on the mild side. As roller coasters go, this one's exciting, but as much for the surrounding scenery—bats, goats, a flooded mining town—your runaway mine train races past as for the ride itself. Big Thunder Mountain Railroad is not nearly so fast or turbulent as Space Mountain, and nothing in its four-minute series of reverberating swoops and jerky turns comes even close to Splash Mountain's intimidating plunge. For a bigger thrill, ride it after dark, when you can't see what lies ahead even from the first car.

But Frontierland's appeal extends beyond its two high-profile attractions. The **Country Bear Jamboree**, a 17-minute musical variety show put on by 20 impossibly corny Audio-Animatronics bears in Grizzly Hall, is the perfect attraction to hit when you're feeling a little punchy. If your schedule can accommodate an entire hour's worth of song, cancan dancing, and corniness, the **Diamond Horseshoe Saloon Revue** doesn't disappoint. While **Tom Sawyer Island**, a short raft ride away, provides a nice break from the more structured parts of the park, it tends to attract lots of kids.

Adventureland

When you hear the beating of drums and begin to notice the presence of tropical plants such as palm trees and bougainvillea, you've crossed over into Adventureland, the Magic Kingdom's most exotic place. Among Adventureland's four attractions are the immensely popular Pirates of the Caribbean and Jungle Cruise, best visited during the early morning and evening.

Here, **Tropical Serenade** showcases Disney's earliest Audio-Animatronics figures—chirping, whistling birds—which, while quite animated, are most interesting as a point of comparison to the more recent creations. Remember **Pirates of the Caribbean** as an elaborate, engaging, not-to-be-missed boat ride in which you watch pirates attack and raid a Caribbean village. A classic attraction, it provides plenty of leering, jeering examples of how wonderfully, frighteningly realistic Disney's Audio-Animatronics have become. The unsavory scenes in this ride are offset by upbeat choruses of "Yo-Ho-Yo-Ho, a Pirate's Life for Me." Note that Pirates of the Caribbean includes a small dip and some loud cannon blasts.

Jungle Cruise is an extremely popular attraction that transports passengers on a steamy ten-minute boat trip through the Nile valley and the Amazon rain forest. Although the flora is quite beautiful, the lines for this ride can be prohibitively long. Finally, if you feel up to climbing some serious stairs, **Swiss Family Treehouse** is a fascinating replica of the Robinsons' ingenious perch that's worth the effort, even though the tree itself is a product of the prop department's imagination.

Ears to the Ground

Woman in mid-thirties pleading with her companions in the midst of serious Adventureland foot traffic: "But I LOVE It's A Small World." About ten minutes later, the group was doubling back toward Fantasyland.

EPCOT

Epcot's hours are staggered. Whereas Future World is usually open from 9 A.M. to 7 P.M., World Showcase is generally open from 11 A.M. to 9 P.M. Spaceship Earth and Innoventions in Future World both stay open until World Showcase closes. Epcot's hours are extended during holiday periods and the summer months; call 824-4321 for up-to-the-minute details. One-day park admission is $39.27 for adults (see *Planning Ahead* for ticket options). Prices are subject to change.

Think of Epcot as an extraordinary balancing act. This park is huge—bigger than the Magic Kingdom and the Disney MGM-Studios put together—and it performs two rather ambitious feats simultaneously. While the part of Epcot known as Future World offers a multi-faceted look at what lies ahead for humankind, its alter ego, World Showcase, transports guests (at least in spirit) to 11 different countries. This division of labor works well, and it certainly keeps things interesting here in Disney's "experimental prototype community of tomorrow." While the more serious-minded Future World is striving to spark the imagination, illuminate the technological future, and heighten environmental awareness, lively World Showcase is serving forth Oktoberfest, traditional English tea, and panoramic views of France, China, and Canada. As Future World is ushering visitors through a 21st-century greenhouse and into the mind of a 12-year-old boy, World Showcase is escorting others along a calm river in Mexico and over a stormy Norwegian sea. Together, the two entities stimulate guests to discover new things about people, places, and, indeed, their own curiosity.

If Epcot boasts a tremendous following among legal voters, it's because it has more of the things adults appreciate—live entertainment; quiet gardens; beers, wines, and frozen drinks; tasteful shops and galleries; international cuisines; sophisticated restaurants; and specialty coffees; and that's just the supplementary stuff. Epcot also woos the older crowd by making Mickey a little more scarce, by splicing enrichment of one form or another into the greater part of its amusements. It appeals to adults on a purely aesthetic level as well: World Showcase, wrapped around a vast sparkling lagoon, has a commanding natural and architectural beauty that changes with each border crossing. And Future World more than holds its own with the massive, gleaming silver geosphere of Spaceship Earth. Not surprisingly, we've met a number of Walt Disney World regulars who spend their whole vacations here at Epcot. One couple who confessed as much one afternoon at the *Rose & Crown Pub* couldn't say exactly what they liked so much about Epcot, although they were enjoying their pints of Guinness.

Epcot has its die-hard Future Worlders and its World Showcase fanatics, but most visitors list favorite pavilions

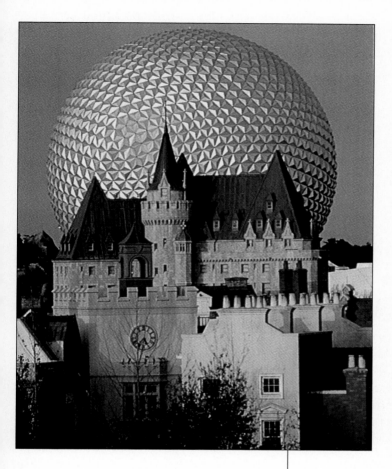

on both sides of the lagoon. Renovations and additions to the Epcot landscape over the past couple of years make this especially true today. You won't find a "New! Improved!" banner pasted to Spaceship Earth or flying from the Eiffel Tower, but Disney has made smart changes in Epcot's entertainment mix that have lightened up Future World, livened up World Showcase, and in the process, earned the park a fresh crop of admirers.

These new and improved attractions are described below so that we might present The Official Five Things We Bet You Didn't Know You Could Do At Epcot List: (1) You can get some terrific gardening tips. (2) You can simultaneously break a sweat and split the 100th annual Rose Bowl Parade right down the middle. Pedaling

Hidden Mickey

A constellation in the overhead star field within Spaceship Earth outlines Mickey with diamonds.

91

against the tide, and seemingly catching floats, bands, majorettes, and horses quite by surprise, we got a Wonder Cycle up to 15½ miles per hour. (3) You can drink fresh watermelon juice. (4) You can watch a butterfly open its wings for the first time. If you want, you can be nipping on a fresh spearmint leaf while that orange-barred sulphur butterfly decides when to flee the hatching box. (5) You can drive a Lamborghini. We took a rip-roaring spin and, when our time was up, turned from the computer screen to discover that a large crowd had gathered. Even the Innoventions attendant was impressed. "I've never seen anyone actually *flip* one!"

The most important thing to know about Epcot is that it is no small undertaking. Even the choosiest visitor will need two full days to cover the park effectively at a comfortable pace.

Since Future World and World Showcase keep different hours, strategically minded guests will take in a couple of key Future World pavilions during the hours before World Showcase opens; explore World Showcase during the afternoon, when Future World is most congested (one day, begin with the United Kingdom and work your way counterclockwise, the other, start at Mexico and proceed clockwise); return to Future World during the relatively uncongested hours immediately preceding its official closing time; and revisit World Showcase during the exceptionally pleasant evening hours to experience Illumi-Nations and the beauty of the park at night.

GUIDING PRINCIPLES: The following section is designed to offer a telling preview for first-time visitors and a timely update for returnees. Structured as a guided walking tour through the 9 themed pavilions of Future World and the 11 countries of World Showcase, it provides a geographical orientation to the layout of the park. Running commentary takes stock of all pavilions (and the attractions located therein) and their place in the adult world, highlighting the essentials, pointing out the redeeming qualities of less compelling attractions, and noting recent additions to Epcot.

For at-a-glance cues, the Touring Priorities list included in this section ranks the park's best adult bets. Note: This book's evaluations of attractions are based on the quality of the experience and the entertainment value for an adult with average interest in the topic; but if you have a serious fascination with the subject at hand—

Coming Attractions

Big change is afoot for Future World. An updated (and streamlined) Universe of Energy show is scheduled to open by year's end. A ride on the wild side of automobile testing is slated to debut at the World of Motion in mid-1997. Rounding out the Future World makeover is a completely transformed Horizons, due to follow shortly thereafter.

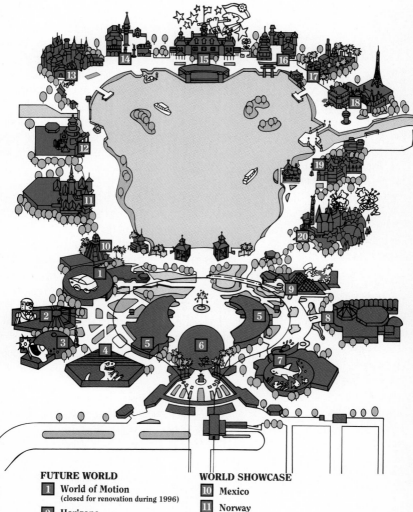

N
↓

FUTURE WORLD

1 World of Motion
(closed for renovation during 1996)

2 Horizons

3 Wonders of Life

4 Universe of Energy

5 Innoventions

6 Spaceship Earth

7 The Living Seas

8 The Land

9 Journey Into Imagination

WORLD SHOWCASE

10 Mexico

11 Norway

12 China

13 Germany

14 Italy

15 The American Adventure

16 Japan

17 Morocco

18 France

19 United Kingdom

20 Canada

Touring Priorities

DON'T MISS

Wonders of Life*
The Land*
The Living Seas
Journey Into Imagination*
France
The American Adventure**
Canada
Germany
United Kingdom

DON'T OVERLOOK

Innoventions
Spaceship Earth*
World of Motion***
Horizons***
China
Norway*
Mexico
Italy
Morocco

DON'T KNOCK YOURSELF OUT

Universe of Energy***
Journey Into Imagination
Ride*
El Rió del Tiempo boat ride

* Long lines; visit in the early A.M., late P.M.

** Pay close attention to performance schedules.

*** Closed for renovation sometime in 1996 (call 824-4321 for status).

gardening or farming, say—you should find the attraction and the pavilion (in this case, the Greenhouse Tour in The Land pavilion) all the more satisfying.

To learn the most efficient strategies for exploring Epcot, look to the Hot Tips in the margins of this section, and the flexible touring plans provided in the *Planning Ahead* chapter. For information about getting to Epcot via Walt Disney World transportation (monorail, bus, and boat) or car, consult the "Getting Around" section of the *Planning Ahead* chapter. For tips and recommendations on dining at Epcot, refer to the "Restaurant Guide" in the *Dining & Entertainment* chapter. To find out about behind-the-scenes tours of World Showcase, or about Epcot's shopping scene, turn to the *Diversions* chapter.

GETTING ORIENTED: It's helpful to think of Epcot as the park with the hourglass figure. In this conception, the gleaming silver ball of Spaceship Earth is the head and northernmost point; the pavilions of Future World are arranged on either side of Spaceship Earth in southward arches that form the outline of Epcot's "upper body"; the promenade of World Showcase pavilions connects to Future World at Epcot's "waist" and, tracing the lines of a long, full skirt, wraps itself around the World Showcase Lagoon; and The American Adventure pavilion, located due south of Spaceship Earth along the bottom hem of the World Showcase skirt, serves as the foot of Epcot.

Visitors should come prepared to do a great deal of walking, as the World Showcase Promenade itself is 1.3 miles around (and the World Showcase visitor with wanderlust will easily log double that distance). Avid walkers and the simply health conscious will be interested to know that a person typically covers more than two miles in a full day of touring Epcot, burning plenty of calories in the process. Don't be dismayed, though; Epcot is equipped with plenty of pleasant resting spots (see the margins of this section for tips to the whereabouts of said nooks) as well as some key foot-saving alternatives. Double-decker buses shuttle guests around World Showcase, and water taxis link Showcase Plaza at the foot of Future World with Germany and France, located at the farthest corners of World Showcase. Many seniors who choose to tour the smaller theme parks on foot rent a wheelchair or a self-driven electric convenience vehicle here at Epcot.

A WALKING TOUR

Our tour begins at the main entrance. This is where you take care of logistics while the gleaming ball of Spaceship Earth offers a 16-million pound hint (to you and, on a clear day, to airplane passengers flying along either Florida coast) as to the precise direction of Future World. Epcot's monorail station is right outside the gates here, as is the park's sole ATM (the latter is located on the far left just before you enter the park). On the far right side of the entranceway, also outside the gates, you can claim lost articles, pick up any cumbersome purchases you arranged to have forwarded here during your visit, and exchange currency. An important note: If you need to use the ATM or any of these other services mid-visit, remember to have your hand stamped upon exiting the turnstiles so you can reenter the park.

As you close in on the big ball, remember that there are still more services here in its shadows. If you want to avail yourself of storage lockers, pass around Spaceship Earth's right side. Otherwise, keep left. This course will lead you past the wheelchair and stroller rentals and on to Guest Relations. The primary resource for Epcot information, Guest Relations is equipped with park maps, entertainment schedules, and representatives who can provide answers to most anything that's got you confused. If you haven't made lunch or dinner reservations for the day and know you'd like to dine here at Epcot, head for Guest Relations' wall of touch-sensitive TV screens straightaway to make your arrangements. Video attendants "stand by" all morning to take your reservations. If you'd like to peruse a few menus first, note that Guest Relations has a book of current offerings. Also, when the screens are not being used to book dinner tables, they can call forth encyclopedic information about Epcot. For the really tough questions, do as we do: Follow the teachers to the **Epcot Discovery Center** in the Innoventions building on the west side of the plaza. The staff here is thoroughly steeped in Epcot-ology and the database is, as far as we can tell, bottomless. So if there's anything at all about the park or specific attractions that has you curious, just stop in and ask. In the center of the plaza, you'll find the **Epcot Tip Board**, a blackboard listing current waiting times for popular attractions.

HOT TIPS

■ On Tuesdays and Fridays, guests staying at WDW resorts may enter Epcot 1½ hours before the official opening time and get an early crack at attractions in selected Future World pavilions, usually The Living Seas, The Land, and Spaceship Earth. Early-entry days and attractions are subject to change.

■ Not coincidentally, Tuesdays and Fridays now tend to be the most crowded days at Epcot.

FUTURE WORLD

You know you're in Future World when you see a thunderous fountain that acts like it owns the place; something resembling an oversize golf ball that would require a club roughly the size of the Empire State Building; kaleidoscopic fiber-optic patterns in the walkway; abstract gardens that could pass for modern art; and freewheeling water fountains that do swan dives and geyser imitations.

This highly conceptual land makes a striking first impression, and no wonder—it's awash in the sort of grand music that might trumpet the credits of an Academy Award–winning film. And it wears its sleek architecture and futuristic landscaping like a power suit. The nine themed pavilions that comprise Future World collectively document humanity's progress in this world and offer intriguing visions of our technological fate. Such broad concerns as communications, health, and the environment serve as springboards for the attractions here, which make positively stimulating experiences of topics that commonly make boring conversation.

The recent tweaking spree has truly invigorated Future World. The croissant-shaped buildings formerly occupied by CommuniCore have a lively new tenant in Innoventions, an area devoted to interactive exhibitions that escort guests to the technological frontier. An updated Spaceship Earth now journeys well into the next century of global communication. The Land has a new raison d'être in the form of an environmental film that takes its cue from *The Lion King,* and Food Rocks, a nutrition-oriented concert that really swings. And Journey Into Imagination has a runaway hit in Honey, I Shrunk the Audience, a 3-D flick with special effects that are not to be believed. Even more exciting: Major redesigns on tap for the World of Motion, the Universe of Energy, and Horizons suggest that Future World's self-improvement kick is no passing phase.

A reminder: This tour is designed to provide a sense of place, not a plan of attack. Pavilions are described here as you would encounter them geographically, beginning with Spaceship Earth, the park's northernmost pavilion. Innoventions, which cradles the west (right, as you face World Showcase) and east (left) sides of the central plaza, is next, followed by a counterclockwise exploration of the remaining pavilions, from The Living Seas in the northwestern corner southward to The Land and Journey Into

Entertainment

Epcot offers a litany of shows and live performances throughout the day, but entertainment varies daily, so pick up a schedule at Guest Relations upon arrival.

In Future World, a resident drum and bugle corps performs several times daily at Innoventions Plaza. And every 15 minutes the immense Fountain of Nations erupts into a computer-choreographed water ballet.

Imagination, and then across the central plaza to the eastern flank of pavilions, beginning with World of Motion and proceeding to Horizons, Wonders of Life, and Universe of Energy. **Note:** World of Motion will close in January for a major renovation that should be completed by mid-1997. Universe of Energy will be closed for at least six months during 1996 while its show is updated. And Horizons will open periodically in 1996 to supplement Future World's mix. For information on the status of these pavilions during your visit, call 824-4321.

Spaceship Earth

This 180-foot-tall geosphere sticks out like a wayward planet come to roost. You may be interested to learn that the silver exterior comes from layers of anodized aluminum and polyethylene, and is composed of 954 triangular panels, not all of equal size or shape (although it takes an awfully keen eye to discern any differences). Or maybe you'd rather hear how the gleaming exterior funnels every raindrop that hits it into World Showcase Lagoon. Strange, but true.

While outward appearances can be deceiving, that is not the case here. Spaceship Earth is visually arresting to the core. The recently revamped **Spaceship Earth** ride inside the geosphere winds past exquisitely detailed scenes, tracing the evolution of human communication with Audio-Animatronics figures that here, in their element, seem more natural than many sitcom actors. There is a Benedictine monk asleep at his desk who is so realistic people hush their companions out of courtesy. Anyway, in 14 minutes you've gone from Cro-Magnon grunts all the way to the fabled information superhighway. New narration by Jeremy Irons adds drama. An astute fan might notice the attraction's fresh musical score. The new finale provides a hip, forward-looking finish for Spaceship Earth; take away the lasers and it would still be the ride's biggest head-turner. This attraction—your worst bet first thing in the morning—is least crowded during the hours just prior to park closing.

Outside, in the **Global Neighborhood**, you can dabble in interactive activities, from viewer's choice sporting events to video shopping and games.

In World Showcase, each pavilion has a cast of roving performers, any of whom *could* be appearing during your visit. Among the possibilities: bagpipe players in Canada, puppeteers in the United Kingdom, belly dancers in Morocco, drummers in Japan, singers in Italy, oompah musicians in Germany, acrobats in China, and mariachi bands in Mexico. The American Adventure features the expected fife and drum players, plus the outstanding Voices of Liberty a cappella group, and various stage shows at the America Gardens Theatre.

Epcot's grandest entertainment—a spectacle of fireworks, lasers, symphonic music, and dancing fountains known as IllumiNations—provides an extraordinarily dramatic and memorable finale every night at closing time. IllumiNations is centered around the lagoon and visible from any point on the World Showcase Promenade.

Did you know...

Epcot opened on October 1, 1982—11 years to the day after the Magic Kingdom debuted—with six Future World pavilions and nine World Showcase nations. Since opening day, The Living Seas (1986), Wonders of Life (1989), and Innoventions (1994) have been added to Future World, and Morocco (1984) and Norway (1988) have become part of World Showcase.

Innoventions

You might think of Innoventions as a boarding house for the next generation of lust objects. This is a huge technological showcase of new and forthcoming goodies for home, entertainment, and office. Within the 100,000-square-foot area, you will find an ever-changing array of hands-on exhibits and displays presented by such major manufacturers as IBM, AT&T, Apple, General Electric, Sega, Honeywell, and General Motors. If you are a devout techie or a gadget hound, this is your Consumer Electronics Show. If you are a partial or total technophobe, this is your opportunity to check out things like CD-ROM or electronic shopping in a fun, friendly, pressure-free environment. The company representatives are knowledgeable and unobtrusive; they're quick to answer any questions you might have about a product or to talk you through a computer program, but they are just as quick to honor your wishes if you'd prefer to be left alone.

Innoventions is a bright (meaning beige stands out, screaming yellow blends in) labyrinth of activity that's difficult to pass through quickly even if you cannot stand video games. (Sega runs quite an "arcade" here, however, with more than 140 new and proposed video games set out for sampling.) You should know that this Future World pavilion is housed in two structures, one on the east side of the plaza and the other on the west side. Within each building, most exhibit areas are organized by company. What you'll see here is constantly changing, just as Walt Disney envisioned.

Of course, some exhibits are more compelling than others. Your highest priorities: Start with **Eclectronics**, a sprawling area reigned over by an Audio-Animatronics figure in the buff who is quite a crackup. Here you can view high-definition television, hear for yourself the difference between $1,500 and $50,000 sound systems, redecorate the Oval Office, try snowboarding via CD-ROM, take a virtual reality tour of St. Peter's Basilica, interact with a Lamborghini, you name it. In the small corner of Innoventions occupied by Oracle, you can use an interactive television to find out what awful weather you're missing back home, preview the settings and entrées at a few of New York City's most elegant restaurants, and at least pretend to buy several thousand dollars' worth of designer clothing right off the backs of runway models. The **Walt Disney Imagineering Laboratory**—located in an out-of-the-way hallway behind the *Pasta Piazza Ristorante*—provides a fascinating behind-the-scenes preview of a future attraction and a flying carpet perspective on virtual reality.

Other areas of interest: Hammacher Schlemmer's lair is always worth browsing through, especially if the noise-reduction headphones are still around. Both IBM and Apple feature personal digital assistants and opportunities to check out the latest software on their most current computer models.

The keys to an enjoyable experience at Innoventions:
■ Adjust your touring plans if you need to, but visit when you're feeling fresh—this is no place for a zombie.
■ Take advantage of the fact that this pavilion is split between two buildings; plan to check out the one on the east side of the plaza one day and explore the one on the west side the next.
■ Check the large maps placed on stands just inside both entrances to familiarize yourself with exhibit locations.
■ Give the exhibits some time. If you breeze through, you'll miss a lot.
■ If you're not sure where to start, begin by looking over people's shoulders or taking in a show. The film *Bill Nye, the Science Guy* offers a particularly good introduction, and screenings run continually throughout the day.
■ Finally, don't hold back. Whether you're highly skeptical or curious about something you see, ask the question.

Hungry?

See the *Dining & Entertainment* chapter for restaurant recommendations and advice on reservations.

The Living Seas

The Caribbean is not as far away as you think. If you want to catch a wave, some mammoth lettuce-munching manatees, and a richly stocked coral-reef environment (pop.: 5,000) that even a scuba diver would find extraordinary, look no further. This pavilion dedicated to the study of oceanography and ocean ecology ranks among Future World's most inspired and compelling areas. During the toasty summer months, it's particularly refreshing to ogle The Living Seas' pièce de résistance, a 5.7-million-gallon tank in which a simulated Caribbean Sea and man-made reef support a glorious array of life including sharks, dolphins, barracuda, sea turtles, rays, and crustaceans.

There are two paths to this not-to-be-missed underwater vista, where in addition to colorful sea life you can observe one-person submarines and humans conducting marine experiments.

To immerse yourself thoroughly, take the **Caribbean Coral Reef Ride**. This three-pronged journey features a waterlogged film about the relationship between humankind and the seas, a simulated descent to the ocean floor (the elevator-like capsules actually plunge only an inch), and a quick taxi through an underwater viewing tunnel to the main event, **Sea Base Alpha**. Here, you can linger all you like in front of enormous eight-inch-thick windows to the undersea world (be on the lookout for sharks, moray eels, barracuda, butterfly fish, grunts, cowfish, and puffers). You needn't know a parrot fish from an angelfish to spot the ever-amphibious Homo sapiens. Scuba divers enter the tank via a floor-to-ceiling lock-out chamber, and can be observed conducting experiments (wireless radios allow them to explain their work even before they emerge, dripping, from the chamber). Exhibits offer insight to marine research methods, additional display tanks, and—unless you encounter those endangered, impossibly animated sea barges known as manatees frequently in your travels—compelling reasons to stick around awhile.

If you're hungry for more than oceanic knowledge, every table in the *Coral Reef* restaurant (located around the bend from the pavilion's main entrance) has an unobstructed view of the main reef environment.

Of course, no high-seas adventure is complete without the opportunity to shout "Land ho!" so it's only right that The Land is the next pavilion on the horizon.

Epcot Unplugged

Insight to the inner workings of Epcot is easier to come by than you might think. The passwords:

- Greenhouse Tour (at The Land pavilion)
- Gardens of the World (described in the *Diversions* chapter)
- Hidden Treasures of World Showcase (described in the *Diversions* chapter)

The Land

This popular six-acre plot, surpassed in size only by Innoventions (or the manatees at The Living Seas), explores themes related to food and farming while planting seeds of environmental consciousness. Underneath this pavilion's dramatic, skylit roof, you'll find a well-balanced slate of attractions, a bountiful food court, and a lazy susan of a sit-down restaurant, the *Garden Grill*, which rotates *very* slowly past several of the ecosystems featured in the pavilion's boat ride. All things considered, The Land merits two green thumbs up as the purveyor of one of Future World's strongest lineups.

The **Living with the Land** boat ride is a beautifully informative 13½-minute journey that escorts you through a stormy prairie, a windswept desert, and a South American rain forest en route to experimental greenhouses and an area given over to fish farming. The dripping, squawking rain forest is so realistic you'd need to chomp on a fern to truly believe it's all plastic. The

narration is an interesting commentary on the history and future of agriculture. The impressive greenhouses show futuristic technology at work on real crops (many of which are served here at Epcot), with NASA experiments and cucumbers in desert training among the highlights. This popular attraction is best visited in the morning or during the hours just prior to park closing.

If you're an avid gardener, or a farmer, or the Living with the Land has you intrigued, we heartily recommend the 45-minute **Greenhouse Tour**, which covers the same terrain in a much more intimate, detailed, and behind-the-scenes fashion. Reservations are necessary and must be made in person on the day you wish to tour (behind the Green Thumb Emporium shop on the lower level). Spots fill up quickly, so reserve yours first thing.

The Land's newest attraction, **Circle of Life**, packages ecological concerns in a fable featuring Timon and Pumbaa, the wisenheimer meerkat-warthog duo from *The Lion King*, as developers, and Simba as the environmentally

Knock on Plastic

While they're good enough to fool any lumberjack, every last tree in the Living with the Land boat ride's ecosystems is plastic to the core. Disney artists molded the trunks and branches from live specimens, then snapped on polyethylene leaves one at a time. So be sure to see the trees for the forest.

On Pins and Needles

On a recent visit, we observed a couple in their mid-forties so fixated by an exhibit at Journey Into Imagination's Image Works that they wouldn't lift their eyes to acknowledge the other's spontaneous artistry. Standing on either side of a table whose surface was composed entirely of long, soft-edged pins, they stood, running their hands along the bottom of the table as if playing a harp. As their hands plied the pins, they pushed up to form fleeting patterns, and the one-upmanship began. He made a perfect fish. She made a dolphin. He made a school of fish. She made a swooping gull and a fish. We didn't stick around to see the finale.

sensitive lion. The 20-minute 70mm movie also features the Oscar-winning song "Circle of Life."

Remember **Food Rocks**—a so-called musical tribute to good nutrition that turns out to be more of a nutrition-oriented salute to great music—as a notable new arrival that makes a satisfying snack. This 15-minute concert performed by endearing Audio-Animatronics lip-synchers is Disney showing its sense of humor. Among the reasons you'll be an instant groupie are your charming host, Füd Wrapper, a rapper after Tone Loc's heart; Pita Gabriel singing "I wanna be your high fiber"; The Refrigerator Police with "Every bite you take, every egg you break" (guess who is a milk carton with dark sunglasses?); and the Get-the-Point Sisters with a revised "Respect." It's nearly always possible to get into the next show. But wander around the muraled pre-show area for a bit and you'll learn all kinds of interesting food facts, like what Ethiopian goats have to do with your morning coffee.

Journey Into Imagination

While you'd think that glass buildings would leave very little to the imagination, the glass pyramids that house Journey Into Imagination have quite the opposite effect. Fronted by wonderfully unpredictable fountains that seem to have agendas of their own, this pavilion is, predictably, one of Future World's most whimsical.

The attraction at Journey Into Imagination that earns a solid high five is **Honey, I Shrunk the Audience**. If you had time to visit only a few attractions at Epcot, this spectacle of a 3-D movie (which debuted in 1994) should be high on your list. The 17-minute film is so riddled with

World of Motion

You won't see Disney Imagineers rolling this shiny, wheel-shaped pavilion away to any garage, but come January 1996 it will effectively become a World of Suspended Motion, at least so far as guests are concerned. The reason: The pavilion formerly devoted to chronicling the past, present, and future of transportation is being overhauled. It's not *going* anywhere, but when it reopens (e.t.a.: mid-1997), there will be a new attraction inside. Gear up for an exciting introduction to automobile testing. Ride vehicles will barrel up steep hills, zip down straightaways, squeak around hairpin turns, and slam on the brakes (and not always in the best road conditions). Until then, visions of Corvettes and Firebirds will be dancing in our heads.

sensational special effects that the audience is consistently reduced to a shrieking, squirming, giggling mass. The experience is not rough, but the effects *are* heightened with a little suspense, so we won't say any more. This popular attraction is least congested in the morning.

On the other side of the priority spectrum, ironically enough, is the pavilion's title attraction. The **Journey Into Imagination Ride**—a 14-minute trip in which an adventurer named Dreamfinder and his purple dragon, Figment, explore the creative process—is cute and lighthearted. Better yet, head upstairs to sample the interactive offerings of **Image Works**. (On your way, be sure to check out the terrific photography display, located just outside the entrance. The images are winners of Kodak's International Newspaper Snapshot Awards.) In Image Works, amuse yourself by trying your hand at conducting the Electronic Philharmonic orchestra. Basically, you step up to a console that has panels representing woodwind, string, percussion, and brass sections. To raise and lower the volume of a section, you raise and lower a hand over the appropriate panel. Another highlight is Stepping Tones, a floor endowed with such dazzling sound qualities (step here, it's a fiddle; there, it's a drum roll) you'll wish you'd brought a vacuum cleaner.

A Healthy Crop

If you're eating your vegetables (and fruits) at Future World's *Garden Grill, Coral Reef,* or *Sunshine Season Food Fair,* odds are good that you're sharing in The Land pavilion's bounty. Some 30 tons of produce are harvested each year from The Land's greenhouses. Talk about fresh local ingredients!

Have Q, Get A

Exactly how does the sphere of Spaceship Earth catch rainwater and funnel it into World Showcase Lagoon? Where do the laser beams come from in IllumiNations? What sort of computers are used to choreograph the dancing fountains? Who was the composer for the score of *Impressions de France* in World Showcase? How can I set up a hydroponics garden at home?

Epcot has a way of stimulating an almost childlike curiosity in adults, and the Epcot Discovery Center, located upstairs in the Innoventions building on the west side of Innoventions Plaza, has more answers than anyone could ask for.

Horizons

The three-acre pavilion is nothing if not forward thinking. Here you can do a little time travel and, depending on how you and your compatriots vote at the climactic moment, zoom o'er land, sea, or space. The cars tilt back and vibrate, accompanied by sound effects and close-up visuals that make it seem almost plausible that you're traveling at warp speed.

But first, you'll recall the future of yesteryear in Looking Back at Tomorrow. Then the suspended, continuously moving vehicles will transport you into the Omni-Sphere Theatre, where in-your-face scenes of a Space Shuttle launch and of growing crystals are projected onto a pair of hemispherical screens 80 feet in diameter.

The voyage continues to Nova Cite and its advanced transportation and communication systems, which include holographic telephones and trains that operate by magnetic levitation; then it's on to Mesa Verde, where voice-controlled robots harvest genetically engineered fruits and vegetables in a once-arid desert. In Sea Castle, still other robotic devices try their hand at kelp farms; and in the free-floating space colony of Omega Centauri, all manner of far-out things occur. Zero-gravity basketball, anyone?

Note: This pavilion is scheduled to be open periodically in 1996 while the World of Motion and the Universe of Energy are undergoing renovations. When it is not "covering" for these other pavilions, Horizons will be busy reinventing itself, as a completely new attraction is expected to open here in the near future.

Wonders of Life

While the 72-foot-tall steel DNA molecule certainly marks the territory of this mostly whimsical pavilion devoted to health and fitness concerns, the sculpture also provides a visual reminder of the uniqueness of this area. Wonders of Life has three basic things currently found nowhere else in Epcot—a true thrill ride, a health food bar, and (believe it or not) exercise equipment.

First, the main attraction: **Body Wars**, a frenetic five-minute trip through the human body in a flight simulator, could be the fraternal twin of Star Tours, the rocky ride through space located at Disney-MGM Studios, but for a couple of things. It is a year older and a couple of notches rougher than its counterpart at the Studios. The premise

Did you know...

■ If the 75-foot DNA sculpture standing in front of Wonders of Life were a real DNA molecule, the human whose genetic information it carried would stand millions of miles tall.

■ At the time of its construction in 1982, the Universe of Energy was the largest privately funded solar-power installation in the world.

of Body Wars is that you are along for the ride on a routine medical probe to remove a splinter (from the inside) when things get out of hand. Before you know it you are barreling through the human lungs, heart, and brain. Body Wars is a tremendously exciting journey, both visually and physically, that rates among Walt Disney World's biggest thrills—but it is also a turbulent ride that encompasses a lot of very jerky movements.

Note that if you're especially squeamish, you may find the visual content too much in this context. If you are pregnant, you will not be permitted to board this ride. You should also bypass Body Wars if you've recently eaten, have a back problem or a heart condition, are susceptible to motion sickness, or have other physical limitations. While crowds flock to this attraction, it is generally least congested first thing in the morning and during the hours just prior to park closing.

Another Wonders of Life attraction that merits not-to-be-missed status is **Cranium Command**, an utterly

Like Child's Play

As Walt Disney once said, "Laughter is no enemy to learning." And so it is that Future World is blessed with attractions that make great fun of enlightenment. For entertainment so whimsical you're barely conscious of any information intake, consider the following amusements:

- Cranium Command and Body Wars at Wonders of Life

- Innoventions

- Food Rocks at The Land

- Honey, I Shrunk the Audience and Image Works at Journey Into Imagination

tame, utterly delightful 17-minute journey into the mind of a 12-year-old boy. This is an attraction so good Billy Crystal would have a tough time making it funnier. The setup, basically, is that the commander of a specialized corps of brain pilots is issuing assignments, and our pal Buzzy is dealt the unlucky task of piloting an adolescent boy. The show follows a day in this boy's life, with Buzzy calling the shots. Celebrity cameos include George Wendt (Norm from "Cheers") manning the stomach.

For a little more whimsical fun, explore the audio and visual challenges of the Sensory Funhouse, located just outside Cranium Command. And don't neglect the stable of Wonder Cycles, computerized stationary bicycles that let you pedal (headlong into traffic) through the Rose Bowl parade and Disneyland.

While Wonders of Life ranks with Journey Into Imagination among Future World's most lighthearted pavilions, it does have a serious side. This is best evidenced in the far-left corner of the pavilion at Frontiers of Medicine, a timely exhibit that showcases recent medical advances.

Universe of Energy

Behind this unassuming mirrored facade lies a popular pavilion on a serious power trip (it draws some of its own electricity from photovoltaic cells mounted on the roof). Universe of Energy is notable primarily for its life-like dinosaurs, some of the largest Audio-Animatronics animals ever created.

The pavilion is given over entirely to a multi-tiered show that explores the origins of fossil fuels and muses about energy alternatives. It begins in a large, (intentionally) musty-smelling theater, where arresting visuals are shown on a montage of triangular panels that rotate in perfect sync with changing images. At one point, the seating area rotates and splits into six 97-passenger vehicles, which then travel through parted curtains into the warm, clammy, sulfur-scented air of the primeval world. Here, you encounter erupting volcanoes, an eerie fog, and loud, lifelike prehistoric creatures locked in combat, rearing up suddenly from a tidal pool, and gazing down at you like vultures.

Note: This pavilion will be closed for renovation for at least six months during 1996. The attraction is expected to reopen later in the year as an updated, streamlined version of its former self, with dinosaurs intact.

Leave Future World by walking back through its central plaza past the fountain that aspires to be Niagara Falls (in an odd case of confused identity or perhaps an attempt at foreshadowing, it's called the Fountain of Nations). As you head south over the walkway that leads to World Showcase, be sure to look to each side: On the right, a spontaneously erupting fountain is delivering a merciless soaking (mostly to children); farther down to the left, the resident flock of flamingos is bathing in the canal. Welcome to the flip side of Future World.

WORLD SHOWCASE

Think of World Showcase as a handful of gourmet jelly beans, the sort so flavorful they make your taste buds believe you're actually putting away strawberry cheesecake, Champagne punch, and chocolate pudding. You know they're just jelly beans, of course, but you pretend, fully savoring the essence of that piña colada. In the same way, World Showcase cajoles your senses into accepting its 11 international pavilions at face value, enveloping you in such delectable representations of, for example, Germany, Japan, and Mexico, that you are content to play along.

This parade of nations, a cultural thoroughfare wrapped around a lagoon the size of 85 football fields, is

International Gateway

Think of this second entrance as Epcot's back door. The turnstiles here provide a direct "in" to World Showcase, depositing guests between the France and United Kingdom pavilions. Because the International Gateway is connected via walkway and water launches to the *Yacht Club, Beach Club, Dolphin, Swan*, and (once it opens in mid-1996) *Disney's BoardWalk*, guests at these properties have exceptional access to Epcot. Be aware that:

■ Wheelchairs are available for rent at this entrance.

■ If you plan ahead, you can make a surprisingly quick exit from here after IllumiNations.

■ Nothing in World Showcase opens until 11 A.M., so guests arriving earlier must walk to Future World at the opposite end of the park.

marked by dramatic mood swings. The atmosphere changes markedly with each border crossing, going from positively romantic to utterly serene, toe-tappingly upbeat, patriotic, festive, wistfully Old World, or cheerfully relaxed in a matter of yards.

Of course, the World Showcase pavilions are not simply outstanding mood pieces, but occasions to get uniquely acquainted with the people, history, and beauty of nearly a dozen nations. Each has a strong, unmistakable sense of place that announces itself with painstakingly recreated landmarks (among them, Doge's Palace in Venice, and a Norwegian stave church) and faithful landscaping that ensures bougainvillea in Mexico and lotus blossoms in China. Each contributes its culinary specialties to an apple-tart-to-zabaglione smorgasbord that makes World Showcase one of Walt Disney World's hottest meal tickets.

To transport yourself totally, try to supplement the smattering of "attractions"—panoramic films, theater and dinner shows, boat rides, and the nightly not-to-be-missed fireworks extravaganza known as IllumiNations—with the legions of less structured pursuits. Start by making a point of trying to catch one street performance per country. So frequent they're practically ongoing (check your schedule for exact times), these live entertainments encompass everything from mariachi bands to acrobatics, belly dancing, and bagpipes—and they make a great accompaniment to a mobile wine tasting. Take time, too, to chitchat with the "locals" in each village (nearly all of whom claim the represented country as their homeland) and to talk with visiting artisans as they demonstrate their crafts. To personalize your journey even more, make a mission of snacking, drinking, shopping, gallery hopping, or even bench warming your way around the World.

Structurally, World Showcase is perhaps the most user-friendly area of Walt Disney World's theme parks. You may get tired walking along the 1.3-mile promenade that leads past all pavilions as it encircles the lagoon, but you won't lose your sense of direction. While locations of countries here don't correspond at all to their placement on the planet, the landscape offers a wealth of Eiffel Tower–like clues that *almost* preclude use of a map. Because World Showcase is less attraction driven (5 of the 11 countries have no attractions, per se), it requires less strategical maneuvering.

Snacking Around the World

When your stomach's growling, head for World Showcase, where every country has a little something to hit whatever spot you're looking to fill. Here's an inkling of what we have (happily) sampled.

Near the Canadian border, it's frozen yogurt at the *Refreshment Port*. In the United Kingdom, we like the stuffed baked potatoes outside the *Rose & Crown Pub*. In France, we appreciate the *Boulangerie Pâtisserie's* fine snacking sensibility, particularly the pastry known as the Marvelous. In Morocco,

If World Showcase came with an instructions booklet, it might say:

■ Touring is a clockwise or a counterclockwise proposition that's most pleasant when begun as soon as this part of Epcot opens.

■ Shops are optimally saved for the afternoon, when the throngs from Future World have descended, significantly lengthening lines for movies, rides, and shows.

■ The motion pictures at Canada, France, and China are often better appreciated when spaced out over two days.

■ IllumiNations, the amazing spectacle of fireworks, lasers, and music that closes the place down every night, is the biggest draw in all of Epcot. The display is visible from most any point along the World Showcase promenade.

Moving along, this tour describes World Showcase pavilions in the order they're encountered when walking counterclockwise around the lagoon.

Canada

In a marked departure from the real world, a refreshment stand poised a good 50 yards before the border makes it possible to arrive in Canada with Molson in hand. This large pavilion—which merits kudos as the site of an outstanding panoramic film, some interesting shops, and the coolest spot in World Showcase—covers an impressive amount of territory in its bid to capture the distinctive beauty and cultural diversity of the Western Hemisphere's largest nation. An artful ode to the Indians of Canada's northwest (towering totem poles and a trading post) leads to an architectural tribute to French Canada (the Hotel du Canada here is a hybrid of Ottawa's Château Laurier and Quebec's Château Frontenac).

From here, follow the sounds of rushing water to find the cooling sprays of a miniaturized Niagara Falls that's tucked neatly into the face of a Canadian Rocky and usually blessed with a rainbow. A stunning feature film, a visual anthem of sorts appropriately called **O Canada!**, is presented, in all its Circle-Vision 360 glory, inside the mountain itself. Filmed with nine cameras mounted on a 400-pound rig that crews suspended from a helicopter and a B-25 bomber among other things, the 17-minute movie places you smack in the middle of most all things

we go for the baklava. Japan's *Matsu No Ma Lounge* sates when we're in a sushi frame of mind. The American Adventure's *Liberty Inn* provides—what else—apple pie, french fries, and Coca-Cola. Italy's Delizie Italiane offers chocolates, and a nearby cart stands by with gelati. Germany comes through with killer soft pretzels, potato salad, and bratwurst at *Sommerfest*. China squeaks by with egg rolls at the *Lotus Blossom Café*. Norway (specifically *Kringla Bakeri og Kafe*) satisfies sweet and savory instincts most notably with open-face sandwiches and *vaflers* (heart-shaped waffles) made on the spot and topped with fresh preserves. And Mexico surprises with fresh watermelon juice alongside the requisite chips and salsa at the lagoonside *Cantina de San Angel*.

In other words: No reservations? No problem.

Quiet Nooks

- *Fountain View Espresso & Bakery* in Future World

- Plaza de Los Amigos inside Mexico's pyramid

- Stave Church Gallery in Norway

- Benches near reflecting pools in China

- Lagoonside benches near the gondola in Italy

- Rose garden on the side of The American Adventure

- Bijutsu-kan Gallery, hillside gardens, *Matsu No Ma Lounge*, in Japan

- Tucked-away garden with benches in France

- Herb and topiary gardens at rear of United Kingdom pavilion and the *Rose & Crown Pub*

- Waterfall and mountain setting at rear of Canada pavilion

Canadian, including a hockey game, a flock of Canadian geese taking flight, vast reindeer herds, and the Royal Canadian Mounted Police. Because it's a standing engagement, it's best viewed earlier in the day, when the standing's still good. Whatever you do, don't miss it. As you leave, check out the bountiful greenery inspired by the famous Butchart Gardens in Victoria, British Columbia—while not as cool as the falls out back, they're still a great place to lay claim to a bench, especially when the Caledonia Bagpipe Band is performing.

United Kingdom

This cheery neighborhood, which reveals its identity with the bright-red phone booths dotting its quaint cobblestone streets, is clearly a fine place for a spot of tea, a bit of shopping, or making new friends over a pint of ale. What's less obvious: The knotted herb garden tucked behind the thatched-roof cottage (note the spearmint plants), the butterfly hatchery on the hill behind it, and the courtyard at the rear of the pavilion where, in addition to peace and quiet, you'll find a traditional English hedge maze and a Mary Poppins topiary. Also, a table at the *Rose & Crown Pub* is the best perspective from which to view this pavilion, because the cobblestone streets, phone booths, and Tudor, Georgian, and Victorian structures seem all the more real from the window of a friendly English pub. If it's late afternoon and you could use a pick-me-up, try the *Rose & Crown's* traditional English tea (one seating only, at 3:30 P.M.—you'll need a reservation), featuring tasty sandwiches, pastries, and scones.

Architectural enlightenment is a great excuse to dally in the United Kingdom's fine shops. You can cover 300 years of building styles just by walking from the slate floor of The Tea Caddy (a replica of the thatched-roof cottage of Shakespeare's Anne Hathaway) straight through to the carpeted room with the Waterford crystal chandelier, which signals your arrival to the Neoclassical period and the fancy-schmancy Royal Doulton, Ltd., shop known as The Queen's Table. Note how the building that houses the Magic of Wales widens from foundation to roof; this is because property tax in the 1600s was based on square footage at ground level.

Because the United Kingdom has no queue-driven attractions, it is easily explored any time of day.

France

A footbridge from the United Kingdom leads across a picturesque canal to one of the most romantic areas of World Showcase. Petite streets and Eiffel Tower aside, you're looking at Paris during the Belle Epoque ("beautiful age") years of the late 19th century. The one-time Parisian institution Les Halles is recreated here, as is a one-ninth-scale Eiffel Tower that would be infinitely more evocative were it not so obviously perched atop a building (note that the model here is brown, to reflect the Eiffel Tower's original color). Luxurious boutiques, bustling sidewalk cafés, and, of course, pastries that announce their presence *par avion* are among the big draws here, as is the wine-tasting counter at the nicely stocked La Maison du Vin. Beckoning, too, is one of the most peaceful spots in all of Epcot—a quiet park on the canal side of the pavilion that might have leapt off the canvas of Georges Seurat's *Sunday Afternoon on the Island of La Grande Jatte*.

But the biggest lure here is certainly the breathtaking 18-minute film **Impressions de France**, which puts its five 21- by 27-foot screens to terrific use in a tour de France that ranges from Alpine skiing to foothills of buttery pastries. If you know France, you'll love it; if you don't, you'll want to. The superb score featuring French classical composers could stand on its own. *Impressions de France* is least congested during the morning and early-evening hours. A few key words to help you communicate with the locals: Say *bonjour* (pronounced "bohn-zhoor") for good day, *merci beaucoup* ("mehr-see boh-koo") for thank you very much, and *au revoir* ("oh revwar") for goodbye.

Morocco

This enchanting area—arguably the most meticulously crafted of all the represented nations—also happens to be the loudest World Showcase pavilion. The authenticity has something to do with the fact that nine tons of tile were handmade, handcut, and handlaid by Moroccan artisans into the mosaics seen here. The prayer tower at the entrance takes after the famous Koutoubia Minaret in

Tired of Walking?

Double-decker buses shuttle guests around World Showcase, and water taxis link Showcase Plaza at the foot of Future World with Germany and France, located at the farthest corners of World Showcase. Convenient—but keep in mind that it's quicker to walk.

Where the Art Is

Exhibits change periodically, but here's an indication of what you can expect to see.

■ Mexico's "Reign of Glory" exhibit features pre-Columbian pieces, some of which are on loan from the Smithsonian.

■ Norway's tiny Stave Church Gallery contains exhibits on Norwegian explorations of the North and South poles.

■ Japan's Bijutsu-kan Gallery displays traditional Japanese art and carvings.

■ Morocco's Gallery of Arts and History showcases intricate Moroccan tilework and costumes.

■ China's House of the Whispering Willows displays ancient Chinese art and artifacts.

Marrakesh, and sets the scene for the energetic Moroccan musicians and dancers who perform in the courtyard. The Bab Boujouloud gate, patterned after one that stands in the city of Fez, leads to the medina (or old part of the city), a tangled array of narrow passageways where hand-knotted Berber carpets, leather goods, and brass items and basketry are among the wares for sale.

Walk through the bazaar, whether or not you feel like shopping, so you can get a feel for the medina and try out your Arabic. Hello is *salam alekoum* (pronounced "sah-lahm ah-lee-cohm"), thank you is *shokran* ("showk-ran"), and goodbye is *b'slama* ("bs-lemah"). The medina also brings you to the entrance of *Marrakesh* restaurant, notable for its North African menu, its belly dancers, and the fact that it's about the only sit-down restaurant in World Showcase where you can frequently get a table without a reservation. Make a point of checking out the extraordinary tilework and costumes displayed at Gallery of Arts and History, and be on the lookout for visiting artisans demonstrating their craft. It may interest you to learn that the gardens of this pavilion are irrigated by an ancient working waterwheel located on the promenade. Morocco is easily toured any time of day.

Japan

As quietly inviting as Morocco is vibrantly enticing, Japan is a pavilion of considerable beauty and serenity. Its most prominent landmarks are the red *torii* gate (a popular good-luck symbol) that stands close to the lagoon, and the five-tiered pagoda, created in the mold of an eighth-century shrine located in Nara. Note that each level of the pagoda represents one of the elements that, according to Buddhist teachings, produced everything in the universe (from bottom to top: earth, water, fire, wind, and sky).

The most compelling features of this pavilion—restaurants aside—are the entertainment (the One World Taiko drummers), the elaborate detail of its manicured gardens (note the differently patterned fences, the bamboo "scarecrow" contraption in the stream), and the consistently strong art exhibits displayed at the small Bijutsu-kan Gallery. Japan also claims one of the largest shops in all of Epcot. The Mitsukoshi Department Store, housed in a structure reminiscent of a section of the Gosho Imperial Palace that was originally constructed in Kyoto in A.D. 794, counts bonsai, kimonos, and dolls

among its many offerings. This pavilion is easily toured any time of day. Note that good morning in Japanese is *ohayo gozaimasu* (pronounced "oh-hah-yoh goh-zah-ee-mahs"), thank you is *arigato gozaimasu* ("ah-ree-gah-toh goh-zah-ee-mahs"), and good evening is *konban wa* ("kohn-bahn wah").

The American Adventure

This, the centerpiece pavilion of World Showcase, is so devoutly devoted to Americana it can bring out the Norman Rockwell in you even when you're cranky. Housed in a Colonial-style manse that combines elements of Independence Hall, the Old State House in Boston, Monticello, and various structures in Colonial Williamsburg, it's dressed for the part. The 30-minute show inside—an evocative multimedia presentation about American history—is among Disney's best, both for its astonishingly detailed sets and sophisticated Audio-Animatronics figures, and for its ability to rouse goose bumps and chills from unsuspecting patriots. Ben Franklin and Mark Twain lead what's been called "a hundred-yard dash capturing the spirit of the country at specific moments in time."

A talented a cappella vocal group called The Voices of Liberty usually entertains in the lobby before the show begins (so talented are these singers that they are consistently able to get most every person in the place singing "God Bless America"). The wait for The American Adventure can be long because the show itself is lengthy,

HOT TIP

Get to the lobby of The American Adventure at 3 P.M., and you're in for a double treat: Two a cappella groups—the first and second shifts of The Voices of Liberty—sing together, filling the space with the sounds of 16 to 20 (terrific) voices.

so check your schedule for times and plan accordingly. This pavilion also features a fast-food restaurant and the lagoonside **America Gardens Theatre**, where you may very well find worthwhile entertainment. (Check your schedule for current offerings.) Note: The rose garden at the side of The American Adventure pavilion features roses named after U.S. presidents, and can be a relaxing spot—but only between visits from Pocahontas and other characters.

Italy

This little Italy is defined by an abiding, you-are-there ambience and meticulous authenticity that extends from the gondolas tied to striped moorings at the pavilion's very own Venetian island to the homemade (before your eyes) fettuccine and spaghetti at its popular *L'Originale Alfredo di Roma Ristorante*. Look to the very top of the scaled-down Venetian Campanile dominating the romantic piazza here, and you'll see an angel covered in gold leaf that was molded into a spitting image of the one atop the bell tower in the real St. Mark's Square in Venice. The Doge's Palace here is so faithfully rendered that its facade resembles the marbled pattern of the original.

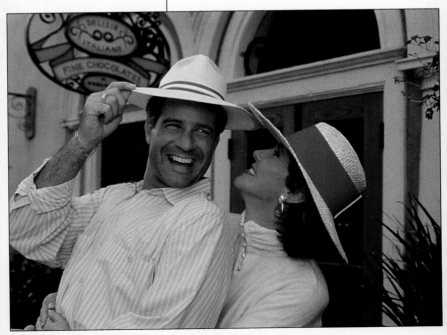

Adding to the effect are tall, slender stands of Italian cypress, authentic replicas of Venetian statues, potted flowers, and olive and citrus trees.

The Italy pavilion is among the most romantic and evocative areas in all the World Showcase. It has no major attractions per se, but between its memorable street performers and the strolling musicians who perform during dinner at *Alfredo's*, it has all the entertainment it needs. The pavilion offers some interesting shopping options, including one of World Showcase's rare clothing stores, and is easily visited at any time of day. When in Italy, note that good day is *buon giorno* ("boo-on jor-no"), thank you is *grazie* ("graht-see-eh"), and goodbye is *arrivederci* ("ah ree-veh-dair-chee").

Germany

In a word: oompah. Arguably the most festive country in all of World Showcase, Germany is immediately recognizable by its fairy-tale architecture. To the rear of the central cobblestone square (which is named for Saint George), you'll see a giant cuckoo clock, complete with Hummel figurines that emerge on the hour. Immediately past this clock lies the *Biergarten*, the vast restaurant and entertainment hall that—thanks to lively lunch and dinner shows primed with German beer, sausages, yodelers, and folk dancers—serves as the pinnacle of this pavilion's entertainment. For a more impromptu beer or piece of Black Forest cake, there's an outdoor counter called *Sommerfest*; a strolling accordionist and trio frequently usher the *gemütlich* atmosphere of *Biergarten* out into the square.

Germany also scores with the Weinkeller, which offers one of two wine tasting opportunities at World Showcase (the other's in France), and with shops that rate among the most tempting of any in the World Showcase pavilions. In Glas Und Porzellan, it's almost always possible to watch a Goebel artist demonstrating the elaborate process by which Hummel figurines are created. Germany is easily toured at any time of day. When in Germany, good day is *guten Tag* ("goot-en-tahkh"), thank you very much is *danke schön* ("dahn-kuh shurn"), and goodbye is *auf Wiedersehen* ("owf vee-der-zay-in").

For the Lovebirds...

Epcot's World Showcase has some great romantic spots, namely:

- The El Rió del Tiempo boat ride and the *San Angel Inn* in Mexico
- The lovely courtyard at the rear of the United kingdom
- Italy's piazza and gondola landing
- Every inch of France

China

This at once serene and exciting pavilion is marked by a dramatic half-scale replica of Beijing's Temple of Heaven set behind stands of whistling bamboo and quiet reflecting pools, where you'll often see an egret posturing on a rock and almost always see floating lotus blossoms. Traditional Chinese music wafts over the sound system. When you're looking for a nice spot to relax, remember the benches near the reflecting pools here. In addition to its arresting gardens, the pavilion features House of the Whispering Willows, an ever-changing exhibit of ancient Chinese art and artifacts from well-known collections that's always worth a look. Live entertainment here is invariably stirring, with performances of the Chinese Lion Dance and demonstrations by the Red Panda Acrobats.

But the main reason to visit China is the spectacular Circle-Vision 360 film shown inside the Temple of Heaven, which is right up there with the extraordinary films presented at Canada and France. Basically, you stand, and ***Wonders of China*** whisks you on an incredible 19-minute, blink-and-you've-missed-the-Great-Wall journey that visits Inner Mongolia, Beijing's Forbidden City, and Shanghai, and provides fascinating glimpses of the people of China. Pay special attention to the fleeting scene of mist-enshrouded Huangshan Mountain if you can; the film crew and 40 laborers had to haul the 600-pound camera nearly a mile uphill for those three seconds of footage. When in China, hello is *ni hao* ("nee how"), thank you is *xiexie* ("shay-shay"), and goodbye is *zai jian* ("sigh jee-ahn").

Norway

This 11th addition to the World Showcase landscape is immediately intriguing. A curious array of buildings ring the pavilion's cobblestone square, including a reproduction of a wooden stave church (an endangered species of sorts, with just 30 remaining in Norway) and a replica of the 14th-century Akershus Castle that still stands in Oslo's harbor. Beside a grassy-roofed, thick-logged structure that harks back to Setesdal, there's a statue of a Norwegian running champion, living legend Grete Waitz. This Land of the Midnight Sun has added some twists to the World Showcase lineup—among them, performances of traditional Norwegian music and Norwegian handicrafts of the gorgeous hand-knit sweater variety. The stave church houses a gallery of artifacts recalling Norwegians' explorations of the North and South poles (don't skip it, if only to see the inside of the church). But Norway really scores with **Maelstrom**, a ride in dragon-headed boats through Viking territory that is undoubtedly among Epcot's best rides. An inspired and technologically sophisticated voyage that surprises you with a troll here, a backward plunge there, a sudden waterfall here, a storm there, Maelstrom doesn't throw big punches; it just keeps you guessing. The ten-minute trip lets you out at a quaint Norwegian village, then finishes up with a brief film on the essence of Norway. This attraction is least crowded in the evening. When in Norway, hello is *god dag* (pronounced "goo dahg"), thank you is *takk* ("tock"), and goodbye is *adjø* ("ahdyur").

Mexico

There's no mistaking this pavilion's identity. A wild thicket of tropical foliage leads past squawking (sometimes shrieking) macaws to a great pyramid. Inside, you wend your way through a brief but consistently engaging cultural exhibit (past displays have included pre-Columbian artifacts on loan from the Smithsonian) to the main event. What you see next—a thoroughly romantic vision of a quaint Mexican village at twilight—is among the most wondrously escapist visions in World Showcase. True to form, there are stands selling colorful sombreros, baskets, pottery, and piñatas (the shop off to the left is your source for higher quality Mexican handicrafts). In the rear of the plaza, note the dimly lit *San Angel Inn* and, behind it, the river and the smoking volcano. Here too, you'll find the embarkation point for **El Rió del Tiempo**, a pleasantly relaxing six-minute boat trip through Mexican history that might be described as a subdued south-of-the-border It's A Small World. If you encounter long lines early in the day, skip it, and check back later. Note, too, that the mariachi bands performing inside and outside of this imposing pavilion are quite good—particularly when you have a margarita in your hand. When in Mexico, hello is *hola* (pronounced "oh-lah"), thank you very much is *muchas gracias* ("moo-chahs grah-see-ahs"), and goodbye is *adios* ("ah-dee-ohs").

a glass of wine from La Maison du Vin in France; a glass of hot mint tea (poured from three feet above) at *Marrakesh* in Morocco; Kirin beer or sake specialty drinks at *Matsu No Ma Lounge* in Japan; wine in Italy, although, true to tradition, you'll have to drink it with a meal or at least dessert at *Alfredo's*; Beck's beer and H. Schmitt Sohne wine in Germany's *Sommerfest*; Chinese wine and beer at the *Lotus Blossom Café*; Ringnes drafts from *Kringla Bakeri og Kafe* in Norway; and what else but margaritas in Mexico's *Cantina de San Angel*.

DISNEY-MGM STUDIOS

L ike an actress who is just right for the part, Disney-MGM Studios is perfectly cast as the vivacious, movie-obsessed theme park that is seemingly incapable of keeping a secret. Since its 1989 debut, this park has worked hard to make the transition from entertaining sidekick to leading lady, and it has succeeded.

Disney-MGM Studios holds its own at Walt Disney World not merely by offering ticket holders a rose-colored reminiscence of 1930s Hollywood, but by resurrecting decades of Tinseltown magic as innovative rides, stage shows, and theater programs, and by baring all manner of backstage secrets. The park immerses guests in showbiz to the point that they can momentarily forget there *is* life beyond television and motion pictures.

You'd do well to think of the Studios as the adult's Magic Kingdom. The place is magical, but in a more meaningful and sophisticated way; it is marked by a whimsicality far more ageless than that which pervades the Magic Kingdom itself. Sure, it has a Beauty and the Beast Stage Show and a 3-D movie featuring the Muppets, but these hardly constitute a satellite Fantasyland. In fact, at times the Studios seems to have even been scripted for a mature crowd, carefully crafted with a wink of the eye by (and for) grownups to elicit knowing laughs and no-holds-barred nostalgia.

Certainly, The Great Movie Ride has greater meaning to an audience steeped in the films of James Cagney, Judy Garland, and Humphrey Bogart. Another case in point: the *50's Prime Time Café,* a nostalgia-fest of a restaurant that harks back to the era of "Father Knows Best" and "I Love Lucy" with a montage of black-and-white television clips, pot roast, Formica tables, fussbudgety moms, and vinyl sofas. It's packed with inside jokes the younger crowd just wouldn't get. Meanwhile, over at the frightful Twilight Zone Tower of Terror, any adult with an inkling of Rod Serling's legacy will appreciate Disney's superbly rendered fifth dimension despite the approaching doom (a 13-story plummet down an elevator shaft). Even the Studios' most child-oriented attraction, Voyage of the Little Mermaid, packs a few lines that whoosh right over kids' heads (sea witch to love-struck mermaid about to be stripped of her voice in exchange for a pair of feet: "Don't underestimate the importance of body language").

The Studios also speaks to adults by offering an intimate brush with Disney's creative and technical prowess, a chance to penetrate and even take part in the magic. The park is so brimming with behind-the-scenes glimpses that a photo of Walt himself sketching a certain fawn nets but quick glances as folks enter The Magic of Disney Animation to meet the next Mickey Mouse–wannabe in its formative stages. Other tours allow you to prowl the catwalks of a television production studio, to feel the power of special effects in a catastrophe-laced demo complete with flash flood, and to learn the gymnastic logistics behind daring film stunts. Audience participation plays a bigger part in attractions here, making experiences dynamic and, if you or a companion are chosen to, say, test your ear for sound effects on a movie sound track, uniquely personal.

While the Studios remains the most manageable of Walt Disney World's major theme parks, it has more than doubled its repertoire over the past seven years. The most dramatic addition, the Tower of Terror, looms over the park's ostensible landmark, a specially endowed water tank commonly known as the "Earffel Tower."

Certain attractions here, such as The Magic of Disney Animation, sometimes don't open until an hour or more after the curtains officially rise. This fact underlines the importance of pausing to align your schedule with the showtimes and crowd patterns listed on the Studios Tip Board. The board will also alert you to any celebrities who will be appearing during your visit. The most strategic

Did you know...

The Disney-MGM Studios opened on May 1, 1989, with five attractions: The Great Movie Ride, The Magic of Disney Animation, the Backstage Studio Tour, SuperStar Television, and the Monster Sound Show. Since then, the park has more than doubled its repertoire of amusements.

Coming Attractions

By late 1997, a spin-off of Fantasmic!—Disneyland's biggest pyrotechnic dazzler—is due to premiere here in a new lagoon-endowed amphitheater built with special effects in mind. The entertainment venue, located behind the Tower of Terror, continues the Studios expansion begun with Sunset Boulevard.

spot to take a catnap: a sofa at the *Catwalk Bar*, which puts you far above the madding crowd with access to such things as frozen drinks and shrimp cocktails. For more cues to pleasantly removed refuges, note the restful and shady nooks described in the margins of this section.

GUIDING PRINCIPLES: The following walking tour is designed to offer a basic overview for first-time visitors and a timely update for returnees. The running commentary highlights the adult essentials, pointing out redeeming qualities of less-than-vital attractions and spotlighting recent additions to the park. For visitors with a limited amount of time, the Touring Priorities list contained in this section ranks the park's best adult bets.

The size of the Disney-MGM Studios is such that it is possible to experience most everything there is to see and do here in a leisurely day, but only if you're efficient. For additional touring tactics, consult the Hot Tips located in the margins of this section and the flexible touring plans in the *Planning Ahead* chapter. For information on how to get to the Studios via Walt Disney World transportation or by car, see the "Getting Around" section of the *Planning Ahead* chapter. To find out about the unique shops and merchandise found at the Disney-MGM Studios, see the "Shopping" section of the *Diversions* chapter. For restaurant recommendations, look to the evaluative "Restaurant Guide" located in the *Dining & Entertainment* chapter.

GETTING ORIENTED: Disney-MGM Studios is about half the size of Epcot, and easily navigated despite the fact that it has no distinctive shape or main artery. You enter the park—and 1930s Tinseltown—via Hollywood Boulevard, a bustling shopping strip. The first major intersection you come to is Sunset Boulevard, an equally starry-eyed venue that branches off to the right of Hollywood Boulevard; this shopping and entertainment strip ends in a cul-de-sac right at the foot of the park's tallest landmark, the 199-foot Tower of Terror.

Hollywood Boulevard ends where The Great Movie Ride begins—at a replica of Mann's (formerly Grauman's) Chinese Theatre. This ornate building is Disney-MGM Studios' most centrally located landmark, and the plaza fronting it, called Hollywood Plaza, is the site of a Hidden Mickey. (From above, the small garden plots in this plaza form Mickey's eyes and nose, the theater entrance is his mouth, and Echo Lake and the building

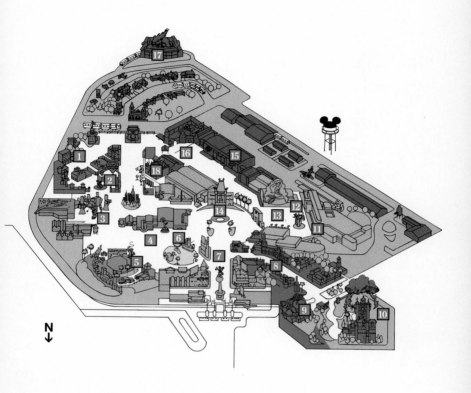

N
↓

1	The Spirit of Pocahontas Stage Show	11	The Magic of Disney Animation
2	Jim Henson's Muppet★Vision 3-D	12	Backstage Studio Tour
3	Star Tours	13	Voyage of the Little Mermaid
4	Monster Sound Show	14	The Great Movie Ride
5	Indiana Jones Epic Stunt Spectacular	15	Working Sound Stages
6	SuperStar Television	16	Inside the Magic: Special Effects and Production Tour
7	Hollywood Boulevard	17	Catastrophe Canyon
8	Sunset Boulevard	18	Honey, I Shrunk the Kids Movie Set Adventure
9	Beauty and the Beast Stage Show		
10	The Twilight Zone Tower of Terror		

Touring Priorities

DON'T MISS

The Magic of Disney
  Animation
Tower of Terror*
Star Tours
Jim Henson's
  Muppet*Vision 3-D
The Great Movie Ride
SuperStar Television
Beauty and the Beast
  Stage Show**
The Spirit of Pocahontas
  Stage Show**

DON'T OVERLOOK

Backstage Studio Tour
Indiana Jones Epic Stunt
  Spectacular**
The Making of...
Monster Sound Show
Special Effects and
  Production Tour

DON'T KNOCK YOURSELF OUT

Voyage of the Little
  Mermaid*
Honey, I Shrunk the Kids
  Movie Set Adventure

* Long lines; visit in the early A.M.,
  late P.M., or during the afternoon
  parade.

** Pay close attention to performance
  schedules.

that houses the *Hollywood Brown Derby* serve as ears.)

If you stand in Hollywood Plaza facing the Chinese Theatre, you'll see an archway off to your right; this leads to Mickey Avenue, a self-contained area with more of a backstage feel to it where tours of working animation and television studios are among the attractions. If (instead of continuing on to the theater) you make a left off of Hollywood Boulevard and proceed clockwise past Echo Lake, you are on course for such attractions as SuperStar Television, Monster Sound Show, Indiana Jones Epic Stunt Spectacular, and Star Tours. Just past Star Tours lies one last entertainment pocket. Jim Henson's Muppet*Vision 3-D theater is the main draw here, together with a facade of a Manhattan block called New York Street. Walk left past the skyscraper end of New York Street, and you're on a quick track back to Hollywood Plaza and the Chinese Theatre.

A WALKING TOUR

Just inside the gates, you may be too distracted by the bright, Art Deco hues of Hollywood Boulevard to notice a building on your left—but this is the site of Guest Relations, where you can go for information, first aid, and a lost and found. Visit Guest Relations first thing in the morning if you'd like to witness the taping of a television show during your visit (tickets are free and

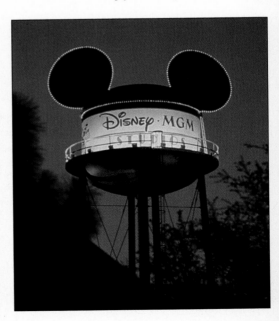

available on a first-come, first-served basis). Stop here or at Crossroads of the World (the gift stand smack in the center of the entrance plaza) to pick up a map and an entertainment schedule. To your immediate right, check out Oscar's Super Service, which has a 1947 Buick parked out front. This is one of several striking and utterly unscratched classic automobiles you'll notice along the streets of the park. (We're not sure how they got through the turnstiles; certainly they must have a multi-day admission pass.) Also remember Oscar's as the site of storage lockers, wheelchair rentals, and the Studios' sole ATM.

Hollywood Boulevard

One look at this main drag, and you have a hunch you're not in Central Florida anymore. The strip oozes star quality with a Mae West sort of subtlety. Movie tunes from Hollywood's Golden Age waft through the air. Palm trees make like Fred and Ginger in the tropical breeze. Streamlined storefronts with neon and chrome Art Deco flourishes line the boulevard like would-be movie sets hoping to get noticed. Don't be surprised if you encounter budding starlets sparring with their agents, paparazzi angling for scoops, or a starry-eyed soul who wants *your* autograph.

Note that the shops along Hollywood Boulevard typically stay open about a half hour after the rest of the park has closed. (Consult the "Shopping" section in the *Diversions* chapter for specifics on our favorite shops; wares generally include a broad range of movie memorabilia and collectibles, plenty of Disney character merchandise that's a cut above T-shirts, and a healthy supply of amazing fudge.)

However you get there, it's important to stop at the corner of Hollywood and Sunset boulevards to check the **Studios Tip Board** (a trusty blackboard that lists current waiting times for popular attractions). This also is the place to make lunch or dinner reservations for any of the Studios' full-service restaurants. Lest you ignore breakfast, the *Starring Rolls Bakery* is constantly auditioning coffee drinkers and croissant and cinnamon roll eaters a few steps away.

HOT TIPS

■ On Wednesdays and Sundays, guests staying at WDW resorts may enter the Disney-MGM Studios 1$\frac{1}{2}$ hours before the official opening time and get an early crack at selected attractions such as The Great Movie Ride, Muppet*Vision 3-D, and Star Tours. Early-entry days and attractions are subject to change.

■ Not coincidentally, Wednesdays and Sundays now tend to be the most crowded days at the Studios.

Quiet Nooks

- *Starring Rolls Bakery*
- *Catwalk Bar*
- *Tune-In Lounge*
- *Sunset Ranch Market*
- Shaded benches around Echo Park
- Brownstone stoops on New York Street

Ears to the Ground

A middle-aged woman removed her eyeglasses but insisted on keeping her Mouseketeer hat intact as she prepared to board a Tower of Terror elevator bound for The Twilight Zone and a 13-story plummet down an elevator shaft. "I've got a bobby pin in it," she said confidently to the attendant. Better make that an industrial-strength bobby pin.

Sunset Boulevard

This newest Studios block is a broad, colorful avenue every bit as glamorous as Hollywood Boulevard. It has the same high-cheekbone style and its own stock of towering palms, evocative facades, and tempting shops. It also has stage presence, in the form of the new 1,500-seat Theatre of the Stars amphitheater, where you can see live performances of *Beauty and the Beast*. Sunset Boulevard begins innocently enough, with Mickey Mouse standing just beyond the Studios Tip Board for photo opportunities, a friendly old-fashioned farmers' market, and a shop called Once Upon A Time that's housed in a replica of the Carthay Circle Theatre where *Snow White* premiered. But none other than the white-knuckle Tower of Terror looms at the end of the road.

Somehow, the **Beauty and the Beast Stage Show**, a wonderful production that was the raison d'être behind the Broadway musical, manages to remain oblivious to its eerie neighbor. The show is 30 not-to-be-missed minutes of rich musicality, delightful costuming and choreography, and uplifting entertainment. While a canopy keeps the sun's heat somewhat at bay, we still try to aim for an evening performance during the summer months.

Then there's **The Twilight Zone Tower of Terror**, a don't-miss attraction. Because few of us have a natural yen to drop 13 stories down a dark elevator shaft, this one requires some bravery. It helps to know a little about the ups and downs in store for you.

Basically, "guests" enter the mysteriously abandoned Hollywood Tower Hotel and are invited into a library, where even the cobwebs appear to be circa 1939. Here, Rod Serling appears on a black-and-white television set to brief you (stormy night, Halloween 1939, lightning strikes, guests disappear from hotel elevator) and welcome you to tonight's episode of "The Twilight Zone." "If you'll just step this way into the boiler room, this is where you'll board our service elevators." You reach a boarding area—Last Call For Chickening Out—and file into an elevator (look at the diagram above the doors to avoid, say, the front row). Once you are seated and the safety bars are secured, the doors shut and the elevator ascends. You're soon so entranced with astonishing special effects—apparitions that appear in a corridor that vaporizes into a dark, star-filled sky, and a gigantic eye straight from the fifth dimension—that dread becomes

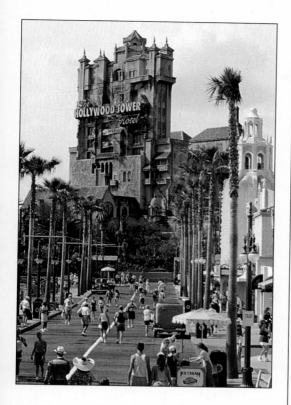

(almost) secondary. When the elevator moves over into a second, pitch-black shaft, anything can happen, since Disney's Imagineers have deviously transformed this ride from a two-screamer into a five-screamer (the bottom *sort of* falls out more than once). One thing's for certain: Your cue to strike a great casual pose—a scream resembling a yawn, perhaps—is when you reach the 13th floor. You want to look good in the group picture, which is taken as a panorama of the park suddenly gives way to a short drop. The big plunge that follows is an incredibly fast downward pull with a surprisingly smooth landing. A terrific scare, yes, but it's over faster than many vocal cords can respond.

A few notes: The jitters tend to stay with you for a bit after the 12-minute drama has ended. If you have back or neck problems, a heart condition, or are pregnant, we suggest that you pass on the Tower of Terror. And *don't* try it on a full stomach.

Tower of Terror Tip

Impending threat of a 13-story plunge in darkness not terrifying enough for you? Disorient yourself further by looking UP into the towering void before the shaft opens to a window on the park.

Exact Replicas

- Chinese Theatre—Mann's Chinese Theatre in Hollywood

- Once Upon A Time storefront—Carthay Circle Theatre in Hollywood, where *Snow White* premiered

- Mickey's of Hollywood storefront—Frederick's of Hollywood

- Jim Henson's Muppet*Vision 3-D theater—the theater from "The Muppet Show"

- *Hollywood Brown Derby—Brown Derby* of 1930s Hollywood

HOT TIP

Don't eat before...

- Embarking on Star Tours

- Visiting the Tower of Terror

- Dropping by the *50's Prime Time Café* or the *Hollywood Brown Derby*

Animation Plaza and Mickey Avenue

Adjacent to Sunset Boulevard and Hollywood Boulevard is the section of the park that takes you under the sea with a diminutive mermaid and into working animation and television production studios. Passing under an archway located off of Hollywood Plaza, you see Animation Plaza immediately in front of you, with Mickey Avenue to your left.

A few words about timing: First, note that The Magic of Disney Animation sometimes does not open until late morning (check the entertainment schedule). And know that the three tours here—The Magic of Disney Animation, the Backstage Studio Tour, and the Special Effects and Production Tour—are most exciting on weekdays before 5 P.M., because glimpses of Disney's magic makers at work stop when they call it a day.

Consider **The Magic of Disney Animation** a non-negotiable must. A tour through working animation studios uproariously hosted by Walter Cronkite and Robin Williams is a chance to learn the facts of life as they relate to Mickey Mouse and to see Disney's next animated film as a work in progress. You don't spend the whole 35 minutes peering over shoulders, however. First, you watch a film that transforms Williams into one of the lost boys from *Peter Pan.* Then you view a terrific video presentation that reveals the creative passion and sometimes zany methods of the people behind the Disney characters. Finally, you are treated to a finale of Disney classics. If you have an artistic bone in your body, you'll be absolutely captivated. To minimize your wait, try to visit the show shortly after it opens.

If you think you'd enjoy a behind-the-scenes look at moviemaking of the "lights, camera, action" sort, take two: The Backstage Studio Tour and the Inside the Magic Special Effects and Production Tour complement each other well. The **Backstage Studio Tour** is a 25-minute tram ride (sit on the right side to stay dry) that starts calmly enough. You visit the wardrobe area (2.25 million bodies clothed); the lights, camera, and props departments; and the back lot neighborhood of facades where you can see "The Golden Girls" house, or at least its exterior. Then suddenly there you are in a special-effects zone called Catastrophe Canyon that specializes in nature's wrath: violent downpours, fiery explosions, flash floods. Just as you're thinking that New York City would seem hospitable compared to this, there it is, a realistic-looking Manhattan block made mostly of fiberglass and Styrofoam. The Backstage Studio Tour can accommodate about 200 people per tram; lines here tend to be shorter in the late afternoon (ask the attendant for an e.t.a., and if it's more than 30 minutes check back later). The tour exits through **Studio Showcase**, a revolving display of props and partial sets that "Home Improvement" fans will want to note as the site to purchase logo T-shirts.

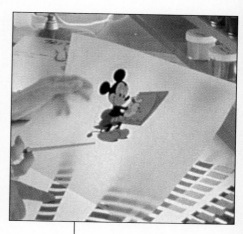

Big footprints painted on the pavement outside Studio Showcase lead right to the **Inside the Magic Special Effects and Production Tour**. The wait for this walking tour rarely exceeds 15 minutes, but you might make tracks to the restroom first; this is a 40-minute gig that takes no breaks. It begins with an entertaining demo of how a realistic sea storm or naval battle might be filmed (two guests are asked to don yellow raincoats and brave the elements). Walking along a soundproof catwalk that overlooks three soundstages, you have an opportunity to witness television shows or movies being filmed. You also view a funny four-minute film starring Bette Midler that was shot here at Disney-MGM Studios (you'll recognize New York Street) and a video revealing how different effects were achieved. All things considered, it's time well spent on even the tightest itinerary.

For an elaborate look at post-production, see the film attraction *The Making of...* (fill in the blank with a recent Disney animated feature). It shows some wacky ways animators got into their characters, as well as how well-known actors created the voices and musicians produced the scores. (You might see *The Making of Pocahontas*, *Toy Story*, or *The Hunchback of Notre Dame*, which is scheduled to open in summer 1996.) Haven't seen the movie yet? Don't worry; you'll enjoy this behind-the-scenes look anyway.

If you can get near **Voyage of the Little Mermaid**— and at this 15-minute musical adapted from the hit movie,

Disney Oscars

Replicas of these 12 Oscars are displayed at The Magic of Disney Animation:

Flowers and Trees	1932
Three Little Pigs	1933
The Tortoise and the Hare	1934
The Orphan Kittens	1935
The Country Cousin	1936
The Old Mill	1937
Ferdinand the Bull	1938
The Ugly Duckling	1939
Lend a Paw	1941
Fantasia	1941
Der Fuehrer's Face	1942
It's Tough to Be a Bird	1969

that's no easy task—don't hesitate. It's not the story line that's so compelling. It's the upbeat music, the amazing puppetry, the occasion to watch children ogle this real, live mermaid *whose tail is moving*, and the mist-infused feeling that you are underwater. This attraction seems to start the day with a 30-minute wait; your best bet is the first show in the morning. Check your entertainment schedule for showtimes.

The Echo Lake Area

Heading back through the archway into Hollywood Plaza, you come upon **The Great Movie Ride.** This drive-through theater of sorts is a classic in its own right and the best ticket we know to a quick video rental decision your next time out. Housed in an artful replica of Mann's Chinese Theatre, this not-to-be-missed 22-minute attraction is bursting with Audio-Animatronics figures that bring motion picture legends and moments of almost every genre astonishingly to life. It's "Chim Chim Cher-ee" meets "Here's looking at you, kid," cigarette-puffing Clint Eastwood meets broom-brandishing Wicked Witch of the West, *Alien* meets *Singin' in the Rain*, and then some—be prepared for surprises. The ride has meticulous detailing and surprising realism. Notice, for example, how Julie Andrews' throat vibrates as she sings. If you think of it, look for the Hidden Mickey in the window above the bank in the gangster scene. The Great Movie Ride draws large crowds all day long. However, with queues that wind past a screening of famous movie scenes, it is also one of the most entertaining waits in Walt Disney World. (Note: It takes about 25 minutes to reach the ride vehicles when the line extends to the theater entrance.)

Heading through Hollywood Plaza toward Echo Lake, the next attraction you encounter is **SuperStar Television**. Remember it as one that simply goes for the laugh and gets it. Good fun whether you're in the limelight or in the audience, the 30-minute variety show merges live action with original film clips to slip audience volunteers into scenes from classic television programs. Most stars are chosen by a casting director in the pre-show area, others in the 1,000-seat theater (situate yourself toward the front to increase your odds). Among the more choice adult roles up for grabs: the Ethel Mertz part in the famous chocolate factory scene from "I Love Lucy" (raise your hand if they ask for a woman with a good sense of humor)

Entertainment

Disney's Tinseltown sticks close to its Hollywood heritage in its roster of live entertainment. Because the marquee is ever-changing, it's essential to pick up a schedule at the entrance plaza or Guest Relations to see what's going on during your visit.

You're sure to see Streetmosphere Characters—budding starlets, gossip columnists, and the like—along Hollywood Boulevard. On any given day you may have and the Al Borlund part opposite Tim "the Tool Man" Taylor in a scene from "Home Improvement" (raise your hand if the emcee asks for a guy who's handy). While the experience changes with the cast, SuperStar Television always weighs in somewhere between a good chuckle and a muffled guffaw on our laughter scale. This attraction can be enjoyed any time of day.

Right next to SuperStar Television is the **Monster Sound Show**, a fun, 15-minute affair in which recruits attempt to create appropriate sound effects for a short film starring Martin Short and Chevy Chase. Even the most diligent volunteers end up making some off notes, like thunderclaps emerging from falling chandeliers and wind whistling through a bookcase. Interestingly, many of the sound-effects gizmos used and displayed here are the creations of Jimmy Macdonald, Disney's man of 20,000 gadgets; he's the guy making a din with David Letterman in the video preview.

Note that the Soundstations booths (located in the small interactive area called SoundWorks, just outside the theater) here are among the coolest things in Walt Disney World. These inconspicuous rooms feature 3-D audio effects so realistic you will swear someone is cutting your hair, placing a newspaper hat on your head, or whispering in your ear. You *have* to try it.

If you are an action-movie connoisseur, it's worth risking life and limb to catch a showing of the **Indiana Jones Epic Stunt Spectacular**. Arrive a good 30 minutes before showtime to snare a seat toward the front of this 2,000-seat amphitheater. The half-hour performance steals its thunder from *Raiders of the Lost Ark* and begins with the selection of a few fearless "extras" (they're put to use during a scene involving a sword fight in Cairo). Nimble stuntpeople perform one death-defying caper after another, leaping between buildings, dodging snipers and boulders, and eluding fiery explosions. You feel the heat of the flames, you fear for the Harrison Ford look-alike. Tricks of the trade are revealed, and you're *still* impressed. The Indiana Jones Epic Stunt Spectacular nearly always plays to capacity audiences, so your best bet for getting a great seat is the first or last show of the day. Keep in mind that seating begins 30 minutes prior to each show.

As exciting as the Indiana Jones Epic Stunt Spectacular

an opportunity to see a celebrity at the park through the "Star Today" program.

Be aware that a new afternoon parade themed to Disney's computer-animated film, *Toy Story*, is expected to roll into the Studios if it hasn't already. Like the movie, the parade will be centered on the adventures of toys that come to life when humans are not around. And last but hardly least: During seasons when the park is open late, Sorcery in the Sky, Disney's best fireworks show, lights up the horizon behind the Chinese Theatre in a ten-minute pyrotechnic gallery complete with narration by Vincent Price and music from Disney's *Fantasia* and other classic films.

Hidden Mickey

In The Great Movie Ride, look at the window above the bank in the gangster scene.

Snacker's Guide

For a healthy nibble, seek out the *Sunset Ranch Market* on Sunset Boulevard for carrot sticks and a great selection of fresh fruit that extends from plums to kumquats, or head for the small fruit stand located between Hollywood Boulevard and Echo Lake.

For a sweet fix, consider the cookies and pastries at *Starring Rolls Bakery* on Sunset Boulevard, and the fudge, marshmallow crispies, and wonderfully addictive Mint Chocolate Cookie Gems at *Sweet Success* on Hollywood Boulevard.

For a frozen treat, try *Catalina Eddie's Frozen Yogurt* on Sunset Boulevard or the strawberry bars and ice cream at *Dinosaur Gertie's* on Echo Lake.

For a savory bite, try the mini, turkey, or foot-long hot dogs at *Rosie's Red Hot Dogs* on Sunset Boulevard.

is, the attraction just around the corner packs even more of a punch. At **Star Tours** you don't sit in an amphitheater, you strap yourself into a flight simulator. You don't live vicariously through professional stuntpeople; you experience the extraordinary sensation of barreling through space at the speed of light for yourself. The premise: Enterprising droids R2D2 and C-3PO are working for a galactic travel agency whose fleet of spacecraft makes regular trips to the Moon of Endor. As luck would have it, you draw a rookie pilot who gives new meaning to reckless abandon. Soon you're spiraling through deep space, dodging lasers and giant ice crystals. Be prepared for an intense five-minute ride that encompasses a lot of bucking, tilting, and other jerky, disorienting movements.

Star Tours is an incredible experience—one of those don't-miss-unless-you-have-a-very-good-reason attractions. (Among the very good reasons: just ate, heart conditions, pregnancy, back problems, susceptible to motion sickness, other physical limitations.) This ride is also a good test of how you'll fare on its Epcot equivalent, Body Wars, a thrilling journey through the human body with visuals that are sometimes even quicker to trigger a yen for Dramamine. Star Tours is frequently mobbed; shortest lines are generally in the morning, with waits of about 30 minutes the remainder of the day.

New York Street

Moving along, you come to the back corner of the Disney-MGM Studios. This is a glimpse of Manhattan as it used to look, with a few alterations having to do with the dimensions of the Empire State Building and the size of the puppet population.

You're here for one thing: the fabulously entertaining, special effects–ridden presentation of **Jim Henson's Muppet*Vision 3-D**. Miss it, and you've deprived your sense of humor. So head straight for the Muppet theater and fill up on a 24-minute stream of amusing Muppet antics that push the creative envelope of 3-D movies with such effects as a cannon blast through the screen, some bubble magic, and a floating banana cream pie. (Yes, the curmudgeons from "The Muppet Show" are in attendance, in their familiar balcony spot, wry and cynical as ever. And yes, we've actually seen a 45-year-old man lift his 3-D glasses several times during a showing.)

Okay, we lied. There's another reason you're here. As

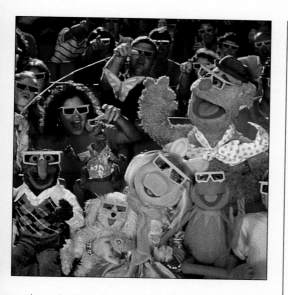

QUIZ: Can you match these animated characters with their real-life voices?

The Genie	Cheech Marin
Mrs. Potts	Nathan Lane
Scar	James Earl Jones
Timon	Angela Lansbury
Rafiki	Jerry Orbach
Lumière	Whoopi Goldberg
The Beast	Mel Gibson
Mufasa	Robbie Benson
Simba (grown)	Robin Williams
Shenzi	Matthew Broderick
Banzai	Robert Guillaume
John Smith	Jeremy Irons

you leave the Muppets, veer right to find the Backlot Theater. Here you'll see special effects and some wonderfully costumed (live) performers, in **The Spirit of Pocahontas Stage Show.** This 25-minute musical brings a magical aura to the famous story of the free-spirited Native American princess and Captain John Smith. Blink and you might miss tree branches cross the stage, winds swirl, and characters appear and disappear in mysterious puffs of smoke and bursts of flame.

From the Backlot Theater, walk straight toward New York Street, where you can take in the skyline or sit down on a stoop. A sign in the window of our favorite brownstone cautions "No Soliciting," but it says nothing about stoop trespassing. So we take a seat, do some people-watching, or simply gaze at the Empire State Building. Disney apparently used a technique called forced perspective to make the four-story version here appear to have 104 floors. (We can't help but think that if the fashion industry applied this forced perspective principle to clothing, the term "petite" would become obsolete.) If passersby ask you for directions, it's good to know that the **Honey, I Shrunk the Kids Movie Set Adventure** playground is behind one of the facades here. And if they want to know where to find the video arcade, tell them it's right across from the Muppet theater.

Answers: The Genie, Robin Williams; Mrs. Potts, Angela Lansbury; Scar, Jeremy Irons; Timon, Nathan Lane; Rafiki, Robert Guillaume; Lumière, Jerry Orbach; The Beast, Robbie Benson; Mufasa, James Earl Jones; Simba (grown), Matthew Broderick; Shenzi, Whoopi Goldberg; Banzai, Cheech Marin; John Smith, Mel Gibson.

Diversions: Sports, Shopping & Other Pursuits

I t's a cool April morning and you are posing for a picture with an eight-pound largemouth bass. You've caught so many fish over the past two hours you're wondering if given more time, you couldn't hook them all. You'd signed on for this guided catch-and-release fishing trip around Seven Seas Lagoon expecting a relaxing morning on the water and a few polite nibbles, but here you are, no more than a few hundred yards from Disney's posh *Grand Floridian* resort, catching bass that require muscle. And this is not an isolated occurrence. Though fishing may not be the first sport that comes to mind when you think of the Royal Mousedom (that would be golf), in angling circles Walt Disney World is fondly known as the theme park metropolis with world-class bass fishing. In lay terms that means big fish (and a lot of them) showing a great time to even the most inexperienced angler who drops them a line.

• • •

It is nearing 10 P.M. on a January night, and a group of sophisticated shoppers are fawning over such things as shortbread baked in the image of Mickey Mouse's shorts. One of them wants Mickey Mouse–shaped pasta, while another has a $100 Mickeyfied teakettle under one arm. A third is off playing credit card bingo with Disney characterized Christmas ornaments and office accoutrements. If the shops at the Disney Village Marketplace don't close the doors soon, their purchases are not going to fit through them. We've made a startling discovery about the shopping scene at Walt Disney World: It can throw unsuspecting adults into a frenzy. The bottom

---

Tee off on your choice of five world-class golf courses; the Magnolia comes with the *Grand Floridian* as a backdrop.

line: Shops here are loaded with nicely evolved character goods and lots more merchandise (labels such as Waterford and Liz Claiborne, for example) that's simply way beyond kid stuff.

It is about half an hour before your lunch reservation comes due in another corner of the World, and you are entranced by a two-day-old lemur that looks like a homemade cat toy, lying on its mom's back. In the last couple of hours you've played nature photographer on the beach with a handsome (and very cooperative) brown pelican, clocked the progress of a 500-pound Galápagos tortoise (unofficial speed: about a hair's width a minute), and witnessed a domestic squabble between first-time-parent storks ("there will be none of *that* in *this* nest"). To think that this terrific wildlife park—Discovery Island—was created by folks whose prior zoological experience was a four-fingered mouse! But it's true, and so Discovery Island becomes one more perfect example of Disney's ability to dazzle in the most unexpected arenas.

Here's the point: The World beyond the three major theme parks offers a slew of terrific diversions. Once you get over the shock of finding such activities here in the first place, you're still pinching yourself because the quality of the experience is so astonishingly good. In other words, even more world-class playgrounds for adults (thoroughly described on the following pages) exist within the world-class playground that is Walt Disney World. We're just hinting at the possibilities when we mention golf courses widely considered among the country's best; state-of-the-art tennis facilities; the world's biggest armada of pleasure boats; and the last word in water parks, including the world's tallest water slide and largest wave pool. If that's not enough, Disney has even gone so far as to make extraordinary fun of learning, with the introduction of The Disney Institute, where adults can dabble freely in radio, animation, cooking, and all manner of other courses completely unburdened of such baggage as pop quizzes and final exams. For a complete inventory of distractions so compelling (the categories: sports, shopping, and other pursuits) you'll wonder why anyone bothers with those theme parks, read on.

"Each one of the Disney courses is unique. You could spend five days golfing and not have the same experience."
—Larry Nelson,
two-time champion of the WDW/Oldsmobile Golf Classic

SPORTS

Okay, sports fans, it's time for our play-by-play guide to Walt Disney World. First and foremost, you can play some of the finest golf courses in the country. There are 99 holes here (available in increments of 9 or 18), and you can take your pick from five designer-name par 72s that both individually and together have earned hosannas from both *Golf* magazine and *Golf Digest*. And as we can personally attest, you need not possess a smidgen of ability in order to enjoy yourself. Whatever your skill or mood, there's a course in Walt Disney World's diverse lineup to suit; each venue is a unique challenge, and opportunities abound to test your mettle on fairways that have humbled the pros.

You also can play some serious (or casual) tennis on the most advanced surface that exists, thanks to recent renovations transforming Disney's Racquet Club into a state-of-the-art facility. You can angle for largemouth bass weighing eight pounds or more (waterways here are teeming with trophy-scale bass). You can rent boats and bikes galore. And, last but not least, you can swim yourself into a waterlogged prune. In other words, you are not lacking for sporting opportunities. All of these playful options plus a few more, including health clubs, jogging, massages, and spectator sports (what can we say, it's a big World out there) are fully detailed in the sections that follow. Of course, you also can choose to play couch potato, although after knowing your options it will doubtless require some willpower.

GOLF

The 99-hole Magic Linkdom—second only to the Mouse in drawing power—is renowned for the challenge, variety, and fairness of its courses. In recent years Walt Disney World has become a familiar name on *Golf* magazine's biennial list of the best golf resorts in the country. *Golf Digest* has tabbed four of the World's five par-72 courses as outstanding ("plan your next vacation around it") or very good ("worth getting off the interstate to play"), and given a high five to the Palm as one of the

Coming in 1997

Big-time athletics will have a place in the World when Disney's multi-million-dollar International Sports Complex opens next year near the intersection of I-4 and U.S. 192. The enormous facility, which spans nearly 200 acres, will host all manner of amateur sporting events, and will doubtless move into the professional sector before long; it will also serve as a training site for both amateur and professional teams. Among the highlights of the new sports center are a 7,500-seat baseball stadium, a 5,000-seat fieldhouse for basketball and volleyball, a track-and-field complex, and 12 clay tennis courts, including a 2,000-seat stadium court.

Tee Time

Want to increase your chances of getting on one of the five WDW courses? Heed the following:

- Try to play on a Monday or Tuesday
- Tee off after 3 P.M.
- Come in the summer (when special rates are available)

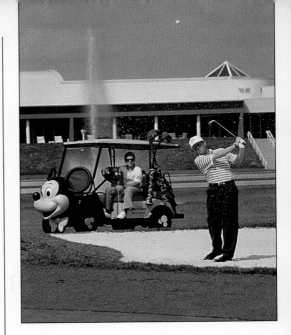

Group Alert

When WDW course calendars are clear, it's possible for civic, corporate, and social groups to arrange a private tournament at no charge beyond normal greens fees. Interested parties should contact Disney's tournament coordinator by calling 824-2275.

country's 75 best resort courses. And noted golf writer Glen Waggoner is hardly alone in giving Mickey Mouse's backyard the nod as America's greatest golfing haven. In Waggoner's words, "Some other places have an individual course that is superior to any in Walt Disney World's lineup, but no other resort in the entire country has five courses this good." With a quarter century of the PGA Tour's Walt Disney World/Oldsmobile Golf Classic already behind it, Disney stepped into the women's arena to host the LPGA HealthSouth Inaugural in January 1995.

Depending upon the tee box chosen, the immaculately kept Disney courses provide challenging or relaxed play; while the layouts are quite distinct in their design, they are all constructed to be especially forgiving for the mid-handicap player. Of the original three Joe Lee–designed courses, the Palm and the Magnolia (located just west of the *Polynesian* resort) get the most attention, but the Lake Buena Vista course (whose fairways border The Disney Institute and the *Disney Vacation Club*) is a popular course that more than holds its own. Tucked into a corner of the Magnolia is Oak Trail, a par-36 walking course especially suited to beginners. Rounding out the offerings are the two challenging courses added in 1992—the Tom Fazio–designed Osprey Ridge and the Pete Dye–designed Eagle Pines, which play from the Bonnet Creek Golf Club located near *Fort Wilderness*.

KNOW BEFORE YOU GO: WDW's peak golfing season extends from January through April. During this period it is especially important to secure reservations well in advance for play in the morning and early afternoon (though starting times after 3 P.M. are usually available at the last minute). Tee times are extremely difficult if not impossible to get during the LPGA HealthSouth tournament (this year, January 19–21); during the third and fourth weeks of January, when some 30,000 truly serious golfers descend on the area for the PGA of America's Merchandise Show; and during the WDW/Oldsmobile Golf Classic (October 5–8). The Citrus Bowl (January) and Daytona 500 (February) also have proven capable of filling the courses rather quickly, and also beware when a Super Bowl is scheduled anywhere in Florida. During such busy periods, the advance reservations and guaranteed tee times afforded by golf packages can be absolutely indispensable (call 934-7639 for package details).

Rates: Greens fees for the 18-hole courses vary according to when you visit (peak versus non-peak seasons), which course you play (Osprey Ridge and Eagle Pines are more expensive, but only during peak season), and your guest status (WDW resort guests and Magic Kingdom Club members get a break). A detailed breakdown of current rates is provided at right. Basically, though, you can count on paying $85 to $100 per round, including the required cart, up to $115 for non-guests at Osprey Ridge and Eagle Pines. The most dramatic savings can be had by teeing off after 3 P.M. (2 P.M. during November and December), when twilight rates afford savings of 50 percent or more. Note that there are no twilight discounts during January, February, and March. At Oak Trail, a nine-hole walking course, play is $23 for one round or $31 for two. From May 1 through December 31, season badges ($50) provide substantial savings by allowing golfers to pay just $35 per round for unlimited play, including cart; badges are also good for admission to the WDW/Oldsmobile Golf Classic.

Reservations: Anyone buying a golf package may reserve tee times up to 90 days ahead. Golfers who book lodging at any on-property resort can secure tee times up to 30 days in advance. For everyone else, the window of opportunity is seven days in advance, or four days during

Walt Disney World Golf Rates

The following greens fees were in effect at press time for the Walt Disney World golf courses. Prices are subject to change.

Palm, Magnolia, Lake Buena Vista

Day Visitor	$95
Resort Guest	$85
Twilight*	$45
Summer Twilight*	$35

Osprey Ridge, Eagle Pines

	Peak 1/1–4/30	Non-Peak 5/1–12/31
Day Visitor	$115	$95
Resort Guest	$100	$85
Twilight*	$50	$50
Summer Twilight*	$35	$35

* Twilight rates begin at 3 P.M. from April through October, and at 2 P.M. during November and December. Summer Twilight rates are in effect from 3 P.M. during June, July, and August.

Slope Scope

The slope ratings for the five Disney courses are: Osprey Ridge, 135; Magnolia, 133; Palm, 133; Eagle Pines, 131; Lake Buena Vista, 128. By way of comparison, an average slope rating is around 115. The famously challenging links at Pebble Beach check in at 139; the formidable TPC Stadium course at Ponte Vedra, at 135.

peak season. The practical effect of these rules is that it's very difficult, if not impossible, for guests staying outside WDW borders to obtain prime tee times during the busiest weeks, for example, the last two weeks in January. Also note that four golfers are assigned to each starting time, so singles and pairs may very well be matched up. To book tee times call 824-2270.

Transportation: Free shuttles escort guests to the Palm and Magnolia from the *Grand Floridian*, *Polynesian*, and *Contemporary* resorts; complimentary taxis (they work on a voucher system) to Osprey Ridge and Eagle Pines are available from all WDW resorts.

Dress: Proper golf attire is required on all courses. Shirts must have collars, and if shorts are worn they must be Bermuda length.

Equipment rental: Good-quality gear, including Titleist clubs ($20), range balls ($5 a bucket), and shoes ($6), is available for rent at all pro shops.

INSTRUCTION: Players looking to discover or improve their game have several options: clinics, one-on-one instruction, swing analysis sessions, and playing lessons. Beginner clinics accommodating up to eight players are held from 9 A.M. to 10 A.M. Saturdays and Sundays at the Palm and the Magnolia; cost is $25. Skill clinics, held at the same time and location Mondays through Fridays, provide forums in which up to eight players can refine specific areas of their game (depending on the day, the focus is putting, chipping and pitching, bunker shots, irons, or woods); participation is $35. Private lessons are available on any of the Disney courses; cost is $30 per half hour with an assistant pro or $45 per half hour with the head pro). At the Walt Disney World Golf Studio, based at the Palm and Magnolia, PGA professionals offer 90-minute sessions that concentrate on improving players' swings through video analysis. These are offered at 10:30 A.M. and 1:30 P.M. every day. Enrollment is limited to four and the cost is $60. Nine-hole playing lessons, in which a PGA pro provides on-course instruction, delve into strategy, club selection, and short game skills, as well as the psychological side of golf; cost is $100. Reservations are required for all lessons; call 824-2270.

TOURNAMENTS: The Walt Disney World/Oldsmobile Golf Classic, which draws top PGA Tour players every fall, is among the most celebrated events on Disney's sports calendar. The tournament has been a major magnet for golf fans since 1971 when, two months after Walt Disney World opened its gates, Jack Nicklaus won the inaugural event. Because the Classic is one of the last regular PGA Tour stops of the year (it's usually held in October), exciting competition is a given; pros are looking to vault themselves into the Tour Championship or secure their spots on the top 125 money list.

Venues for the four-day tournament have traditionally been the Palm, Magnolia, and Lake Buena Vista courses. During the first three days of the competition, the pros play each course once, accompanied by a different three-person amateur team each day. After 54 holes, the field narrows to the low 70 pros, who compete for a cut of the tourney's million-dollar purse in the final round, played on the Magnolia.

This year's Classic will be held October 5 through 8. Practice rounds (October 3 and 4) are open to spectators at no cost. Tickets are available on site each day of the tournament with one-day admissions ranging from $10 for the first or second round to $15 for the final round. Gallery badges for all four rounds are $35. For more information call 824-2250.

Those who are willing to pay big dues (starting at $5,000 for a one-year membership) can play the Walt Disney World/Oldsmobile Golf Classic alongside the pros. In exchange for their sponsorship, card-carrying members of the Classic Club play side by side with a different competing pro each day for the first three rounds of the tournament. Some memberships also include lodging during the tournament, reduced greens fees on Disney courses for a year, and admission to the Magic Kingdom, Epcot, and the Disney-MGM Studios for a week. For additional details, call 824-2250.

Last January saw the debut of women professionals at Walt Disney World. The LPGA HealthSouth Inaugural draws its name from the fact that it's the first full-field event of the year (1996 dates are January 19–21), and as such it draws a constellation of stars. The 1995 edition featured Dottie Mochrie, Michelle McGann, and Laura Davies. The tourney is contested on the Eagle Pines course over three days, with a one-day pro-am preceding the event. For more information call 824-2250.

Chasing the Pros

During the days immediately following the Walt Disney World/Oldsmobile Golf Classic and the LPGA HealthSouth Inaugural championship, the tournament courses are superbly conditioned and the aura of excitement (not to mention the scoreboards and bleachers) surrounding the big events are still there.

In the Rough

"There's a lot of wildlife around the Palm course's property," says Disney pro Kevin Prentice. "People have seen deer, otters, turkeys, bobcats, and even panthers. The other day, someone said he saw a couple of bald eagles."

The 10 Most Humbling Holes

Cumulative toughest-playing Classic holes since 1983:

1. Palm No. 18
2. Palm No. 6
3. Palm No. 10
4. Lake Buena Vista No. 18
5. Magnolia No. 18
6. Palm No. 4
7. Magnolia No. 17
8. Magnolia No. 5
9. Lake Buena Vista No. 11
10. Magnolia No. 15

Turf Talk

The Oak Trail course used to be just six holes long. Until 1989, the greens were made of AstroTurf.

The Courses

PALM: This prickly yet picturesque course (located just west of the *Polynesian* resort with the Magnolia to its immediate north) is marked by tight wooded fairways, a wealth of water hazards, and elevated greens and tees, which bear Joe Lee's unmistakable signature and make for challenging club selections. The par-72 Palm plays shorter and tighter than its mate, the Magnolia, and measures 5,311 yards from the front tees, 6,461 from the middle, and 6,957 from the back. Rated by *Golf Digest* as one of the nation's top 75 resort courses a few years ago, the palm-dotted venue hosts the WDW/Oldsmobile Golf Classic, along with its fellow Lee designs (the Magnolia and the Lake Buena Vista courses). Of the holes garnering the most locker room curses (numbers 6, 10, and 18), the sixth, a 412-yard par 4, is the most notorious. There's a lake on the left, woods and swamp on the right, and more water between you and the two-tier green. The course—whose greens were rebuilt in 1993 from the drainage basin up—celebrates its 25th birthday this year alongside the Magnolia and the Magic Kingdom itself. Facilities shared by the Palm and the Magnolia include two driving ranges, two putting greens, a pro shop, and a restaurant and lounge. The Walt Disney World Golf Studio also is based here. Course record: 61 (Mark Lye, 1984).

MAGNOLIA: Like the Palm, the Magnolia also opened with the Magic Kingdom in 1971, and it received a major face-lift in 1992 (course designer Joe Lee realigned teeing areas, recontoured greens, and replaced their original playing surface with a "faster" grass, among other things). The Magnolia features abundant water and sand, but what really sets it apart—aside from the 1,500 magnolia trees in its permanent gallery and the mouse-eared bunker beside the sixth green—is exceptional length, vast greens, and a flaw-exposing layout requiring precision and careful course management. Meandering over 175 acres of wetlands and gently rolling terrain, the par-72 course measures 5,232 yards from the front tees, 6,642 from the middle set, and 7,190 from the back markers. Among the signature holes is number 17, a long par-4 dogleg left that dares long hitters to bite off the edge of a lake, then avoid more water to the right of the green. It is the Magnolia that has final say in the outcome of the Walt Disney World/Oldsmobile Golf Classic, and it takes full advantage with a final hole that rates among the tournament's testiest. Among facilities shared by the Magnolia and the Palm are two driving ranges, two putting greens, a pro shop, and a restaurant and lounge. The WDW Golf Studio instructional programs also are based here. Course record: 61 (Payne Stewart, 1990).

OAK TRAIL: This nine-hole par-36 walking course ensconced in a 45-acre corner of the Magnolia is worth noting as an unintimidating venue for beginners, yet it's no cream puff for better players. The 2,913-yard layout unleashes plenty of challenges—including two fine par 5s—and boasts especially well-maintained greens.

OSPREY RIDGE: Tom Fazio has taken his signature mounding along fairways and around greens to monumental heights here—most dramatically with a namesake ridge that meanders through the property and elevates some greens as high as 25 feet above the basic grade. The designer counts Osprey Ridge among his best efforts, and the sentiment is echoed in the course's considerable popularity among experienced golfers. The long par-72 layout winds through a beautifully remote and thickly forested part of the property near *Fort Wilderness*; it has a deceptively gentle start, then raises the stakes en route to its three great finishing holes. Along the way, players will confront the signature par-3 third hole, with its elevated tee, and the fierce 14th, a long par 4 with a carry over water. Osprey Ridge plays to 5,402 yards from the front tees, 6,680 from the middle, and 7,101 from the back. Facilities shared by Osprey Ridge and Eagle Pines include a driving range, a putting green, a pro shop, and a restaurant and lounge. Course record: 65 (Daniel Young, 1992).

EAGLE PINES: The subtle contours of this low-lying links provide a decided contrast to the dramatic landscaping of

Beyond the Magic Linkdom

There are at least 70 courses available to the public within an hour's drive of Walt Disney World. Here are a few of the best:

Big Deals: *Hyatt Regency Grand Cypress* resort (45 holes by Jack Nicklaus and a nifty hotel, just north of WDW); Lake Nona (David Ledbetter's school is here, near the Orlando airport); Bay Hill Club (Arnie's place, and a PGA Tour stop).

Good Deals: Falcon's Fire (two years old, in Kissimmee) and Metrowest (a Palmer design, about 25 minutes' drive from Walt Disney World).

The Hottest Tickets in Town

BASKETBALL
The Orlando Magic play at the Orlando Arena from October through April. While games generally sell out in September, there is a cancellation window at the arena, open 1½ hours before each game, where out-of-town hoop fans have a shot at snaring last-minute tickets (896-2442).

BASEBALL
The Orlando Cubs, a Chicago Cubs farm team, play at Orlando's Tinker Field from early April through early September (245-2827). The National League's Houston Astros hold spring training for about six weeks beginning in March at Osceola County Stadium in Kissimmee (933-5500).

ARENA FOOTBALL
The Orlando Predators take the field at Orlando Arena from late May through August (872-7362).

ICE HOCKEY
Orlando's new International Hockey League team, the Solar Bears, plays at the Orlando Arena from late September through April (872-7825).

its companion course, Osprey Ridge, which also plays from the Bonnet Creek Golf Club. Designed by Pete Dye on a (successful) mission to create a unique challenge for players of all levels, Eagle Pines features target fairways, expansive waste areas, and roughs lined with pine needles. True to its rustic environs (it's located on the outskirts of *Fort Wilderness*), the course is sufficiently nestled in foliage and marshlands to summon comparisons to a nature preserve. Although water comes into play on 16 holes, the overall impression is one of great variety, from short par 4s to far sterner challenges—this is one course that lives up to the cliché of making you use every club in the bag. The course measures 4,838 yards from the front tees, 6,309 from the middle, and 6,772 yards from the back markers. Facilities shared by Eagle Pines and Osprey Ridge include a driving range, a putting green, a pro shop, and a restaurant and lounge. Course record: 60 (Bart Bryant, 1993).

LAKE BUENA VISTA: This Joe Lee design is a Rodney Dangerfield of sorts. The shortest of the five 18-hole courses, it features a good amount of water, and its fairways, hemmed in by stands of pine and oak, are the Magic Linkdom's tightest. Lake Buena Vista honors its reputation as a friendly course perfect for beginners. But it is also well equipped to challenge more skilled players (at least those who don't mind the wear and tear inflicted by duffers). As golf writer Glen Waggoner puts it, Lake Buena Vista may be the weakest link in the Disney chain, but it's still head and shoulders above the number two venue at most other golf resorts. The new 16th hole is a par 3 with an island green, and its two toughest holes—the second and ninth—are counted among the ten most humbling tests in the history of the Walt Disney World/Oldsmobile Golf Classic. But perhaps no one has greater respect for the course than Calvin Peete, who during the 1982 Classic blitzed the Palm in a record-breaking 66 strokes, only to give it all back—and more—on little ol' Lake Buena Vista. The course plays to 5,176 yards from the front tees, 6,268 from the middle, and 6,829 from the rearmost markers. Facilities at Lake Buena Vista include a driving range, a practice green, a clubhouse, and a restaurant. Once The Disney Institute opens in February 1996, this course will largely be given over to Institute programming. Course record: 61 (Bob Tway, 1989).

TENNIS

Even if you can't quite picture Mickey with a midsize racquet in his hand, Walt Disney World can still serve up plenty of tennis action for players of any caliber. There are a total of 25 courts scattered around the World, including 8 at the *Dolphin* hotel, which shares them with the *Swan*. You'll find a pair of hard-surface courts at the *Yacht Club* and *Beach Club*, two more at *Fort Wilderness* (watch out for swinging toddlers), and a nice, quiet trio (the courts, not the players) at the *Disney Vacation Club*. The *Grand Floridian's* duo boasts clay surfaces, ditto the new pair at *The Villas at The Disney Institute*; this is a big deal given the daytime heat during much of the year. Courts lighted for night play are available at each resort.

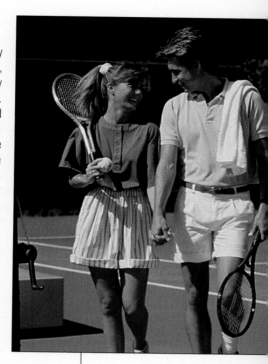

In 1997, tennis will assume a much higher profile hereabouts with the arrival of Disney's International Sports Complex, an array of courts, fields, arenas, and pools big enough to host everything this side of the Olympics. Included in this vast facility will be a dozen state-of-the-art clay courts, and don't be surprised if a major pro tournament shows up soon thereafter. For the time being, however, the most important three words that serious tennis buffs need remember if they're planning a visit are: Disney's Racquet Club (a full-service, six-clay-courts-with-pros-and-pro-shop facility located at the *Contemporary* resort).

Disney's Racquet Club

Reopened in April 1995 after a complete overhaul, Disney's Racquet Club should please even the pickiest players. The six courts, lighted for night play, are state-of-the-art hydrogrid clay, with a subterranean irrigation system that keeps them evenly watered without sprinklers. The pro shop is chock-full of high-quality equipment and tennis fashions, from Wilson's popular Hammer series racquets to those cushy Thorlo socks everyone covets.

Tennis Tips

■ Court fees are $12 at the Racquet Club, the *Grand Floridian,* and the *Dolphin*. All other courts are free.

■ The only on-property courts with a full-time pro (except at the Racquet Club) are those at the *Grand Floridian* and the *Dolphin*.

■ New tennis balls can cost up to $5.50 per can on property. Bring plenty from home.

■ Can't sleep? The courts at the *Dolphin* are illuminated all night long.

Want to Up the Ante?

Try the Beat the Pro program at Disney's Racquet Club. Win two out of three sets, and the match is free. Lose, and you pay the full private-instruction rate.

Fishing Tips

Although the fishing is good here year-round, it's most pleasant from November through May, when temperatures are cooler. As for strategy, one local recommends going with plastic worms, the red-shad-colored ones in particular. To stack your odds, he suggests shiners (about $8 for a dozen; ask for them when you make reservations). Also, top-water baits work well in spring and fall.

KNOW BEFORE YOU GO: Disney's Racquet Club is located at the north end of the *Contemporary* resort, just beyond the Garden Wing to the north of the Tower. Courts are at their busiest during June and July, when tennis camps can take over from 10 A.M. to 4 P.M. Two courts are open to guests at these times, but they are first-come, first-served (so to speak). February, March, and April also tend to be busy, especially around holidays and spring break. January, October, and November should be considered prime time to play. Courts and pro shop are open from 9 A.M. to 8 P.M.; summer hours are 8 A.M. to 9 P.M.

Rates: Court rentals are $12 per hour. WDW resort guests can pay a one-time fee ($40 per family) good for the length of their stay. Ball machine rental is $10 per half hour. Racquets can be rented for $4. Full locker room facilities are available at no charge.

Reservations: Courts may be reserved 24 hours in advance. Call 824-3578. Need a partner? Just ask for the "Tennis Anyone?" sign-up sheet.

Dress: You may think it's hip to look like Andre Agassi on the court, but it's hot down here, so we recommend cool, loose-fitting tennis whites. As for showing up in any footwear other than flat-bottom tennis shoes, note that cross-trainers, running shoes, baseball spikes, etc., tear up clay courts something awful. The pro shop staff will politely, but firmly, recommend you purchase the proper shoes on the spot.

INSTRUCTION: Private instruction from USPTA pros is available for all levels of play and covers everything from strokes to strategy. Rates are $40 per hour, $20 per half hour. Playing lessons also are available for $35 per hour. Video analysis may be added for $10 over the regular lesson rate. Worth checking out is the Stroke of the Day clinic each morning.

TOURNAMENTS: Private tournaments may be arranged through the pro shop at a cost of $40 per hour.

FISHING

Drop a line, it's promptly answered. That's typical fishing at Walt Disney World. Bay Lake, which adjoins man-made Seven Seas Lagoon, was stocked with 70,000 largemouth bass in the mid-1960s. A restrictive fishing policy allowed the fish to swell in both numbers and size. Even today angling is permitted on Bay Lake and Seven Seas Lagoon strictly in the context of guided expeditions, so the fish have gotten only so wise to plastic worm tricks. Bass pro Bob Decker, a longtime WDW fishing guide who has pursued his sport in lakes and tournaments all over Florida, gives Bay Lake his hard-earned vote for the best bass fishing in Florida. On these waters you're not just likely to catch fish, you're apt to catch largemouth bass weighing eight pounds or more (Decker has seen some so-called bucket mouths that tipped the scale at over 12 pounds). And it's not uncommon for a group to catch 15 to 20 fish in a couple of hours or for a first timer to reel in half a dozen good-size bass.

While the guided fishing trips that comb the picturesque waters of Bay Lake and Seven Seas Lagoon generally net the biggest catches, there's more to the WDW fishing scene than boats departing from *Fort Wilderness*. Additional guided expeditions lead anglers to the fish residing in a few of Disney's more scenic waterways. And those who prefer to go it alone have some tempting options in the canals of *Fort Wilderness* and the stocked fishing hole at *Dixie Landings*.

No license is required for fishing on Walt Disney World waterways. Disney's guides know their territory well, keep track of where the fish are biting, and serve in whatever capacity guests prefer—from straight chauffeurs to casting coaches and even all-out facilitators. While the official policy is catch-and-release, anglers equipped with coolers and accommodations with kitchens may keep fish caught on Bay Lake, Seven Seas Lagoon, or *Fort Wilderness* canals.

Guided Fishing Trips

FORT WILDERNESS: Guided expeditions offering some of the finest bass fishing to be found anywhere in the country depart from the *Fort Wilderness* marina at 8 A.M., 11:30 A.M., and 3 P.M. for two-hour adventures on Bay Lake and Seven Seas Lagoon. Trips are made on pontoon-style boats, equipped with trolling motors, and can accommodate up to five people. The fee per boatload is $125 for two hours ($50 for each additional hour) and

Casting About

FRESHWATER

Area lakes teem with bass, speckled perch, bream, and bluegill. Anglers may buy the required Florida freshwater fishing license (about $17 for a seven-day permit) at most local Kmart, Walmart, and sporting goods stores. For info on regulations, call (422-6995).

SALTWATER

Prime spots for surf fishing within 60 miles of Walt Disney World are the Ocean and Sunglow piers of Daytona Beach (904-677-4050), Playalinda Beach (867-4077), and the piers and jetties of Florida's most popular state park, the Sebastian Inlet State Recreation Area (800-872-1969). Deep-sea charters departing from Sebastian Inlet, Ponce Inlet (800-854-1234), and Port Canaveral (868-1108) reel in dolphin, wahoos, sailfish, tuna, and marlins. Florida saltwater fishing licenses (about $15 for a seven-day permit) are required for surf fishing done outside of licensed charters, and are available from the same sources mentioned above for freshwater licenses. For specifics, contact the Florida Marine Patrol (383-2740).

The World's Most Striking Feature

Walt Disney World lies squarely within a band of Central Florida known as the Lightning Capital of the World. Prime striking season runs from May through September, peaking during July and August, when Mother Nature unleashes about 40 thunderstorms over just 62 days according to National Weather Service figures. Most of these storms come and go rather quickly.

To protect yourself, seek shelter (the type with four walls and a roof) the moment you see a storm developing, and wait a good 15 minutes after the last rumble before resuming outdoor activity. Trees and umbrellas do not provide safe refuge. For a weather report, call 646-3131.

includes guide, gear, tackle, and refreshments (coffee and pastries in the morning, soft drinks in the afternoon). Guides will pick up guests at the *Contemporary*, *Grand Floridian*, and *Polynesian* marinas. Reservations must be made at least 72 hours in advance and may be made up to two weeks ahead. Call 824-2621.

DISNEY VILLAGE MARKETPLACE: Guided fishing excursions plying the 35-acre Buena Vista Lagoon and the Disney Village waterways depart three times daily from the marina here—at 7 A.M., 9 A.M., and 11 A.M. The 7 A.M. trips are preferable because anglers have the lagoon, and the largemouth bass therein, all to themselves (after 10 A.M., speedboats and such can infringe on prime fishing territory). The cost for up to five people, including guide, gear, tackle, and refreshments, is $120 for two hours, $145 for three hours, or $175 for four hours. Guides will pick up guests at the *Port Orleans*, *Dixie Landings*, and *Disney Vacation Club* marinas. Reservations must be made at least 48 hours in advance; call 828-2461 or 828-2204.

DIXIE LANDINGS: The two-hour fishing trip that escorts anglers on the bass-infused Sassagoula River and Buena Vista Lagoon every day at 6:30 A.M. is the only excursion that's sold by the seat rather than by the boat. The guided trip accommodates up to five people; includes gear, artificial bait, and soda; and costs $35 per person. While parties of three or fewer will come out ahead, bigger groups will end up paying more than they would for an outing on Bay Lake or a trip on Buena Vista Lagoon departing from the Disney Village Marketplace. Reservations must be made 24 hours in advance; call 934-5409.

Fishing on Your Own

Individuals who prefer to fish solo are permitted to do so on the myriad canals of *Fort Wilderness* and off the dock at the Disney Village Marketplace and resort area. Cane poles may be rented at the Marketplace for $5.50 per hour. While it's also possible to toss in a line right from the shores of *Fort Wilderness*, canoes allow anglers to slip into some truly peaceful and often fruitful channels, yielding bass, catfish, and panfish.

Canoes may be rented from the Bike Barn at *Fort Wilderness* for $4 per hour or $10 per day; also available are rods and reels ($4 per hour or $8 per day, including plastic worms) and cane poles ($2 per hour or $4 per day). Call 824-2742. Note: The canals can be unbearably steamy during the warmer months.

Dixie Landings also has a wonderfully secluded pond called the Ol' Fishin' Hole that's stocked with catfish, bass, and bluegill. Strictly catch-and-release, the peaceful fishing spot features a small dock among tall reeds where, from 9 A.M. to 3 P.M. every day, fishing is returned to its cane-pole-and-worm roots. Pole rental is $3 per hour, including worms. Call 934-5409.

BOATING

Guests looking to cruise, paddle, or even create a small wake on the pristine lakes and waterways of Walt Disney World have nothing short of the largest fleet of pleasure boats in the country at their disposal. Nearly a dozen marinas stand by with sailboats, pontoon boats, canopy boats, canoes, speedboats, and pedal boats, all of which are available for rental on a first-come, first-served basis.

On WDW's most expansive boating forum, the 650-acre body of water comprising Bay Lake and the adjoining Seven Seas Lagoon, watercraft from the *Contemporary, Wilderness Lodge*, and *Fort Wilderness* marinas converge with boats lighting out from the *Polynesian* and *Grand Floridian*. Other areas are more contained. Craft rented at the *Caribbean Beach* cruise around 45-acre Barefoot Bay. As boats on brief loan from the Disney Village Marketplace roam 35-acre Buena Vista Lagoon, small flotillas of rental craft drift in from the upriver marinas of the *Disney Vacation Club*, *Port Orleans*, and *Dixie Landings*. Meanwhile, watercraft from the *Yacht Club* and *Beach Club*, and the *Swan* and *Dolphin*, make ripples on 25-acre Crescent Lake.

All the marinas are open from 10 A.M. until early evening (closing hours vary). No privately owned boats are permitted on any WDW waterways. To rent, day visitors must present a valid driver's license or passport, and Disney resort guests must show their hotel ID. Some rentals carry other restrictions (described below).

Getting Above It All

If the notion of flying like a kite above Bay Lake with a panorama of the Magic Kingdom appeals to you, factor in a contoured chair (called a Sky Rider) that allows you to sit in a reclined position, and you have an idea of the parasailing experience as it exists at Walt Disney World.

The flight lasts seven to ten minutes, and the landing is quite soft, thanks to the parachute and the two-person crew's masterful timing (as one gently reels in the cord, the other is slowing the boat just so).

Parasailing excursions are offered at the *Contemporary* marina, with none other than Mark McCulloh, the man who invented the sport, running the show. The cost is about $40 for a single rider or $65 for two riders, and reservations are required (call 824-1000, ext. 3586).

Running Around the World

Despite pleasant terrain that looks like it's been spread with a rolling pin, Walt Disney World can be a rough place to pursue the world's most mobile form of exercise; from late spring through early fall, comfortable running conditions are fleeting, with early birds getting the best shot at a pleasant run. In cooler seasons, joggers have greater freedom to explore the many compelling options here.

Maps of the jogging trails and footpaths accessible from each WDW resort are available from each hotel's Guest Services desk. Courses range from one mile to just over three, and are typically conducive to early turnarounds and repeats. *Dixie Landings*, the *Disney Vacation Club*, and *Fort Wilderness* offer some of the most extensive and scenic venues.

Outside WDW boundaries, the pathways ringing Lake Eola (in downtown Orlando) and Lake Underhill (just east of town) are popular with local joggers. Competitive runners can catch up with local road races (from 5K to marathons) through a pre-recorded hotline (896-5473) offered by the Track Shack running shop, or by calling the Track Shack directly (898-1313).

SAILING: While Bay Lake and Seven Seas Lagoon offer pretty reliable winds and unparalleled running room, guests may also choose to sail on lakes awash in Caribbean or Nantucket ambience. Sailing conditions are generally best in March and April. A variety of sailboats may be rented at the *Grand Floridian*, *Polynesian*, *Contemporary*, *Wilderness Lodge*, *Fort Wilderness*, *Caribbean Beach*, and *Yacht Club* and *Beach Club* marinas. Among the options are Aquafin (two passengers maximum; $10 per hour), Capris (good beginner boats holding up to six; $14 per hour), and Hobie Cat 14s and 16s (catamarans accommodating two and three people, and costing $14 and $15, respectively; catamaran experience is required).

CRUISING: For groups interested in taking a leisurely sunning, sightseeing, or party excursion on the water, motorized canopy boats and pontoon boats are the only way to go. Sixteen-foot canopy boats accommodating up to eight adults (about $17.50 per half hour) and 20-foot pontoon boats holding ten adults ($20 per half hour) are available for rent at most marinas with the notable exceptions of the *Dolphin* and *Swan*. Cruising of a different sort is offered at the *Dolphin* and *Swan*, where electric-powered SunKats and CraigCats ($15 per half hour) offer lounge-chair-style transport.

CANOEING: Paddling among the narrow channels of *Fort Wilderness* during the cooler and more peaceful morning hours, canoers pass through both forest and meadows, encountering solitary anglers and quacking contingents along the way. Fishing and canoeing are an irresistible combination for many, with fishing gear available for rent right alongside the canoes (which run $4 per hour or $10 per day) at *Fort Wilderness'* Bike Barn. Canoes also may be rented at the *Caribbean Beach*, *Port Orleans*, and *Dixie Landings* marinas. Use of these watercraft is restricted to WDW canals.

PEDAL BOATING: For those who prefer pedal-pushing to paddling, these craft (accommodating two pedaling passengers and two freeloaders) are available for about $5.50 per half hour or $8 per hour at most marinas. Rentals are restricted to Disney resort guests at the *Caribbean Beach*, *Port Orleans*, *Dixie Landings*, and *Yacht Club* and *Beach Club* marinas; the Bike Barn at *Fort Wilderness* follows the same policy.

Biking Around the World

While *Fort Wilderness* is certainly prime territory for leisurely cycling, the World is filled with picturesque roads that wind, relatively untrafficked, within some of its most sprawling and scenic resorts.

Bikes are available for rental (about $4 an hour or $8 per day, with some variation among locations) in precisely the spots where guests will want to ride: *Fort Wilderness* (featuring tons of wooded trails); the *Wilderness Lodge* (with a lakeside pathway leading to *Fort Wilderness*); *Port Orleans* and *Dixie Landings* (for extensive roadways at either end of a waterfront path); the *Disney Vacation Club* (with pleasant neighborhood streets); and *The Villas at The Disney Institute* (for rustic roadways and pathways).

Avid cyclists who bring their own bikes might also spin their wheels with the Florida Freewheelers Club (788-3446). The group leads organized rides from social to race-pace every weekend year-round.

SPEEDBOATING: Among the most enjoyable—and popular—ways to cool off at Walt Disney World is the legion of mini speedboats called Water Sprites. While the boats max out at a paltry ten miles per hour, their small hulls ride a choppy surface as if they were galloping steeds. Disney Village Marketplace offers one of the more uncrowded arenas in Buena Vista Lagoon. (An additional boon: Riders must be 14 to rent Water Sprites here; elsewhere the minimum age is 12.) While Water Sprites ostensibly seat two, adult boaters will reach greater speeds going solo (and creating tiny wakes for one another). Water Sprites are restricted to lakes only, and are available for $15 per half hour at the *Grand Floridian*, *Polynesian*, *Contemporary*, *Wilderness Lodge*, *Yacht Club* and *Beach Club*, *Fort Wilderness*, *Caribbean Beach*, and Disney Village Marketplace marinas.

WATERSKIING: Enthusiasts interested in hitching a ride around Bay Lake and Seven Seas Lagoon will pay $75 per hour for a boat and driver. Up to five skiers can be accommodated at a time, with a two-person minimum. Waterskiing excursions are available exclusively at the *Contemporary*, *Polynesian*, *Grand Floridian*, *Wilderness Lodge*, and *Fort Wilderness* marinas. Reservations are necessary, and can be made up to two weeks in advance (phone 824-2621 for all resorts, 8 A.M. to 4 P.M. daily).

149

Which Way to the Beach?

Walt Disney World resort guests need not set out for the coast to find pretty strands where they can sunbathe and get a little sand between their toes. Between the resorts fronting Bay Lake (the *Contemporary*, the *Wilderness Lodge*, and *Fort Wilderness*) and those on the shores of Seven Seas Lagoon (the *Grand Floridian* and the *Polynesian*), there's over five miles of white-sand beaches. And that doesn't include the powdery white stretches at the *Caribbean Beach*, the *Yacht Club* and *Beach Club*, and the *Dolphin* and *Swan* resorts. The beach fronting the *Polynesian*'s Moorea guest building is among the more secluded shores. All resort beaches are reserved exclusively for guests staying at those properties.

When only a bona fide seashore will do, consider the world-famous Daytona Beach (nominal toll collected per car). Relax at Melbourne beaches (the shortest hop from the Magic Kingdom). Or stretch out on the pristine shores of 24-mile-long Canaveral National Seashore, with its 40-foot dunes, sea grapes, and pristine scalloped shores.

SWIMMING

As if it weren't enough to have an inside track to three water parks (see "Other Pursuits" in the latter part of this chapter), WDW resorts are themselves bursting at the seams with watery playgrounds. With no fewer than 40 pools spread throughout Disney's hotel grounds, guests at each resort can be assured of access to at least one pool. However, it is important to note that due to a policy initiated to prevent overcrowding, WDW hotel pools are open only to guests staying at that resort; pool-hopping is permitted strictly between sister resorts (the *Yacht Club* and *Beach Club*, *Port Orleans* and *Dixie Landings*, and the *Dolphin* and *Swan*).

As a general rule, the hotels with multiple pools afford the most pleasant swimming for adults. This is because one pool is tailored (most often via a delightfully rendered theme) to attract the splashy crowd, thereby freeing up the other(s) for swimmers in search of calmer waters. The *Yacht Club* and *Beach Club* offer the best of both worlds: two secluded pools with whirlpools, and an extraordinary mini–water park called Stormalong Bay that sprawls over three acres and features whirlpools, jets, and a sand-bottomed wading lagoon. The *Dolphin* and *Swan* also do things right; a grotto pool filled with waterfalls and alcoves is punctuated by whirlpools and complemented by two rectangular pools.

Among resorts with one swimming hole, the *Grand Floridian's* pool is vast, unthemed, and open 24 hours; the *Wilderness Lodge's*, beautifully themed yet smallish; and *Port Orleans'*, fun if generally overrun with children (although there's the added option of swimming next door at *Dixie Landings*). Featuring two pools apiece are the *Contemporary*, the *Polynesian*, *Fort Wilderness*, and the *All-Star Sports* and *All-Star Music* resorts. (Note: Both *All-Star* resorts are marked exceptions to the two-pools-means-at-least-one-quiet-pool rule.) The *Disney Vacation Club* features four pools; *Dixie Landings* and *The Villas at The Disney Institute* both have six; and the *Caribbean Beach* resort has seven. Each of the Disney Village Hotel Plaza properties has one pool. Lap swimmers will be happiest with the spacious rectangular pool at the *Dolphin* and *Swan*.

HEALTH CLUBS

Of the eight fitness centers located within WDW hotels, all but two are reserved strictly for guests staying at the resort that houses them. They are the Olympiad Health Club at the *Contemporary* (824-1823; temporary membership is available to any WDW guest) and the Body By Jake Health Club at the *Dolphin* (934-4264; membership is open to anyone).

More generally, the clubs divide into three tiers. Falling into the category of good on-the-road maintenance are the fine but bare-bones facilities at the *Swan* (complimentary to guests). Better equipped—with Nautilus, more current and varied cardiovascular machines, and such pleasant extras as a sauna or massage—are the *Contemporary's* Olympiad ($8 per day, $15 for length of stay); R.E.S.T. at the *Disney Vacation Club* (no fee for resort guests); and St. John's Health Club at the *Grand Floridian* ($5 per day, $10 for length of stay).

The best of the lot are exceptionally pleasant—and uncramped—settings that distinguish themselves by going the extra mile and offering the likes of personal trainers, Gravitrons, and Cybex machines. These are the Ship Shape Health Club at the *Yacht Club* and *Beach Club* ($5 per day, $10 for length of stay; mirrored alcove offers hot tub, steam room, and sauna); the Body By Jake Health Club at the *Dolphin* ($8 per day, $16 for length of stay; aerobics and Polaris equipment offered); and the 300,000-square-foot health and fitness center at *The Villas at The Disney Institute* (complimentary to Institute guests; features aerobics, a gymnasium, Cybex equipment, and a full-service spa).

For a Good Massage Call...

- Olympiad Health Club at the *Contemporary* (824-1823)
- Ship Shape Health Club at the *Yacht Club* and *Beach Club* (934-3256)
- St. John's Health Club at the *Grand Floridian* (824-2433)
- Body By Jake Health Club at the *Dolphin* (934-4264)
- Slappy Joe's Massage Room at the *Disney Vacation Club* (827-1677)

Licensed massage therapists offer massages by appointment only. Fees are $37 for a half-hour session, $55 for an hour at all locations (except Body By Jake and Slappy Joe's, where half-hour sessions are $35).

SHOPPING

There's more to the shopping scene at Walt Disney World than Mouseketeer hats, Mickey Mouse watches, and sweatshirts ad infinitum. Indeed, Disney character merchandise has reached a level of taste and sophistication that will amaze even the most demanding souvenir hunter. The options range from dark chocolate

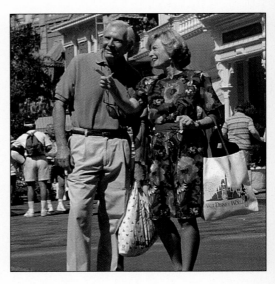

molded in the image of a certain mouse's face to exclusive pieces of Disneyana created by such world-class artisans as Waterford, Goebel, and Georgio Armani. For adults looking to find a grownup forget-me-not, the pickings have never been better. There are henley T-shirts, sweat-shirts, and denim shirts playfully adorned with tasteful character appliqués. Ties, hair scrunchies, and dress socks feature surprisingly subtle Mickey Mouse designs. And product lines earmarked for executives and gour-mands have deftly infused the World's most recognizable silhouette into the likes of black leather portfolios, fine writing implements, and sugar bowls and creamers.

Although much of the commerce here revolves around Disneyana, most shops offer character merchandise within the context of a broader theme (jewelry or books, for instance). Others, such as Olde World Antiques in the Magic Kingdom, eschew the stuff altogether. Yes, that's right, antiques. In the Magic Kingdom. A bit bizarre,

Did You Know...

Enough Mouseketeer hats are sold each year to cover the head of every person in Pittsburgh.

granted. But the fact that such a possibility exists in this prime "Please, Daddy, please!" real estate serves as a nice elbow-in-the-ribs allusion to what fills shelves and racks in more adult corners of the World. When we say that Epcot's World Showcase is no United Nations of Kmarts, no international convention of Disney paraphernalia, we mean (1) merchandise eloquently represents each of the 11 nations; (2) we'd trust the folks who stock some of the shops here to choose a gift for our mothers; and (3) the place is a dangerous buying spree waiting to happen. Then there's the Disney Village Marketplace, an attractive enclave of boutiques and restaurants on the shores of Buena Vista Lagoon that (from 9:30 A.M. to 11 P.M. daily) offers the best one-stop shopping in the World. And it's not just because it boasts the biggest hoard of Disney merchandise on the planet: The whirlwind shopping potential of the Marketplace extends to animation cels, books, country crafts, designer clothing, environmentally themed goods, fine jewelry, and gourmet gifts (and that's just from A to G). The sort of place that inspires shoppers to drag companions by their arm to see this great thing or that, the Marketplace is loaded.

Because it wouldn't be right to send you out into the World without an itemized shopping list, we've pulled together a diverse selection of the best shops—both in the World and in the Orlando area. While particular items may not be in the store when you are, comparable goods should be available.

IN THE DISNEY VILLAGE MARKETPLACE

Stand-Outs

THE ART OF DISNEY: Skip this showroom brimming with limited-edition art pieces, collectibles, and animation cels, and you've missed out on some of the most spectacular ogling to be had at WDW (Disney characters masterfully rendered by the likes of Lladro and Armani). This is one of three such shops at WDW (the others are at the Magic Kingdom and the Disney-MGM Studios); displays vary among galleries.

More Than a Marketplace

In addition to the World's best shopping, the Disney Village Marketplace offers restaurants, lounges, a marina, special events, interactive fountains, and a walkway to Pleasure Island. It's also a scenic place to hang out.

Big Things in Store

When the last nail has been hammered into place on a major Disney expansion project, Pleasure Island and the Disney Village Marketplace will no longer be simply joined at the hip; in fact, the two areas will be united and their collective horde of restaurants, clubs, and shops will have doubled. The entertainment district's transformation is due for completion sometime in 1997. Here's a quick run-through of the coming attractions.

■ There will be three new restaurants: *Wolfgang Puck's Café* (the innovative L.A. chef's Florida premiere); *Lario's* (created by Gloria Estefan and her husband as a taste of Cuba); and *House of Blues* (a bastion of New Orleans cuisine that's part-owned by Dan Aykroyd). *Lario's* and *House of Blues* will double as nightclubs.

■ Add-ons to AMC Theatres will more than double the capacity of the state-of-the-art cineplex, bringing the total number of screens to a whopping 24.

■ A 1,500-seat performing arts theater will provide a venue for concerts and shows.

■ A pair of Disney mega-stores will add considerably to the World's shopping circuit (see opposite page for details).

CHRISTMAS CHALET: Rather than tick off the many delightful trimmings—both traditional and with Disney characters—proffered at this trove of decorative items, ornaments, and collectibles, we'll cut to the chase: Just add eggnog.

GOURMET PANTRY: This Marketplace institution stocks a full line of Gourmet Mickey cookware, including sleek Michael Graves designs (there's a limited-edition Mickey-fied silver teakettle for $100). It is also positively crammed with delectables; while many sweets and savories are meant for instant gratification, others (Mickey-shaped pasta and Mickey Shorts Bread) make good souvenirs.

GREAT SOUTHERN CRAFT CO.: There's no telling what special articles of homespun Americana you'll find in this shop, so don't preclude the possibility of a $325 *American Gothic*–themed chess set in which chickens are pawns and the pitchfork pair serve as king and queen.

HARRINGTON BAY CLOTHIERS: Mickey makes himself very scarce at this upscale spot—a reliable resource for men's sportswear and accessories, branded by the likes of Perry Ellis, Polo by Ralph Lauren, and Nautica.

MICKEY'S CHARACTER SHOP: The most comprehensive collection of Disney character merchandise available anywhere makes this emporium a terrific venue for streamlined souvenir shopping. Large displays vacillate from limited-edition watches to stuffed animals, from nightshirts to office accessories, and from music compilations to books and videos. While conspicuous characters are the rule, there is also a lot of great Mickey Mouse innuendo to be found here.

PLANET HOLLYWOOD: If there are no "Beverly Hillbillies" or *Star Wars* vehicles hanging from the rafters in this satellite shop located just outside the celestial restaurant itself, it's because the place is filled to the hilt with Planet Hollywood–logo clothing—from hats and boxer shorts to denim and leather jackets.

2R'S READING AND RITING: In this terrific book nook, you'll find plenty of best-sellers, children's books, and Disney tomes; gifts such as Cross pens and Disney's

Executive Collection desk accessories, which take Mickey to his sophisticated heights; and a ready supply of stationery, cards, and cappuccino.

RESORTWEAR UNLIMITED: With classic separates from such labels as Liz Claiborne and Adrienne Vittadini, the largest selection of swimwear at WDW, and a choice stash of accessories (shoes, handbags, and jewelry), this spot is equipped to plug most any hole in a woman's travel wardrobe. It also has a Lancôme cosmetics counter.

TEAM MICKEY'S ATHLETIC CLUB: This shop specializes in sport-specific Disney character apparel and gear that runs the gamut from Goofy golf club covers to Tigger thong leotards.

Good Bets

24KT PRECIOUS ADORNMENTS: An elegant showroom in which unique designer jewelry gleams alongside good-quality Disney character charms and watches.

THE CITY: Disney proves worthy of outfitting and accessorizing the young and hip.

CRISTAL ARTS: Don't ask us why it's spelled with an *i*. This is crystal city. Items similar to those at Crystal (with a *y*) Arts on Main Street in the Magic Kingdom may be engraved on site.

DISCOVER: A natural for the ecologically minded set, this shop tenders such wares as wooden wind chimes and character T-shirts made of unbleached cotton.

EUROSPAIN: Decorative ceramic masks are among the more unusual possibilities at this bastion of breakables specializing in fine porcelain figurines.

YOU & ME KID: Here's looking at a landslide of toys, clothing, and other items suited for children of all ages.

...Really Big

The World of Disney Superstore will supersede Mickey's Character Shop (by a long shot) as the keeper of the largest collection of Disney character merchandise available anywhere. And the Team Mickey Superstore will make a huge production of sports.

Carved in Stone

Some guests let people walk all over them—for posterity's sake. Actually, they allow fellow guests to step on a hexagonal brick bearing their name, one of the many forming a walkway at the entrance to the Magic Kingdom and around Seven Seas Lagoon. The ten-inch bricks—engraved with Mickey Mouse and up to three lines of text, including name(s), city, and state or country—are carefully numbered and mapped for easy location. Special designs are available to commemorate weddings and anniversaries. The bricks may be purchased for $96 at the Magic Kingdom entrance or by calling 800-36-BRICK (362-7425) anytime.

IN THE PARKS
Magic Kingdom Stand-Outs

BRIAR PATCH (Frontierland): Specialties of the house are stuffed animals from Disney's *Song of the South* and a distinctive batch of character merchandise.

CRYSTAL ARTS (Main Street): This shop offers cut-glass bowls and vases, and clear-glass mugs and steins similar to those available at the Disney Village Marketplace's Cristal Arts. Items can be engraved on site, and guests have the opportunity to observe an engraver or glass-blower at work.

DISNEYANA COLLECTIBLES (Main Street): One of three WDW showrooms featuring limited-edition art pieces, collectibles, and animation cels (an extraordinary eyeful that should not be missed). Displays are different at each gallery; the other venues are found at the Disney Village Marketplace and the Disney-MGM Studios.

DISNEY CLOTHIERS (Main Street): Souvenir clothing earns big style points here, as various Disney characters appear on silk scarves, ties, and leather goods, and are appliquéd on golf shirts, denim shirts, sweaters, and nightshirts. Selection is small but choice.

EMPORIUM (Main Street): The Magic Kingdom's largest gift shop offers an array of Walt Disney World logo and character merchandise (including lots of stuffed animals, T-shirts, sweatshirts, and hats) whose variety is eclipsed only by that found at the Marketplace.

THE KING'S GALLERY (Cinderella Castle): You'll pay a king's ransom to walk off with some of the treasures at this richly appointed shop filled with tapestries, suits of armor, Spanish-made swords, and chess sets. Or at least you'll be tempted.

MAIN STREET ATHLETIC STORE (Main Street): It wasn't exactly sleight of hand, but one day—poof—the magic shop and arcade were gone and in their place was a nifty stash of sport-related character apparel. If you want to score some unique team-logo items, don't pass.

MAIN STREET CONFECTIONERY (Main Street): Sweet tooths fall in line for delicious peanut brittle, fudge, and marshmallow crispies made on the premises. For milk chocolate golf balls and an amazing find called Chocolate Mint Cookie Gems, this is the source.

OLDE WORLD ANTIQUES (Liberty Square): Pretty linens, collectible dolls, and made-to-order perfumes hold their own with the antiques and reproductions here.

SILVERSMITH (Liberty Square): The sort of single-minded spot where delicate sterling silver ornaments share the spotlight with silverware chimes and gold-for-saking jewelry.

UPTOWN JEWELERS (Main Street): If you're shopping for a character watch or good-quality souvenir charms, earrings, and pendants, this elegant catchall is the place. The full line of Mickey-suggestive Cross writing implements is represented. There is also a large selection of ceramic character figurines.

YANKEE TRADER (Liberty Square): A front porch with a rocking chair sets the tone for this cozy niche chock-full of country kitchen wares.

The Mouse Delivers

Arrive home with one T-shirt or stuffed animal too few? Call 800-237-5751 for the Disney Catalog. Have a sudden, not-to-be-denied yearning for a certain music box, watch, or tie that you saw in a shop during your visit? Call WDW Mail Order at 800-272-6201.

Window on the World

Browsing takes on new meaning in the international marketplace that comprises Epcot's World Showcase, for there's more to eyeball in this thoroughfare than a cornucopia of goods from far-away places. In each pavilion, there's a chance to watch visiting artisans at work. Among the handicrafts you might see as works-in-progress are hand-knotted carpets (Morocco), Lissi dolls and M. I. Hummel figurines (Germany), paper fans (China), and jewelry (Mexico). Be sure to lift your eyes from the merchandise itself long enough to take it all in.

Epcot Stand-Outs

THE AMERICAN ADVENTURE (World Showcase): Heritage Manor Gifts waxes patriotic with pre-1940s Americana. Highlights include decorative throws, quilted items, and political campaign buttons.

CANADA (World Showcase): A tempting array of Canadian handicrafts and Indian artifacts puts the Northwest Mercantile on the essential shopping circuit.

CENTORIUM (Innoventions, Future World): Epcot's best address for Disney character merchandise also stocks futuristic gizmos such as talking calculators and Seiko pendulum clocks that fairly beg for attention.

CHINA (World Showcase): The Yong Feng Shangdian Shopping Gallery is so huge it's almost a province; and the montage of paper fans, Chinese prints, silk robes, antiques, vases, and tea sets is truly something to behold.

FRANCE (World Showcase): Spellbinding boutiques offer things beautiful and French. Our favorites are Plume et Palette (oil paintings upstairs, and crystal, porcelain, and collectible miniatures downstairs); La Maison du Vin (fine wines, cookbooks, and hand-painted dishes); and La Signature (fragrances, lotions, and linens).

GREEN THUMB EMPORIUM (The Land, Future World): Do not be misled. While this great little shop is flush with seeds, garden kits, and garden-themed kitchen accessories and knickknacks, gardening prowess is not for sale here. Repeat: No green thumbs change hands.

GERMANY (World Showcase): This pavilion's irresistible lineup may be Epcot's best. Volkskunst (bursting with cuckoo clocks, beer steins, nutcrackers, and wood carvings) could hold down the fort by itself. Instead it jockeys for attention with Der Teddybär (a delightful toy shop brimming with Steiff stuffed animals, colorful wooden toys, and Lissi dolls); Weinkeller (featuring about 250 bottlings from H. Schmitt Söhne, one of Germany's oldest vintners); and Glas und Porzellan (a boutique wall-to-wall with Goebel's cherubic M. I. Hummel figurines, where an artist demonstrates the process by which the rosy-cheeked creations are painted and finished).

ITALY (World Showcase): When in this multi-shop pavilion, we gravitate toward Delizie Italiane for fine chocolates, and Il Bel Cristallo for the brilliant array of Venetian glass paperweights, ceramics, and lead crystal bowls.

JAPAN (World Showcase): In this pavilion's vast emporium, Mitsukoshi Department Store, kimono-clad dolls (priced from $3.50 to $3,000) merit special attention, as do kimonos, origami kits, and bonsai.

MEXICO (World Showcase): While the vibrant piñatas, baskets, and ponchos presented in the central plaza are great for effect, the ceramics and other handicrafts at adjacent Artesanias Mexicanas tend to be marked by a more enduring appeal.

MOROCCO (World Showcase): At least half the fun of shopping in this pavilion's maze of Berber bangles, basketry, clothing, and hand-knotted carpets is never knowing just what awaits around the bend. Carpet-making demonstrations are ongoing.

NORWAY (World Showcase): The Puffin's Roost is undoubtedly Central Florida's best source for trolls and gorgeous Norwegian ski sweaters (bargains when compared to flights to Oslo). Exquisite miniature wood carvings and handcrafted jewelry add to the eclectic mix.

UNITED KINGDOM (World Showcase): Some of Epcot's finest shops lie within this pavilion's borders. There's The Toy Soldier (a primarily Paddington Bear and Peter Rabbit affair); Lords and Ladies (a British free-for-all complete with fragrance products and dartboards); Pringle of Scotland (a bounty of cashmeres, woolens, and all things plaid); The Queen's Table (with Royal Doulton collectibles from $5 to $12,500); and The Magic of Wales (featuring handcrafted gifts from the land of Diana). And of course, there's a prime spot for tea lovers—The Tea Caddy.

Bonsai to Go

When we tell you the Mitsukoshi Department Store in Japan has a bounty of beautiful, reasonably priced bonsai for sale, we mean the collection approximates a miniature forest. Even better: You can leave your purchase with a salesperson for shipping, and let the teensy tree-of-choice meet you back at the homefront.

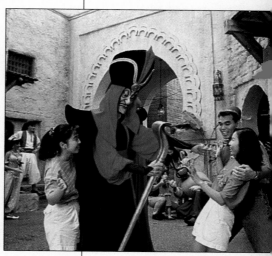

Talk About an Eclectic Mix ...

The unique array of merchandise found in shops at the Disney-MGM Studios is best quantified by example. At last check, the theme park could fill the following unlikely shopping list:

- Scarlett O'Hara doll and Elvis doll
- Limited-edition Disney animation cel
- "Brady Bunch" and "Munsters" T-shirts
- Videotape of *Casablanca*
- Big Bad Wolf mask
- Autographed photo of James Dean
- Grumpy serving dish
- Original invitation to a Disney movie premiere
- Plastic "quacking" whistle (with neck cord)
- Mickey Mouse golf shirt
- Musical snow globe with "When You Wish Upon a Star"
- Something once worn by Mel Gibson

Disney-MGM Studios Stand-Outs

ANIMATION GALLERY: This sophisticated shop is one of three Walt Disney World venues showcasing limited-edition art pieces, collectibles, and animation cels (a spectacular eyeful that is not to be missed). While gallery displays vary, there's always a mix of contemporary and classic styles, and a fair representation of characters from both current and vintage Disney films. The other show-rooms are found at the Magic Kingdom and the Disney Village Marketplace.

CELEBRITY 5 & 10: A low-budget Elvis, Marilyn, *Wizard of Oz*, James Dean, *Star Trek*, Betty Boop, "Munsters," and "Brady Bunch" o-rama.

THE COSTUME SHOP: Disney villains reign supreme in rubber masks, T-shirts, and other merchandise here (though the children's costumes stick to the fairy princess side of the fence).

KEYSTONE CLOTHIERS: Characters turn up on adult fashions. While we've seen a couple of sequined bustiers, clothing more typically replicates that found in Disney Clothiers at the Magic Kingdom. The selection includes appliquéd golf shirts, nightshirts, and chambray shirts, plus ties, silk scarves, and other accessories.

LEGENDS OF HOLLYWOOD: The type of shop where one might stumble upon a Scarlett O'Hara doll (though, as Miss O'Hara so eloquently put it, "Tomorrow is another day"). Credits include movie posters, books, and stills, plus a nice array of classic films and Disney animated features on video.

ONCE UPON A TIME: There was a little shop that offered one of the classiest souvenir collections the World over—musical snow globes featuring artfully rendered Disney characters, wooden and ceramic character figurines, and (at last look) extraordinary Pinocchio and Mickey marionettes, and a fine Grumpy serving dish. It seemed sure to live happily ever after. The End.

SID CAHUENGA'S ONE-OF-A-KIND: Celebrity encounters abound in this den of movie and television memorabilia. There are scads of autographed photos, original movie posters, and, for just $5, much belated premiere invitations to Disney animated films. There's also ample opportunity to snap up hand-me-downs direct from the stars, so when someone compliments your handbag, you can say, "Yeah, Mae West liked it, too." Closet contents turn over too frequently to allow for specifics, but we suspect a certain custom-made pink suit with matching platform boots ($500; courtesy of Sonny Bono) might stick around awhile.

SWEET SUCCESS: Compelling reasons for an intermission include fresh-made chocolates, fudge, candies, and marshmallow crispies.

BEYOND THE WORLD
Local Stand-Outs

BELZ FACTORY OUTLET WORLD (5401 W. Oak Ridge Rd., Orlando; 352-9600): Shoppers with endurance can save up to 75 percent on wares from 180 brand-name merchants when they test their limits at the two giant malls and four shopping centers that make up Central Florida's largest outlet center. Among the notable presences: Pfaltzgraff, Oneida, Anne Klein, Geoffrey Beene, Calvin Klein, London Fog, Levi Strauss, and Reebok. Also check out Everything but Water for women's bathing suits (sizes petite to 26), and the Character Warehouse, which sells Disney merchandise that is discontinued or out of season. Open daily.

EDWIN WATTS GOLF SHOPS (Four area locations including 7501 Turkey Lake Rd., Orlando; 345-8451; and 7048 International Dr., Orlando; 352-2535): This chain stokes the local obsession with golf attire, clubs, and gear, sporting all the big labels (Ping, Callaway, Taylor Made). The Turkey Lake Road store is the flagship; the International Drive location is the clearance center (with discounts of up to 50 percent on discontinued lines). Open daily.

FLEA WORLD (U.S. 17-92, Sanford; 330-1792): This 350,000-square-foot open-air market is no fly-by-night affair. With 1,700 vendors under one roof, it's the largest covered flea market in the country (if it gets any bigger it'll

Crossroads of Lake Buena Vista

The main attraction at this conveniently located shopping center, across from the Disney Village Hotel Plaza, is a huge Gooding's supermarket, notable because it's open 24 hours a day and because it has a pharmacy. Other shops specialize in casual clothing, swimwear, athletic shoes, and electronics. Restaurants include such familiar entities as *Perkins* (open 24 hours) and *T.G.I. Friday's*, plus a local favorite, *Pebbles*.

Between Shops in Winter Park?

■ For the most glorious "window-shopping" on Park Avenue, visit the Charles Hosmer Morse Museum of American Art (644-3686), which boasts one of the world's largest collections of Tiffany glass.

■ A one-hour pontoon cruise plying Winter Park's lakes and canals (644-4056) passes historic Rollins College and offers a breathtaking perspective of the community's exquisite gardens and estates.

need public transportation). Among the myriad offerings: country crafts, fresh Florida citrus, and power tools. Open Fridays, Saturdays, and Sundays. Free parking.

INTERNATIONAL DESIGNER OUTLETS (5211 International Dr., Orlando; 352-3632): The uptown cousin (and close neighbor) of Belz Factory Outlet World boasts 45 outlets, including Donna Karan, Coach, Saks Fifth Avenue, Waterford/Wedgwood, and (go figure) Black & Decker. Discounts up to 40 percent. Open daily.

MOUNT DORA (For information call the Mount Dora Area Chamber of Commerce, 383-2165): This lakeside village is the unofficial antiques capital of Florida, with more than a dozen antiques shops dotting its quaint downtown streets. Shops closed Sundays.

PARK AVENUE (For information call the Park Avenue Area Association, 644-8281 or 740-5660): Scores of upscale shops purveying everything from designer clothing to jewelry, housewares, and handicrafts line this tony retail district in downtown Winter Park, sometimes referred to as Little Europe. Parking is scarce. Most stores closed Sundays.

RENNINGER'S ANTIQUE CENTER (Just east of Mount Dora, off U.S. 441; 904-383-8393): This venerable institution—Florida's largest antiques and collectibles emporium—features 150 furniture, jewelry, glass, china, doll, and oriental rug vendors. Open only on Saturdays and Sundays.

RON JON SURF SHOP (4151 N. Atlantic Ave., Cocoa Beach; 799-8888): The sort of 24-hour convenience store where one can rent a boogie board at 3 A.M., Ron Jon's is the ultimate beach shop. The door is always open for shoppers seeking sunglasses, swimwear, active wear, and water sports equipment. Beach bikes, surfboards, and in-line skates also are available for rent. Open daily.

SEMINOLE TOWNE CENTER (State Road 46 just off I-4, Sanford; for information call the Sanford Chamber of Commerce, 322-2212): This state-of-the-art mall—brand-spanking-new in fall 1995—is anchored by Dillard's, JC Penney, Parisian, Burdines, and Sears, and features 100 specialty stores. Open daily.

OTHER PURSUITS

You're at Walt Disney World, but you're not in the mood for a theme park, don't feel much like swatting a little white ball or sitting by the pool, and have already shopped (and dropped). You're up for something, but lacking inspiration. What do you do? Don't despair. Disney's got this one covered.

Perhaps you'd like to select from the aquatic side of the adventure menu. Disney has channeled its usual creative flair, and no less than 4.3 million gallons of H_2O, into three parks that are to water what Liberace was to music. There's River Country, an old-fashioned swimming hole with several water slides and a Huckleberry Finn sense of fun; Typhoon Lagoon, where tsunamis are the specialty of the house; and Blizzard Beach, the new park with all the trappings of a ski resort, from its chairlift to its ski jump–style centerpiece, the world's tallest water slide.

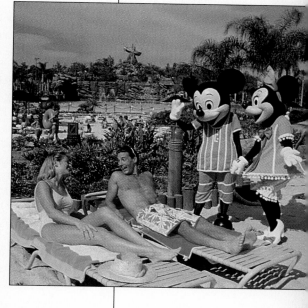

Or, perhaps you'd be interested in something more nature-oriented. For a lot of greenery and a little wildlife, there's *Fort Wilderness*, 700 acres of woodland rife with picturesque trails and canals, and plenty of ways (including biking, canoeing, fishing, and horseback riding) to explore them. For glorious foliage and a litany of unusual animal encounters, the zoological park called Discovery Island is the natural distraction of choice.

If you're thirsting for something deeper, perhaps you'd enjoy a horticultural seminar or a tour that reveals the cultural and architectural underpinnings of Epcot's World Showcase. For the ultimate Disney learning adventure, there's the new Disney Institute, where the curriculum runs from topiary making to radio broadcasting.

163

WATER PARKS
River Country

Disney's original watery playground holds its own with the sort of old-fashioned swimming hole Tom Sawyer would have tried to keep a lid on: a walled-off cove of Bay Lake furnished with rope swings and a ship's boom that swimmers may also enter via two fast-moving water flumes. A white-water raft ride deposits passengers into the swimming hole a bit more gently. River Country's other swimming area possesses charms of its own. A 330,000-gallon pool ensconced in man-made boulders, it is fitted out with two steep chutes that stop seven feet above the water's surface; unlike the swimming hole, it's heated during cooler months. River Country honors its rustic *Fort Wilderness* location with a short-but-sweet nature trail along the lake's edge that offers a peaceful retreat among egrets and a telescopic perspective of Discovery Island.

KNOW BEFORE YOU GO: River Country is located in the northwestern corner of *Fort Wilderness* on a shore of Bay Lake directly opposite Discovery Island. The park is usually closed for refurbishment for at least one month in winter (call 824-4321 for exact dates). During the summer, crowds may push capacity as early as 11 A.M.; when the magic number comes up, only guests arriving with tickets in hand will be admitted, until crowds subside later in the day.

How to get there: Buses from the TTC and the *Wilderness Lodge*, and boat launches from the Magic Kingdom and the *Contemporary*, deliver passengers within walking distance. Buses transport all other guests from the *Fort Wilderness* parking lot to the park entrance.

Where to eat: Guests may bring their own food and nonalcoholic beverages. *Pop's Place* is the main snack stand. Shaded picnic areas are available.

Vital statistics: Hours vary, with extended hours in effect during the summer (call 824-4321 for current times). Adult admission is $15.64; a One-Day Water Park Hopper Pass ($23.85) includes admission to River Country, Typhoon Lagoon, Blizzard Beach, and Discovery Island. River Country admission also is included with a Length of Stay Pass and a Five-Day World Hopper Pass. Dressing rooms are available, and lockers and towels may be rented.

River Country Tip

Don't arrive expecting to find a water park of Typhoon Lagoon or Blizzard Beach proportions. River Country (just one-seventh the size of Typhoon Lagoon) is much more quaint and contained.

Typhoon Lagoon

The centerpiece of this 56-acre state-of-the-art water park—ostensibly a small resort town transformed by nature's wrath—is a surf lagoon larger than two football fields that incites happy pandemonium with every 4½-foot wave it unleashes. But there are also two speed slides (which drop 51 feet at 30 miles per hour), three quick and curvy body slides, and a trio of white-water raft rides (one of which accommodates foursomes) that send tubers rollicking through caves and waterfalls. It's all encircled by a lazy floatable river in which swimmers—or more accurately, inner-tube innards—leisurely beat the heat.

KNOW BEFORE YOU GO: Typhoon Lagoon is located near the Disney Village Marketplace off Buena Vista Drive. Pools are heated during the winter, and the park is typically closed for refurbishment for at least one month in winter (call 824-4321 for exact dates). During warmer months, the throngs arrive early, often filling the parking lot before noon; when this happens only guests staying at WDW resorts using WDW transportation will be admitted, until crowds subside later in the afternoon.

How to get there: Direct buses from the TTC, and all WDW resorts except the *Grand Floridian*, *Contemporary*, *Polynesian*, and *Wilderness Lodge* (which require transfers at the TTC).

Where to eat: Guests may bring food and nonalcoholic beverages into the park. Of the two main snack stands, *Leaning Palms* offers a larger selection than *Typhoon Tilly's Galley & Grog*. Shady picnic areas are close at hand.

Vital statistics: Hours vary, with extended hours in effect during summer months (call 824-4321 for current times). Adult admission is provided with a One-Day Water Park Hopper Pass ($23.85 or $16.96 after 3 P.M. in summer), which includes admission to River Country, Blizzard Beach, and Discovery Island as well. Entry to Typhoon Lagoon also is included with a Length of Stay Pass or a Five-Day World Hopper Pass. Dressing rooms are available, and lockers, towels, and (personal) rafts may be rented. Singapore Sal's stocks beach basics.

Typhoon Lagoon Tips

■ The arrival of Blizzard Beach has meant easier access to Typhoon Lagoon for guests willing to settle for Disney's second-biggest and second-newest aquatic theme park.

■ Tidal conditions in the lagoon change every hour, alternating (with warning) between gentle waves and surf city.

■ For time checks, look to the shrimp boat marooned atop Typhoon Lagoon's makeshift mountain; it sounds its horn and shoots a 50-foot flume of water into the air every 30 minutes.

■ Women will find that one-piece suits stay in place better on the speed slides here.

Blizzard Beach

Disney legend has it that this 66-acre water park—Walt Disney World's newest and largest—is the melted remains of a failed Disney ski resort. Call it a not-so-little white lie. The bottom line on this place built around a "snow-covered" man-made peak called Mount Gushmore: It has some amazing runs. Chief among them is a ski jump–turned–speed slide that sends riders feet-first down the watery equivalent of a double-black-diamond run (a 120-foot-drop at a 66-degree angle, in which speeds reach 60 miles per hour). A second speed slide plunges from 90 feet. Less intimidating highlights include an extra-long white-water raft ride accommodating five people per raft, an eight-lane "racing" water slide, and flumes that slalom. For cool yet calm, there's a lazy floatable creek that encircles the park (though it does at one point run through a cave dripping with ice-cold water) and a free-form pool with gently bobbing waves.

KNOW BEFORE YOU GO: Blizzard Beach is located near the Disney-MGM Studios. All pools are heated during the winter; the park will be closed for refurbishment for at least one month in winter (call 824-4321 for exact dates). During the warmer months, the throngs descend upon Blizzard Beach early in the day, and the parking lot frequently closes before noon; when this happens, only guests staying at WDW resorts using WDW transportation will be admitted, until crowds subside later in the afternoon.

How to get there: Buses from the TTC and all Walt Disney World resorts.

Where to eat: Guests may bring their own food and nonalcoholic beverages. Of the three main snack stands, *Lottawatta Lodge* is the largest and most centrally located. Picnic areas are nearby.

Vital statistics: Hours vary, with extended hours in effect during the summer months (call 824-4321 for current times). Adult admission is provided with a One-Day Water Park Hopper Pass ($23.85 or $16.96 after 3 P.M. in summer), which includes admission to Typhoon Lagoon, River Country, and Discovery Island as well. Entry to Blizzard Beach also is included with a Length of Stay Pass or a Five-Day World Hopper Pass. Dressing rooms are available, and lockers, towels, and (personal) rafts may be rented. The Beach Haus stocks fun-in-the-sun essentials.

Blizzard Beach Tips

■ The chairlift that transports guests to the summit of Mount Gushmore affords a wonderful view, as does an observatory located at the summit itself.

■ Women will find that one-piece suits fare better on the speed slides here.

NATURAL DISTRACTIONS

Fort Wilderness

Simply put, no place on WDW property is better equipped to satisfy yens related to the great outdoors than this campground and recreation area, set on 700 forested, canal-crossed acres on the shore of the World's largest lake. (For information about campsites and other accommodations at *Fort Wilderness*, see *Checking In*.) Between its wonderfully canoe-worthy canals and its guided fishing excursions, *Fort Wilderness* gives anglers unparalleled access to the lake's largemouth bass. A marina invites guests to strap on waterskis and to rent all manner of boats for explorations of the lake. (See "Sports" earlier in this chapter for more details on fishing and boating). Escorted trail rides and a ¾-mile hiking trail deliver nature lovers into peaceful areas where it's not uncommon to see deer, armadillos, and wild birds. Myriad pathways provide inspiring venues for joggers and cyclists (bikes are available for rent), and tennis, volleyball, and basketball courts are scattered about the property. While the pair of swimming pools and the white-sand beach are open only to campground guests, River Country (described earlier in this chapter) is close at hand. In the evenings, hayrides and the World's best dinner show, the Hoop-Dee-Doo Musical Revue (see *Dining & Entertainment* for details), keep things humming.

KNOW BEFORE YOU GO: *Fort Wilderness* is located east of the *Contemporary* on a 700-acre wooded plot stretching south from Bay Lake to Vista Boulevard. It is open year-round.

How to get there: Preferably by car, for efficiency's sake. Guests at WDW-owned properties and those with admission tickets to River Country or Discovery Island may take boat launches from the Magic Kingdom and the *Contemporary*. Buses from the TTC and the *Wilderness Lodge* transport guests with a WDW resort ID or a multi-day admission pass.

Getting around: Only vehicles bound for campsites are permitted beyond the guest parking lot. *Fort Wilderness* is serviced by an internal bus system that links all

Fort Wilderness Tip

Because getting to and from this area can be a chore, it's worthwhile to combine a visit to *Fort Wilderness* with an excursion to Discovery Island or River Country.

Worth the Detour

FOR THE BIRDS

The Merrit Island National Wildlife Refuge in Titusville (861-0667) is a bird-watcher's paradise. Self-guided walking tours and a six-mile driving tour are available year-round. More than an avian haven, the 220-square-mile sanctuary is also home to one of the country's most diverse populations of threatened and endangered species (manatees, bald eagles, and loggerhead turtles).

ON THE GATOR TRAIL

Airboat tours of Lake Jesup in Oviedo let curious visitors ogle the lake's huge alligator population from a comfortable distance (365-1244).

UP THE RIVER

The unspoiled Wekiva River, part of the Florida State Canoe Trail, offers runs ranging from 6 to 19 miles, and its lower basin has been designated "scenic and wild." Contact Katie's Wekiva River Landing (628-1482).

recreation areas and campsites (buses circulate at 20-minute intervals from 7 A.M. to 2 A.M.). Guests who prefer greater independence can rent bicycles or electric carts from the Bike Barn.

Where to eat: The Settlement Trading Post and the Meadow Trading Post stock staples; for sit-down meals, there's *Trail's End Buffet* (all-day dining) or *Crockett's Tavern* (dinner only).

Vital Statistics: Admission to *Fort Wilderness* is free. Reservations for waterskiing trips ($75 per hour) should be made two to three days in advance (call 824-2621). The Bike Barn, located in the Meadow Recreation Area, is the place to pick up trail maps and to rent bikes ($3 per hour, $8 per day); canoes ($4 per hour, $10 per day); rods and reels ($4 per hour, $8 per day); fishing poles ($2 per hour, $4 per day); and electric carts ($35 for 24 hours; reservations required, call 824-2742). Hayrides depart twice nightly from Pioneer Hall and last about an hour ($5; call 824-2900). Trail rides depart four times daily from the Tri-Circle-D Livery near the guest parking lot; reservations are recommended ($17; call 824-2621 up to five days in advance).

Discovery Island

This lush landfall for nature lovers—an 11½-acre wildlife sanctuary smack in the middle of Bay Lake—allows guests to come face-to-face with Disney's most animated cast of characters. A zoological Who's Who, it features upwards of 100 species of birds, reptiles, and mammals; some roam freely about the island, and all can be observed in the course of an exquisitely shaded (self-guided) ¾-mile footpath. Among the island's most intriguing sights are families of small busybody primates (young can often be observed clinging like tiny puffballs to their mothers' backs); a lagoon full of honking, posturing hot-pink Caribbean flamingos; a walk-through aviary bespeckled with impossibly vibrant scarlet ibis; and prehistoric-looking Galápagos tortoises weighing up to 500 pounds (these endangered creatures move with such astonishing subtlety they could conceivably transport glass houses on their backs).

NEW AND NOTABLE: The island's best entertainment—a 20-minute avian extravaganza called Feathered Friends—has been reconfigured and now incorporates parrots, birds of prey, and a few of their feathered peers in one show that makes impressive use of the birds' natural behaviors. Featured performers include nimble macaws, a baby kookaburra that croons karaoke-style to a (kookaburra) tape, and a king vulture with a five-foot wingspan that at one point swoops from behind and skims right over guests' heads. Feathered Friends is one of two demonstrations offered several times daily on the island. The other show, Reptile Relations, is more educational, revealing how to tell alligators from crocodiles, for example (hint: look at their teeth).

Discovery Island's huge new South American exhibit features both primates and birds in an innovative setup that effectively blurs the lines between habitats while preserving the animals' separate domains. The island's most extraordinary newcomer—a fishing cat from India—will before long provide informal (if inapplicable) fishing lessons from its own stocked stream. And not new, but notable, is the island's big gray Malay Argus pheasant, which (more outgoing now that its tail feathers have come in) greets onlookers with a rousing and unbelievably human "woo-woo" sound best described as the catcall to end all catcalls.

KNOW BEFORE YOU GO: Discovery Island is located in the center of Bay Lake and linked to the rest of the World only by boat. Despite its isolated feel, the island is just minutes away from the resorts fronting Bay Lake and adjoining Seven Seas Lagoon, and from the Magic Kingdom itself.

How to get there: Boat launches from the *Contemporary*, *Wilderness Lodge*, *Fort Wilderness*, and River Country are the fastest means, with watercraft from the Magic Kingdom, the *Polynesian*, and the *Grand Floridian* slightly slower. A Discovery Island admission ticket or WDW resort ID is required for boarding. Last boats to the island depart about an hour and 15 minutes before closing.

Where to eat: Guests may bring food and nonalcoholic beverages to Discovery Island, or grab a bite at the *Thirsty Perch* (the main snack stand) or the *Outback* (an outpost). We suggest bypassing the picnic area located near the *Thirsty Perch* for the quiet alcove of tables tucked back by the toucan exhibit.

FOR THE DIVING AND THE MANATEES

From late November through early March, the 72-degree spring at Blue Spring State Park (904-775-3663) is a magnet for manatees, hosting as many as 70 of the mammoth endangered mammals at one time. The head spring's caverns also offer some of the best scuba diving around (certification and dive partner required).

TURTLE WATCH

Florida's eastern coastline from Spessard Holland Park south to Sebastian Inlet is the largest sea turtle nesting area in the country. Loggerheads, greens, and leatherbacks lumber ashore from May through August to lay eggs; hatchlings struggle back to the ocean through late October. Guided walks are held from May through July (call 676-1701 from noon to 3 P.M.).

Did you know...

Discovery Island has two bald eagles, but displays only one at a time because the pair simply do not get along.

Discovery Island Tips

■ Although it's possible to make a circuit of the island in about 45 minutes, we recommend allowing at least a couple of hours; pushing through the exhibits any quicker inevitably undercuts the experience.

■ While showtimes for Feathered Friends and Reptile Relations vary depending upon the season, the two performances are generally scheduled back-to-back from 11 A.M. to 12:30 P.M. and from 2 P.M. to 3:30 P.M.

■ Bring your camera, plenty of film, and, if you think you might want to sit out on the island's short beach, a towel; this is not lounge chair territory. If you decide to check out the beach, walk down toward the shipwreck at the end (a holdover from the isle's original Treasure Island days) and see whether the shaded settee there is open for roosting.

■ Expect the unexpected (peacocks and long-legged rabbitlike animals called Patagonian cavies) to run across your path.

■ Peek into the animal care facility (back by Toucan Corner), where Discovery Island's professionals may sometimes be observed treating and feeding some of their charges.

Vital Statistics: Discovery Island is open from 10 A.M. to 5 P.M. except during summer months when hours are extended to 7 P.M. Admission for adults is $10.60; Discovery Island admission also is included with a One-Day Water-Hopper Pass, a Length of Stay Pass, and a Five-Day World Hopper Pass.

CLASS ACTS
Adult Learning Seminars

Folks who find themselves consumed by a desire to know more about Walt Disney World can get a running start with programs that offer insight to one of Disney's more enlightened creations—Epcot's World Showcase. Current offerings include Hidden Treasures of World Showcase (which examines the key design elements of each of the international pavilions) and Gardens of the World (which reveals the methods and meaning behind World Showcase's meticulous landscaping). Both programs devote the better part of three hours to curiosity-sating inspections of World Showcase pavilions; tours begin before this area officially opens, so participants get to duck under the ropes and experience the beauty of World Showcase without the crowds.

In Hidden Treasures of World Showcase, an overview of how this international promenade evolved is followed by a walking tour in which the instructor stops just short of turning pavilions inside out to illuminate their scrupulous detailing and sometime trompe l'oeil design. Suddenly you know such things as why the Eiffel Tower here is brown (that was the original color), why the art and tile-work in the Morocco pavilion doesn't depict people (so as not to imitate Allah by creating life), and how to walk through several centuries' worth of British architecture in 20 steps or less (start in the United Kingdom pavilion's Tea Caddy shop, modeled after Anne Hathaway's cottage, and keep your eyes peeled for the Neoclassical period). Hidden Treasures of World Showcase also includes a backstage stroll through the Epcot wardrobe facility (where aisles are so thick with costumes it feels like you're walking through a sound vacuum).

In Gardens of the World, hosted by a Disney horticulturist, things start off with an enlightening introduction to WDW's horticultural history ("Everything you see was brought in") and philosophy ("It's quite a bit of work, but

Walt loved roses, so we've gotta have roses"). On a walking tour of the beautifully distinctive gardens of World Showcase, you learn just how seriously Disney takes its landscape (gardeners report for duty at 4:30 A.M.); discover the lengths to which Disney has gone to create authentic-looking landscapes for each international pavilion (species are either indigenous to the country or good look-alikes); and find out how to apply clever techniques employed here at home (if you have a shallow front yard, plant pale-colored flowers near the porch to give the lawn greater depth). By tour's end you have intimate knowledge about how topiaries are made, what the curved lines of Japan's stone garden mean, and where in World Showcase you can find a butterfly hatchery and a sprig of spearmint—which is to say, you know an awful lot.

VITAL STATISTICS: Both Hidden Treasures of World Showcase and Gardens of the World are offered three days a week, and both use Epcot Guest Relations as their rendezvous point. While starting times differ (Hidden Treasures of World Showcase begins at 10:15 A.M. and Gardens of the World at 9:15 A.M.), both programs run for about three hours, including short breaks. The tour programs cost about $25 apiece, not including the required Epcot admission. While schedules are subject to change, Hidden Treasures of World Showcase is typically slated for Sundays, Wednesdays, and Fridays, with Gardens of the World taking over on Mondays, Tuesdays, and Thursdays. Reservations are necessary and can be made several months in advance (call 939-8687).

The Disney Institute

Insatiable souls looking to take home fresh perspective, newfound skills, and fascinating experiences as souvenirs can go to town at this innovative vacation resort, scheduled to open in February 1996. With more than 80 participatory programs that immerse guests in everything from animation to hydroponics, rock climbing, interior design, and showbiz, it is uniquely configured to provide fun and meaningful dabbling for grownup vacationers. Designed exclusively for adults and families with older children (ten years and up), The Disney Institute gives

Really Smelling the Roses

During the International Flower and Garden Festival (this year, April 18–June 2), Epcot is a virtual perfumery, with some 30 million blossoms ensuring that World Showcase and Future World look their showy best, and the Gardens of the World horticultural tour is offered daily to allow guests to learn about the many special garden displays.

A second opportunity presented by the festival is the Backstage Horticultural Tour (described in the "Special Events" section of *Dining & Entertainment*), which escorts guests behind the scenes through WDW's nursery areas and greenhouses ($20; call 939-2223).

It's a Blast

At Kennedy Space Center's Spaceport USA Visitor Center (452-2121), visitors can walk through a full-size Space Shuttle replica and check out real launch pads. Complimentary car passes are available for launch viewing within six miles; requests must be made three months in advance (call 867-4636 for shuttle launch dates, then write to NASA Visitor Services; Mail Code: PA-PASS; Kennedy Space Center, FL 32899).

guests free rein to explore whatever programs in the eclectic mix interest them most. Each day, they can choose up to four sessions from about 60 different workshops; an instructor-guest ratio of 1 to 15 ensures personal attention.

As an indication of the possibilities, consider: You might experiment with improvisational comedy, make your radio debut, create topiaries, or become the anchor or roving reporter for the Institute's television news team (news programs are broadcast on the Institute's closed-circuit channel). Or you might work alongside Disney animators (brainstorming story ideas, writing scripts, color-

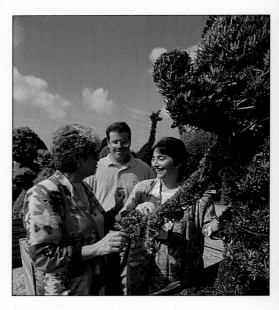

ing cels, or mixing sound) to produce animated shorts to be used as public service announcements. Complementing (and facilitating) such programs is an extensive Artists-in-Residence program that brings noted talents in all kinds of fields (sports, music, film, design, and culinary arts) to the Institute to interact with guests and do some cross-cultivating of their own. As an example of how this works, imagine members of the (visiting) Pilobolus modern dance troupe bringing guests into play in freshly choreographed dance numbers; practicing in open rehearsals; staging an evening performance in the Institute's recital hall; and, in their spare time, learning how to make soufflés, record their family stories, or care for an organic garden right along with the rest. Morning fitness activities (including nature walks, tai chi, and slow stretching on the village green) and nightly film screenings and performances at the recital hall help to establish a sense of community within the rustic lakeside retreat.

VITAL STATISTICS: The Disney Institute is located near the Disney Village Marketplace on the reconstructed site of Disney's former *Village Resort*. Designed by noted architect Tom Beeby, the lakeside resort takes after a small town, with its main structures clustered around a village green. Disney Institute guests may enjoy such traditional amenities as a fitness center with spa, clay tennis courts, swimming pools, and privileged access to 18 holes of golf (at the adjacent Lake Buena Vista course). The self-contained community also features program studios, a recital hall, an outdoor amphitheater, a state-of-the-art cinema, and closed-circuit television and radio stations. The *Seasons* family-style restaurant offers four seasonally themed dining rooms. The Institute is designed for guest arrival on Mondays and Fridays, but can accommodate those who prefer to arrive on other days of the week.

Rates: Programs and accommodations are entwined. Rates are based on double occupancy and a minimum three-night stay, and include accommodations at *The Villas at The Disney Institute*, unlimited program participation (excluding spa treatments and private golf and tennis lessons), taxes, and baggage gratuities, plus a one-day theme park ticket. An optional meal plan is offered.

Bungalows (with one bedroom and separate sitting room) are $582 for three nights or $690 for four nights ($184 for extra nights). One-bedroom Town Houses with fully equipped kitchens run $694 for three nights or $839 for four nights ($221 for extra nights). Fully equipped two-bedroom Town Houses are $738 for three nights or $897 for four nights ($235 for extra nights). Cost per additional adult sharing the same accommodation is $340 for three nights or $366 for four nights. All prices are subject to change.

Reservations: Stays at The Disney Institute must be booked separately from other Walt Disney World resort arrangements. Advance reservations are necessary and may be made by calling 800-496-6337. Note that it's possible to reserve a place in specific programs at the time accommodations are booked.

Learning Seminar Tips

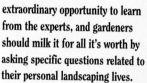

■ **Gardens of the World is an** extraordinary opportunity to learn from the experts, and gardeners should milk it for all it's worth by asking specific questions related to their personal landscaping lives.

■ **For both programs—Hidden Treasures of World Showcase and Gardens of the World—be sure to** wear comfortable shoes and sunscreen; you will be spending a few hours out on the promenade.

Dining & Entertainment

I t's late in the book and we're sure you must be dying of hunger by now, so we'll begin by quickly running through the food specials. But first, you'll be happy to hear that the outfit you are wearing at this moment, plus shoes, will be just fine for most any WDW restaurant (assuming that you didn't get all gussied up to read this chapter, and that you're not in your pajamas or reading on the job). And second, atmosphere—the sort that mere ambience wouldn't recognize—is a specialty of the house (you won't simply dine on seafood here, you'll do it cheek-to-cheek with a bustling coral reef or within the effervescent context of a New England clambake). Sampler platters include such unfamiliar cuisines as Norwegian and Moroccan. And if you're looking for some sophisticated eats, you're in luck. In response to patrons' demands for fresher, more imaginative fare, Disney recently revised its purchasing system to give its chefs greater freedom. With WDW's chefs doing their own grocery shopping (more accurately, blanketing the country to find the most flavorful ingredients) and having more fun, not to mention flexibility, in the kitchen, the World's menus have finally closed their historic gap with discriminating taste buds. As an example of the quality of dining that can now be found all over Walt Disney World, consider *Artist Point* restaurant, which features the likes of just-hooked king salmon, creatively prepared and served with hard-to-get pinot noirs from the Pacific Northwest. But we're getting carried away, and you're hungry and need to make a decision. Our "Restaurant Guide" will help; it cuts to the chase and describes the best dining opportunities for adults in and around the World.

From french toast at breakfast to Champagne toasts at midnight, Disney dining offers a delicious world of possibilities.

Of course, you also need to be thinking about what you want to do later, so let us quickly outline the basics. For your nighttime entertainment, you will not simply find a tremendous variety of nightclubs; you will find them shoulder-to-shoulder in a complex called Pleasure Island that takes the hassle out of club-hopping. The place gets going early and doesn't turn into a pumpkin until 2 A.M.; dress is weekend casual. You will also discover resort lounges that defy their ho-hum genre and make events of nightcaps by evoking such locales as

Polynesia and the Old West, and by specializing—there's an outstanding wine bar, a beer lover's paradise, and several enterprising lounges that offer custom-made microbrews or beer by the yard.

Please, take your time, and when you're ready to think about after-dinner entertainment, know that this chapter's "Nightlife Guide" provides the complete scoop on Pleasure Island as well as on compelling lounges and clubs in the theme parks, the resorts, and beyond WDW borders. You'll see that we've also slipped in an after-dinner mint of sorts—a listing of special events and celebrations that have proven capable of raising the entertainment ante at Walt Disney World.

Bon appétit!

Calling Cue

Unless otherwise noted, all phone numbers are in area code 407.

RESTAURANT GUIDE

The dining scene at Walt Disney World has evolved into a vast array of possibilities that spans the price, cuisine, and atmosphere spectrums. It stretches from the theme parks to the resorts and beyond, encompassing the Disney Village Marketplace and Pleasure Island, as well as some promising off-property options. Memorable dining experiences abound for adults who prefer meals to fast-food fixes. Peruse the World menu, and you'll find such diverse combos as meat loaf with a side of "Father Knows Best," tiramisù served with an aria, and a sumptuous six-course splurge complete with harpist and Royal Doulton china.

Collectively, WDW's many eateries can satisfy most any craving. The key is to think with your stomach as you plot your days and nights at the World. Take note of the fact that the Magic Kingdom is the weakest culinary link among the theme parks. Recognize Epcot's World Showcase as a gastronomic stronghold, and plan to arrive with appetite and reservations. Note that the Disney Village Marketplace and Pleasure Island have some mouthwatering distractions—including *Planet Hollywood*—that you might want to figure into your meal plan. Be sure to look beyond the restaurants at your own hotel to consider mealtime pilgrimages to others, since the resorts contain some of the World's most pleasant dining rooms and most enticing menus. And there are some exciting new options with the opening of the *Contemporary's California Grill*, the *Polynesian's 'Ohana*, and an entirely new dining frontier at the *BoardWalk*.

We're happy to report that Walt Disney World has more tempting cuisine for the sophisticated palate than ever before, as behind-the-scenes improvements—from fresher, more flavorful ingredients to stronger wine lists—have quietly pushed the epicurean envelope. Also, healthier, more interesting grazing options in the theme parks (see our snacking suggestions in the *Theme Parks* chapter) can provide inexpensive treats that help subsidize the sit-down meals.

To ease the task of deciding among the World's innumerable eateries, we've whittled down the list to a

Fare Thee Well

This restaurant guide is not a comprehensive listing of the World's eateries, but a selective roundup of the best adult dining and noshing venues. Those restaurants designated as "Stand-Outs" are dining rooms and fast-food places whose exceptional flair, distinctive fare, and/or terrific setting have earned our highest recommendation. "Good Bets" are additional locales that offer consistently rewarding dining experiences.

The Last Word on Reservations

Unless otherwise noted, the number to dial is 939-3463 (WDW-DINE); reservations may be made up to 60 days in advance.

■ **FOR THEME PARK DINING:** Reservations are necessary for nearly all full-service restaurants at Epcot, and either suggested or accepted for full-service eateries at the Magic Kingdom or the Disney-MGM Studios (see individual entries). Make them through WDW-DINE. If you are unable to secure a table in advance, try making reservations in person on the day of your visit (preferably first thing in the morning). To make same-day dining arrangements for the Magic Kingdom, report directly to the restaurant; for Disney-MGM Studios, go to the kiosk at the

diverse selection of full-service restaurants and more casual noshing spots that we recommend as the best adult bets. The intention is not to diminish the value of establishments not included, but to underscore the greater appeal certain restaurants hold for adults.

Our dining recommendations, which touch down all over the World and provide options for all taste buds and budgets, are presented within four distinct contexts—in the theme parks, in the resorts, elsewhere within WDW boundaries, and off-property. Within each of these locales, we have roped off for extra consideration those restaurants that offer some of the most consistently rewarding dining experiences. Under the heading "Stand-Outs," you'll find stellar places to grab a great bite on the quick; moderately priced restaurants with exceptional flair; and extra-special havens worth every hard-earned dollar for their distinctive food and setting. Under the designation "Good Bets," we've corralled additional locales, also highly regarded, that we've come to know as fine places to take a meal. Because Walt Disney World's theme parks are unique terrain calling for both firm restaurant reservations and flexible eating plans, we have included recommendations for fast food as well as full-service options.

Individual entries characterize each restaurant and provide such essential information as location, price, and the meals (represented by B, L, and D for breakfast, lunch, and dinner, with S symbolizing availability of snacks) served there. As an indication of what you can expect to spend for a meal, we have classified restaurants as very expensive (dinners $50 and up); expensive (lunches over $25, dinners $30 and up); moderate (lunches $15 to $25, dinners $20 to $30); or inexpensive (lunches under $15, dinners under $20). The prices represent an average meal for two, not including drinks, tax, or tips.

We have also indicated those restaurants for which reservations are necessary or suggested. For everything you need to know about making dining reservations in and around the World, consult our at-a-glance guide in the adjacent margins. For the rundown on dinner shows, some strategies to eating your way around the World, and the scoop on where to find traditional afternoon teas, dining rooms with terrific views, late-night bites, great wines by the glass, and more, check the margins of this chapter. A final world of advice: You might *not* want to read this section on an empty stomach.

IN THE THEME PARKS
Full Service

Stand-Outs

AKERSHUS (Norway, Epcot's World Showcase): In a world in which many international cuisines have gone from trendy to almost trite, this is an alluring taste of the unfamiliar. The ambience of a medieval Norwegian fortress—marked by dramatic cathedral ceilings, stone archways, iron chandeliers, leaded-glass windows, and the occasional red carpet—is not to be denied. Nor is the delicious novelty of the all-you-can-eat Norwegian smorgasbord served here. Known as *koldtbord* (or "cold table"), the buffet includes both hot and cold selections. There's plenty for the unadventurous palate, from creamy potato salad to savory Norwegian meatballs; but don't stop there. This is your chance to sample well-prepared signature dishes that don't often leave Scandinavia; there's smoked mackerel, herring prepared every which way, mashed rutabagas (don't wince, they're good), and a whole lot more. It all washes down quite nicely with a tall draft of Ringnes beer. Wine selection is limited. Reservations accepted. Moderate to expensive. L, D.

BISTRO DE PARIS (France, Epcot's World Showcase): An intimate bistro that puts on romantic airs rather than the usual bustle. If you think the decor, with its evocative interplay of brass sconces, milk-glass chandeliers, mirrors, and leaded glass, is convincingly French, wait until you swallow your first morsel. The sophisticated menu—created by three of France's top chefs (Paul Bocuse, Roger Vergé, and Gaston Lenôtre)—is executed with a rich authenticity that will astonish any unsuspecting gourmand. This is hearty dining of the sort that inspires a sudden need for a nap, so we recommend sticking to dinner, even during busy seasons when the *Bistro* serves lunch. Although lunch does have its advantages: lower checks and the opportunity to walk off your lobster bisque, rack of lamb, and chocolate soufflé. The impressive wine list is *très* French. Reservations necessary. Expensive. L (during busy seasons), D.

corner of Hollywood and Sunset boulevards; and for Epcot, use the WorldKey Information System screens at Guest Relations. Arrangements may also be made at the restaurants themselves.

■ **FOR WDW RESORT DINING:** Reservations for all WDW resort restaurants may be made by calling WDW-DINE (see individual entries to determine necessity). To secure a table at any of the full-service eateries at the *Dolphin*, call 934-4025; for the *Swan*, call 934-1609.

■ **FOR DINING AT THE DISNEY VILLAGE MARKETPLACE:** Any necessary reservations may be made through WDW-DINE with the exception of *Fireworks Factory*, for which guests should contact the restaurant directly using the number provided.

■ **FOR DINING AT THE DISNEY VILLAGE HOTEL PLAZA:** Any necessary reservations may be made by calling the number included with the individual restaurant entry.

■ **FOR DINING OUTSIDE WDW:** Make reservations by phoning the number given in the restaurant listing.

50'S PRIME TIME CAFÉ (Disney-MGM Studios): In a word: cool. This good-humored retreat to the era of "I Love Lucy" is an amusing amalgam of comfort food, kitschy 1950s-style kitchen nooks, and attentive servers of the "No talking with your mouth full" ilk. Expect that Mom or her favored offspring will meddle in your affairs here ("Did you wash your hands? All right then, what color was the soap?"). And recognize that the best fun is

had by doing some regressing of your own. One *Prime Time* regular we know—a troublemaker appropriately in his early fifties—has gotten major entertainment mileage from such lines as "Mom, she says I'm a tattletale!" and "Mom, can I sleep over at Susie's house? Her parents aren't home and she's afraid to be alone." As for the fare, it's tasty home cooking as it used to be (heavy on the meat and potatoes), served forth in generous-to-the-point-of-grandmotherly portions. Most guests find it honors their memory of pot roast, s'mores, and root beer floats. In fact, order a peanut butter sandwich, and you could very well be asked if you'd like a side of Marshmallow Fluff. Beer and wine are served. Reservations necessary. Moderate. L, D, S.

GARDEN GRILL (The Land, Epcot's Future World): As your reservation comes due at this lazy susan–turned–dining area—it rotates slowly above the rain forest, desert, and prairie scenes visited by the Living with the Land boat ride below—you are politely informed by a "farmhand" that you have some chores to do. Bessie has been milked,

Smoker's Alert

All restaurants in the theme parks and Walt Disney World–owned resorts are strictly nonsmoking, except in outdoor seating areas. However, Pleasure Island offers refuges for smokers.

apparently, but the table hasn't been set. And so it is that you are directed first to the silverware, plates, and glassware, and then to your table—a cozy, U-shaped booth fitted out with a bovine-print table cloth. As the meal and the setting progress, you steal through a squawking rain forest, observe a strong wind kicking up desert sand, watch buffalo graze on a prairie, and visit a farmhouse (request a table on the lower tier for the best view). It's the evocative, ever-changing scenery and the farm-fresh fare that make the *Garden Grill* perhaps the best spot for adults to dine in the company of Disney characters. Farmers Mickey and Minnie make rounds at each meal. The full country breakfast is served family-style, as are lunch and dinner, which feature vegetables grown in The Land's greenhouses, catfish (also cultivated here), and rotisserie chicken. When all's said and done, you're glad you did your chores. Reservations are necessary for all three character meals. Expensive. B, L, D.

HOLLYWOOD BROWN DERBY (Disney-MGM Studios): The Studios' most gracious dining is found at this faithful revival of the original cause célèbre, which opened on Hollywood and Vine back in 1926. Dressed to the nines in chandeliers, palm trees, and celebrity caricatures, the restaurant stokes the appetite with its signature Cobb salad, fabulous grapefruit cake, and main dishes along the lines of meaty crab cakes, grilled steaks, and light pasta dishes. The wine list is excellent. Reservations suggested. Expensive. L, D.

LIBERTY TREE TAVERN (Liberty Square, Magic Kingdom): This homey restaurant—the best in the Magic Kingdom—revives the spirit of Colonial America so fully in its sprawling dining rooms that you're apt to wonder how many kettles it's got going in the kitchen. The beamed ceilings are hung with candelabras, the floors are made of wide oak planks, and the paned windows were fashioned using 18th-century casting techniques. Interestingly, many of the period paintings on the walls were commissioned for use in the historical film shown at The Hall of Presidents. It all has a way of inspiring a taste for New England clam chowder, roast turkey and mashed potatoes, or maybe beef braised in red wine.

HOT TIP

Walt Disney World restaurants can accommodate special dietary requirements (low-sodium, lactose-free, and kosher meals, for example) if requests are made at least 24 hours in advance. Make your personal needs known when you make your dining reservations (by calling WDW-DINE).

Oversize salads and sandwiches are the call for lunch. Don't miss the apple butter and honey margarine served with the rolls. Reservations are suggested for lunch. Aim for an early or late seating to best experience this restaurant's charms. Dinner is a character affair requiring reservations. Expensive. L, D.

L'ORIGINALE ALFREDO DI ROMA RISTORANTE
(Italy, Epcot's World Showcase): Adorned with massive murals that evoke the Italian countryside, this elegant restaurant inspires a "when in Rome" frame of mind from the outset. You suddenly hear an Italian grandmother's voice in your head, urging you to "eat, eat." But do you go with the specialty of the house, fettuccine Alfredo (wide, flat noodles in a rich butter and Parmesan cheese sauce)? Perhaps the chicken cacciatore? The veal sautéed with black truffles and wine, accompanied by fresh asparagus and mushrooms? It's hard to go wrong at *Alfredo's*, as fresh pasta is made right on the premises and fine Italian wines are in ready supply; of course, you could blow it and neglect to save room for dessert. This restaurant stands out, too, for its atmosphere, which is at once romantic and festive. Between arias, roving Italian singers have been known to choreograph a napkin-twirling tarantella. Reservations necessary. Expensive. L, D.

TEPPANYAKI DINING ROOMS
(Japan, Epcot's World Showcase): It's not exactly an authentic dose of Japanese cuisine (*Tempura Kiku* next door gives a closer approximation with its sushi, sashimi, and tempura), but it offers a great time and a terrific meal. Guests sit around a large, flat teppan grill and watch as a nimble, white-hatted chef deftly demonstrates just how quickly enough chicken, beef, seafood, and vegetables to feed eight people can be chopped (knives fly at speeds that could dust a food processor), seasoned, and stir-fried. Entrées are flavorful and sizzling. Because smaller parties are seated together, *Teppanyaki* becomes a social affair, and it's a fine place for singles. Reservations necessary. Expensive. L, D.

TONY'S TOWN SQUARE
(Main Street, Magic Kingdom): We have nothing against the main dining room (it's quite charming), but the bright and airy atrium at this Victorian-style Italian restaurant rates among the most pleasant dining environs in the Magic Kingdom.

Secrets to Success

Hungry and in no mood to wait in line? To avoid the inevitable crunch, plan to eat an early (or late) breakfast, lunch, or dinner. Selected theme park restaurants offer discounted early-bird specials from 4:30 P.M. until 6 P.M. Sit-down restaurants that offer table service are usually less crowded at lunch than at dinner, so you might want to make that the main meal of the day. But if it's a dinner spot you relish, choose one of the handful of restaurants that accept reservations (call WDW-DINE, the earlier in the day, the better).

Something about the terrazzo floors, hanging plants, ceiling fans, and the view of Town Square beckons. The *Lady and the Tramp* theme is endearingly subtle, and the fare is reliably good, from the waffles to the salads (tossed tableside), pizzas, lasagne primavera, and shrimp scampi. There's a huge kiwi and strawberry dessert with yogurt sauce that, with cappuccino or espresso, could almost be a meal in itself. Reservations suggested. Moderate. B, L, D.

Good Bets

AU PETIT CAFÉ (France, Epcot's World Showcase): Order a niçoise salad with a side of passersby; this Parisian sidewalk café is the best scoping spot in all of World Showcase and a great primer for the pastries of *Boulangerie Pâtisserie* around the corner. No reservations translates here as "don't arrive famished." Moderate to expensive. L, D, S.

BIERGARTEN (Germany, Epcot's World Showcase): Prepare for the best of the wurst. Hearty portions of traditional German cuisine (don't miss the potato salad, red cabbage, or sauerbraten) and rousing oompah-style performances are the main attractions in this vast yet charming makeshift courtyard. Adding to the fun are long communal tables, 33-ounce steins of Beck's beer, and a selection of German wines and liqueurs. Reservations suggested. Moderate to expensive. L, D.

CHEFS DE FRANCE (France, Epcot's World Showcase): With three of France's best chefs—Paul Bocuse, Roger Vergé, and pastry guru Gaston Lenôtre—keeping tabs on this elegant restaurant's nouvelle French kitchen, the broth is far from spoiled. Modest wine list. Reservations necessary. Expensive. L, D.

CORAL REEF (The Living Seas, Epcot's Future World): It's all about sneaking bites of fresh fish and shellfish under the watchful eyes of sea turtles, dolphins, and gargantuan groupers. Every table has a panoramic view of the living coral reef, and some are right up against the glass. Reservations necessary. Expensive. L, D.

Cheap Eats

Here are our suggestions for spur-of-the-moment fast food:

- *Sleepy Hollow* (Liberty Square, Magic Kingdom)
- *Cosmic Ray's Starlight Café* (Tomorrowland, Magic Kingdom)
- *Sunshine Season Food Fair* (The Land, Epcot's Future World)
- *Cantina de San Angel* (Mexico, Epcot's World Showcase)
- *Kringla Bakeri og Kafe* (Norway, Epcot's World Showcase)
- *Sommerfest* (Germany, Epcot's World Showcase)
- *Backlot Express* (Disney-MGM Studios)

Late Bites at Future World

Epcot's Future World attractions close at 7 P.M., but three of its counter-service restaurants stay open until the park shuts down, usually at 9 P.M. The *Electric Umbrella* and *Pasta Piazza Ristorante*, both in Innoventions, serve meals, while the *Fountain View Espresso & Bakery*, next to Innoventions, hits the spot with cappuccino, espresso, pastries, and desserts.

KING STEFAN'S BANQUET HALL (Cinderella Castle, Magic Kingdom): This majestic dining room is named for a friend of the family—Sleeping Beauty's father. Go for the grand medieval setting rather than the American fare. Reservations necessary for daily character breakfast, and suggested for lunch and dinner. Expensive. B, L, D.

MAMA MELROSE'S RISTORANTE ITALIANO (Disney-MGM Studios): A pleasantly removed bastion of red-checkered tablecloths and thin-crust designer pizzas baked in wood-burning ovens. Reservations accepted. Moderate to expensive. L, D (during busy seasons).

MARRAKESH (Morocco, Epcot's World Showcase): It's not every day that you can slip into an exquisitely tiled Moroccan palace and expect to be entertained by belly dancers and musicians as you polish off a sampler plate of distinctive Moroccan cuisine such as couscous or kebabs. The volume of the music here can be a drawback. Reservations accepted. Expensive. L, D.

ROSE & CROWN PUB & DINING ROOM (United Kingdom, Epcot's World Showcase): The menu ventures only a tad beyond fish-and-chips or chicken-and-leek pies, but the pleasant dining room offers a front-seat view of the lagoon, and the pub's downright neighborly. Afternoon tea is served daily (see Two for Tea on page 192 for details). Reservations suggested for dining room, necessary for tea. Moderate to expensive. L, D, S.

SAN ANGEL INN (Mexico, Epcot's World Showcase): The lights are low, the mood is romantic, and there is a smoking volcano poised almost tableside. If that's not enchantment enough, there's a mystical pyramid and a moonlit river. The menu? You may need to bring the table candle closer to read it, but you'll find Mexican fare from margaritas to chicken mole. Don't miss the chips and salsa. Reservations necessary. Expensive. L, D, S.

SCI-FI DINE-IN THEATER (Disney-MGM Studios): The dishes are more creative than those at your average drive-in theater (huge salads, sandwiches, and the Cheesecake that Ate New York, for instance), but it still takes a backseat to the campy moonlit setting. Tables resemble 1950s-era convertibles and are parked next to working drive-in theater speakers. Science fiction and horror trailers play on a large screen. Wine and beer are available. Reservations accepted. Moderate to expensive. L, D.

Fast Food

Stand-Outs

BACKLOT EXPRESS (Disney-MGM Studios): Shady and inconspicuous (it's tucked away by the Indiana Jones Epic Stunt Spectacular theater), this is a sprawling spot with both indoor and outdoor seating and unusual potential for quiet. Paint-speckled floors and assorted auto debris give you an idea of the decor. Salads, soft tacos, carrot cake, and chocolate chip cheesecake are among the more tempting fare. Beer and wine are available. Inexpensive. L, D, S.

BOULANGERIE PÂTISSERIE (France, Epcot's World Showcase): The chocolate croissants, blueberry tarts, apple turnovers, and such here are timeless. Follow your nose, and don't neglect to notice the sweet temptation aptly know as the Marvelous. Kronenbourg beer and French wines also are offered. Inexpensive. S.

CANTINA DE SAN ANGEL (Mexico, Epcot's World Showcase): Forget for a moment the churros, the frozen margaritas, the chicken tostadas, and the Dos Equis drafts—this place has fresh watermelon juice. Inexpensive. L, D, S.

Grape Expectations

Grownups who are surprised by the fine dining (and snacking) all over the World will be absolutely delighted at the new and improved selection of wines to accompany their food. From the pavilions of World Showcase to the lounges and restaurants of the on-property resorts, here are our favorite ways to sample the fruit of the vine.

■ **Weinkeller** (Germany, Epcot's World Showcase): Daily tastings from the shop's 250 varieties. Don't miss the rich, flowery dessert wines, gloriously sweet (and not inexpensive).

■ **La Maison du Vin** (France, Epcot's World Showcase): Tastings and sales from the country synonymous with wine. Another chance to sample top-quality vintages before you buy a whole bottle.

Victoria & Albert's (Grand Floridian): The World's most upscale dining room boasts an equally grand wine list. Best bet: For $25, you can get four glasses of wine specifically chosen to complement individual courses on the prix fixe menu.

Artist Point (Wilderness Lodge): Want to know why everyone says pinot noir and grilled salmon are a match made in heaven? Here's where to find out.

Martha's Vineyard Lounge (Beach Club): Two-ounce samples from a well-chosen list of vintners are a delicious way to explore wine regions across the country.

California Grill (Contemporary): A great selection of California wines by the glass, special wine-and-food pairing dinners. Real zinfandel is red, not white, and they've got the Ravenswood to prove it.

COSMIC RAY'S STARLIGHT CAFÉ (Tomorrowland, Magic Kingdom): A one-size-fits-all establishment that's the choicest spot to get fast food in the Magic Kingdom for two reasons: variety and elbow room. Burgers, salads, and rotisserie chicken all have a place on the menu. Inexpensive. L, D, S.

FOUNTAIN VIEW ESPRESSO & BAKERY (Innoventions Plaza, Epcot's Future World): This ode to pastries, desserts, and specialty coffees is a veritable adult oasis any time of day. Wine and beer also are available. Inexpensive. B, S.

HOLLYWOOD & VINE (Disney-MGM Studios): An Art Deco–style cafeteria with Tinseltown flourishes, this is the ticket when you want to make it quick. Expect standard cafeteria fare, and the heartiest breakfast at the Studios. Beer and wine are available. Inexpensive to moderate. B, L, D, S.

KRINGLA BAKERI OG KAFE (Norway, Epcot's World Showcase): Simply a super place for a sweet fix or a light lunch. Among the tasty morsels to be had here are potato salad, yogurt, open-face sandwiches (roast beef, turkey, salmon, and chicken salad), sweet pretzels called *kringles*, and *vaflers* (heart-shaped waffles fresh-made as you wait and topped with powdered sugar and preserves). Ringnes beer is on tap. The outdoor seating area is shaded by a grass-thatched roof. Inexpensive. L, D, S.

LE CELLIER (Canada, Epcot's World Showcase): If you've forgotten the charms of cafeteria-style dining, this wine cellar–like spot serves up lots of savory reminders. You can eat a hearty meat-and-potatoes meal (plus pie) with no need for reservations. And there's the pie quotient itself—maple-syrup pie and apple-berry-rhubarb pie. Operates seasonally. Moderate. L, D, S.

MAIN STREET BAKE SHOP (Main Street, Magic Kingdom): This dainty spot is renowned for quick breakfasts (from bagels to fresh-baked cinnamon rolls) and enormous fresh-from-the-oven cookies. Inexpensive. B, S.

SLEEPY HOLLOW (Liberty Square, Magic Kingdom): This pleasantly removed alcove with outdoor patio seating serves fast food on the sophisticated side. There are sandwiches made with whole wheat pitas or Norwegian potato bread, avocado salad, vegetarian chili served in a bread bowl, and bagel chips. An untraveled spot of shade with tables and chairs is just steps away. Inexpensive. L, D, S.

SOMMERFEST (Germany, Epcot's World Showcase): Here, quick sustenance takes such classic forms as bratwurst, soft pretzels, Black Forest cake, German chocolates, Beck's beer, and German wine. The shaded outdoor seating area sports a festive mural. Inexpensive. L, D, S.

STARRING ROLLS BAKERY (Disney-MGM Studios): Have croissant and cappuccino, will travel. This is the place in the Studios to get the day off to a sweet start or to take an impromptu cookie or coffee break under umbrella-shaded tables. Inexpensive. B, S.

SUNSHINE SEASON FOOD FAIR (The Land, Epcot's Future World): This bumper crop of food stands, located directly beneath the hot-air balloons on The Land pavilion's lower level, is the best place in Epcot to strap on the ol' feed bag and graze. It's a finicky eater indeed who can't find temptation among this court's countless soups, salads, baked goods, pasta, sandwiches, barbecue, baked potatoes, ice cream, and refreshing libations. The eating's significantly more peaceful here outside prime dining hours. Inexpensive. B, L, D, S.

Fast Food

Good Bets

AUNTIE GRAVITY'S GALACTIC GOODIES (Tomorrowland, Magic Kingdom): A good pit stop for frozen yogurt and health-conscious snacks. Inexpensive. S.

CATWALK BAR (Disney-MGM Studios): This cool loft of a prop-storage area is more than a lounge; it's a great place to prop yourself above the madding crowd for a plate of chilled shrimp. Inexpensive. S.

COMMISSARY (Disney-MGM Studios): Fast food with a conscience—stir-fried veggies, chicken breast sandwiches, and teriyaki burgers, for example. Inexpensive. L, D.

No Reservations Required

If you're caught without reservations in the theme parks, you can usually snag a table at one of these recommended full-service spots (especially if you're willing to wait a bit):

- *Tony's Town Square* (Main Street, Magic Kingdom)

- *Au Petit Café* (France, Epcot's World Showcase)

- *Mama Melrose's Ristorante Italiano* (Disney-MGM Studios)

S.O.S. for Sweet Tooths

The following theme park spots are sure to satisfy:

- *Main Street Bake Shop* (Main Street, Magic Kingdom)
- Main Street Confectionery (Main Street, Magic Kingdom)
- *Fountain View Espresso & Bakery* (Epcot's Future World)
- *Boulangerie Pâtisserie* (France, Epcot's World Showcase)
- Delizie Italiane (Italy, Epcot's World Showcase)
- Süssigkeiten (Germany, Epcot's World Showcase)
- *Kringla Bakeri og Kafe* (Norway, Epcot's World Showcase)
- *Starring Rolls Bakery* (Disney-MGM Studios)
- Sweet Success (Disney-MGM Studios)

CRYSTAL PALACE (Main Street, Magic Kingdom): Cozy nooks needn't always be small, as this bright, sprawling cafeteria overlooking flower beds and courtyards proves. Food is straightforward and wide-ranging (spit-roasted chicken, pasta, and salads). For a full breakfast at the Magic Kingdom sans Cinderella, this is the place. Moderate. B, L, D, S.

LOTUS BLOSSOM CAFÉ (China, Epcot's World Showcase): The menu's on the short side, but what's there—basic Chinese takeout—is a good call when hunger strikes and you're in the neighborhood. Outdoor tables line the sidewalks. Inexpensive. L, D.

PLAZA ICE CREAM PARLOR (Main Street, Magic Kingdom): Simply the park's most bountiful stash of ice cream. Head here when you want a choice of flavors, not a Mouseketeer Bar. Inexpensive. S.

PURE & SIMPLE (Wonders of Life, Epcot's Future World): The place merits attention by offering healthy pickings along the lines of smoothies, multigrain waffles with fruit toppings, tuna pitas with reduced-calorie mayo, and papaya juice. Another plus: This eatery's rarely mobbed. Inexpensive. B, L, S.

YAKITORI HOUSE (Japan, Epcot's World Showcase): Perched among Japan's hillside gardens, this spot (named for the specialty of the house, skewered chicken) is one of the most relaxing settings for a quick and satisfying bite in Epcot. Kirin beer and sake also are available. Inexpensive. L, D, S.

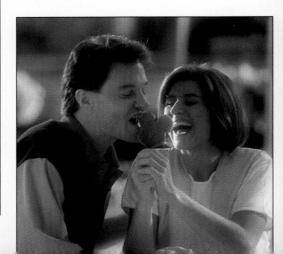

IN THE RESORTS

Stand-Outs

ARTIST POINT (*Wilderness Lodge*): The Pacific Northwest theme of this restaurant is beautifully announced in two-story-high landscape murals, while tall, red-framed windows look out to Bay Lake. And although something about the dining room's clean lines evokes Frank Lloyd Wright, the concept still holds together. *Artist Point's* hallmark is its knack for translating the fresh seasonal ingredients from the Pacific Northwest into flavorful creations. An excellent example is the wild steelhead salmon marinated in whiskey then roasted and served with winter squash. The smoked corn and crab soup, and espresso bean barbecued free-range chicken also are quite good. The berry cobbler is heavenly, and takes so perfectly to vanilla ice cream that you make room no matter how full you think you are. The wine list features some of the best pinot noirs coming out of Oregon right now. The cumulative effect is an artist's palette for the sophisticated palate. Reservations necessary for breakfast (a character affair) and suggested for dinner. Expensive. B, D.

BEACHES & CREAM SODA SHOP (*Yacht Club* and *Beach Club*): Every inch a classic soda fountain, it's the site for egg creams, malts, and milk shakes, plus burgers we happen to think are the best in the World. Continental breakfast also is offered. First-come seating. Moderate. B, L, D, S.

BONFAMILLE'S CAFÉ (*Port Orleans*): This restaurant offers an absolutely endearing introduction to Creole cooking in a casual courtyard setting that neatly evokes New Orleans' French Quarter. The menu offers a story of Memere, the fictional matriarch who inspired *Bonfamille's;* its parting words—"Loosen up your belt and enjoy what you've put past your tongue"—are all the more relevant after you've experienced the portions served here. Try the jambalaya or a roast beef po'boy with a bottle of Dixie Blackened Voodoo Lager or try something else, but do loosen your belt a little beforehand. Dinner reservations accepted. Moderate. B, D.

Best Burgers

The juiciest, tastiest burgers in the World are served up at *Beaches & Cream Soda Shop*, between the *Yacht Club* and the *Beach Club*.

189

The Inside Scoop

Chefs at the *California Grill* use such fresh ingredients that there's not a thing in the restaurant's freezer. Except ice cream.

CALIFORNIA GRILL (*Contemporary*): At this casual, new, wood-toned place on the *Contemporary's* 15th floor, you can mingle with the chefs in an exhibition kitchen that lets you keep a close eye on the action in the wood-burning pizza oven, on the rotisserie grill, and in the bakery oven. The West Coast theme shines through in such market-fresh dishes as alderwood-smoked salmon with whole roasted onions, and oak-fired beef tenderloin with Sonoma foie gras and a zinfandel glaze. The *Grill* bakes a mean California-style pizza, and the star-studded wine list, ranging from traditional chardonnays to new-wave viogniers, hails from California, too. Home-baked desserts along the lines of citrus soufflé provide the finishing touches, as do sweeping views of the Magic Kingdom and Seven Seas Lagoon. Reservations suggested. Expensive. D.

CAPE MAY CAFÉ (*Beach Club*): The all-you-can-eat New England clambake held every night in this whimsical, beach-umbrella-decked dining area is among the best values at Walt Disney World. The groaning board includes mussels, fish, peel-and-eat shrimp, corn-on-the-cob, ribs, red-skin potatoes, chowders, and salads. Lobster is available for an extra charge. If you like, dessert can be milk and cookies. Breakfast is a reservations-required character affair; at dinner, reservations are suggested. Moderate to expensive. B, D.

NARCOOSSEE'S (*Grand Floridian*): Within the conspicuous octagonal building (with veranda) that looks out over Seven Seas Lagoon, you'll find a casual restaurant whose open kitchen presents such not-so-casual fare as double lamb chops, blackened gator steaks, and filet mignon. You'll also discover knockout seafood chowder, Florida stone crab claws, and fried onion straws. For dessert, try the chocolate chip pecan pie. Note: This is not your secluded romantic retreat; there are yards of beer being downed and children are not scarce. But the food is excellent, and the wine selection quite good. Reservations suggested. Expensive. L, D.

'OHANA (*Polynesian*): The beauty of this new family-style dining experience—a South Pacific feast prepared in the restaurant's prominent 16-foot-long open-fire cooking pit—is that the hickory-grilled skewers of pork, shrimp, chicken, beef, and Hawaiian sausage just keep coming.

Lamb is carved tableside. While lo mein noodles, rice, and *siu mai* dumplings are among the accompaniments, this is not a great place for vegetarians. For dessert, try the passion fruit crème brûlée. For special occasions you may want to consider reserving a spot at King Kamehameha's Ceremonial Table, where (among other things) you will be serenaded with traditional Polynesian songs. Reservations are suggested for dinner, required for breakfast (a character affair). Expensive. B, D.

OLIVIA'S (*Disney Vacation Club*): We like the Key West manner with which *Olivia's* approaches its theme; certainly, the enthusiastically laid-back setting and menu convey the spirit of Key West. Oh, there are menu selections that work the theme hard—a toasted bagel with Key lime cream cheese, salads with Key lime–honey Dijon dressing, conch fritters, and Key Lime Kooler, a creamy blend of rum and Key lime juice—but there are just as many offered strictly for fun. Cases in point: turkey pot pie, mango crab cakes, and frozen strawberry margarita pie. All things considered, this spot is worth a detour. Wine, beer, and specialty drinks are served. On Wednesdays and Sundays, breakfast comes with characters and requires reservations; otherwise it's first-come seating. Moderate. B, L, D.

SUM CHOWS (*Dolphin,* 934-4025): The exquisitely prepared and stylishly presented regional Asian dishes served here are the sort you'll be talking about for a long time. *Sum Chows* is a rarity—an elegant restaurant that's serious about food and yet extremely user-friendly. The menu, best described as artfully eclectic, includes dishes with seafood, beef, pork, lamb, and fowl. In addition to a selection of sushi, it provides such flourishes as snow crab claws with lemongrass batter and spicy macadamia sauce, and honeycomb red snapper with a fiery sauce. There's an extensive wine list, excellent desserts, and a side dish known as flash-fried spinach that's positively addictive. For special occasions, consider making a reservation to have a "chef's table" dinner in the heart of the culinary action (no dishwashing required). Smoking permitted. Usually closed Tuesdays and Wednesdays. Reservations suggested. Very expensive. D.

The Wine Line

Got a question about wine? The "Grapeline" at the *Contemporary's California Grill* will answer any and all queries daily from noon until 10 P.M. Call 824-1576.

VICTORIA & ALBERT'S (*Grand Floridian*): Indulgent without being too haute to handle, stunningly luxurious without being pretentious, this grande dame of the Walt Disney World dining scene is in a class all its own. The six-course prix fixe menu changes daily, always offering an array of fish, poultry, beef, veal, and lamb selections as well as a choice of soups, salads, and desserts. The delectable $80-per-person adventure begins with the arrival of hors d'oeuvres from the chef. As an example of what could follow, consider Oriental shrimp dumplings, chicken consommé with pheasant breast, poached Maine lobster with passion fruit butter, mixed greens with raspberry–pinot noir vinaigrette, Stilton cheese with pears poached in burgundy wine, and a dark chocolate and strawberry soufflé. Perfect portions keep it all surprisingly manageable. The beautifully appointed room is well designed for intimate dining. The strains of a harp or violin provide a romantic backdrop. The wine list is encyclopedic, and the wine pairings (you'll pay about $25 more for four selected glasses) provide fitting complements. In sum, an extremely expensive, extremely special experience. Jackets are required for men. Reservations necessary. Very expensive. D.

YACHTSMAN STEAKHOUSE (*Yacht Club*): Our stomachs couldn't possibly be as big as our eyes at this carnivore's paradise, where on at least one occasion a server has kindly saved us from ourselves. The generous portions begin with truly massive rolls and continue with the imperative spicy fried onion skillet and the signature garlic-and-cheese "smashed" potatoes; of course, there's no skimping on the excellent and expertly prepared aged beef entrées (prime rib, filet mignon, and chateaubriand, to name a few), so good luck finding room for a piece of white-chocolate macadamia nut pie or chocolate mousse cake. While the menu emphasizes steak, it also includes seafood and chicken dishes (guests also may order selections from the predominantly seafood menu from *Ariel's*, next door at the *Beach Club;* see below). This atmospheric

Two for Tea

Teatime with all the trimmings—scones, dainty sandwiches, and pastries served on bone china—is 3:30 P.M. at the *Rose & Crown Dining Room* in Epcot's World Showcase. Reservations are necessary; call WDW-DINE, or drop by and make them in person. The *Garden View Lounge* at the *Grand Floridian* also offers an extensive selection of teas and tasty accompaniments during its afternoon tea, held every day from 3 P.M. to 6 P.M. (reservations are accepted; call WDW-DINE).

restaurant is possessed of country club elegance, and is filled with intimate dining nooks perfectly suited for special occasions. Both the wine and beer lists are extensive. Reservations suggested. Expensive. D.

Good Bets

ARIEL'S (*Beach Club*): What the *Yachtsman Steakhouse* does for landlubbers this pretty dining room (which somehow gets away with fish-and-bubble chandeliers) does for seafarers. Lobster is the house specialty and successfully works its way into surf and turf, paella, and pasta dishes. Wine is a big deal here, and perfectly matched wine pairings (called flights) are offered in conjunction with your meal. Note that diners may also order selections from the *Yachtsman Steakhouse* menu. Reservations suggested. Expensive. D.

BOATWRIGHT'S DINING HALL (*Dixie Landings*): Moderately priced Cajun specialties are the draw at this unique eatery, where the centerpiece is a riverboat under construction, boat-making tools are mounted on the walls, and tables are set with condiment-filled tool boxes. Try the baby-back ribs with Cajun dirty rice. Full bar. Dinner reservations accepted. Moderate. B, D.

CONCOURSE STEAK HOUSE (*Contemporary*): If homemade potato chips speak to you, you'd like to sample the best mashed potatoes in the World, or you just want a quick, civilized bite one step removed from the Magic Kingdom, here you have it. Reservations accepted. Moderate. B, L, D.

CONTEMPORARY CAFÉ (*Contemporary*): Dinner here—an all-you-can-eat international buffet served adjacent to the tracks on which the monorail zips quietly through this resort—is one of the World's best values. Breakfast is a reservations-required character affair; for dinner, reservations accepted. Moderate. B, D.

GRAND FLORIDIAN CAFÉ (*Grand Floridian*): Tall, wall-length windows incorporate the hotel's central courtyard into this inviting restaurant's potted-palm greenery. It's a

Only-at-WDW Microbrews

- Lodge House Brew at *Territory Lounge* (*Wilderness Lodge*)

- Monorail Ale at *Outer Rim Cocktail Lounge* (*Contemporary*)

- Harry's Safari Beer at *Harry's Safari Bar* (*Dolphin*)

- And one more that will arrive on the scene with Disney's newest resort complex in mid-1996 (*Disney's BoardWalk*)

We (Almost) Never Close

The following resort eateries are open 24 hours during busy seasons:

- *Roaring Forks (Wilderness Lodge)*
- *Tubbi's Buffeteria (Dolphin)*
- *The Plaza Diner (Royal Plaza)*
- *Crumpets Café (Grosvenor)*
- *Captain Cook's Snack and Ice Cream Company (Polynesian)*
- *B-Line Diner (Peabody Orlando)*

Hours are subject to change.

---

pleasant spot morning, afternoon, and evening, and a reasonably priced way to check out the World's poshest resort. The café's tasty dishes have a southern flavor, and the menu includes many light selections. Try the citrus french toast with cinnamon, the fried chicken, the Caesar salad with grilled shrimp, or the chocolate caramel brownie cake. Excellent wine selection. First-come seating. Moderate. B, L, D.

JUAN & ONLY'S CANTINA (*Dolphin*, 934-4025): It'll cost you a few pesos, but for Texas-size portions of exceptional Mexican fare, head for this colorful spot. Whether you take a white-corn tortilla chip to the Seven Sins Dip is up to you. There's cerveza, margaritas, and both red and blond sangria by the pitcher, and the bar stocks rare tequilas. Smoking permitted. Reservations suggested. Expensive. D.

KIMONO'S (*Swan*): This is the call for good sushi (prepared as you watch) and tempura in a peaceful lounge styled with bamboo and kimono accents. A respectable wine selection is complemented by sake, Japanese beers, and specialty cocktails. The calm is occasionally interrupted with karaoke. Smoking permitted. First-come seating. Moderate to expensive. D, S.

PALIO (*Swan,* 934-1609): An elegant, spirited Italian trattoria worth noting as a trusty source for imaginatively prepared homemade pasta, tasty pizzas baked in wood-fired ovens, and traditional veal and seafood dishes. Peroni and Moretti beers are featured in addition to Italian wines. Coffees hit the spot. Smoking permitted. Reservations suggested. Expensive. D.

WHISPERING CANYON CAFÉ (*Wilderness Lodge*): For savory eating that doesn't stop until you say "when," consider this casual family-style restaurant a delicious candidate. Particularly at dinner, when apple-rosemary rotisserie chicken, maple-garlic pork spareribs, and smoked beef brisket are certain to satisfy. But don't stuff yourself too silly—the berry cobbler is awesome. First-come seating. To minimize your wait, aim for either the early or late side of prime meal times (check in with the hostess, then park yourself in front of the lobby's immense fireplace with a drink or hang out in the adjacent *Territory Lounge*). Moderate. B, L, D, S.

OTHER WORLD OPTIONS

Stand-Outs

ARTHUR'S 27 (*Buena Vista Palace*, 827-3450): In the imposing check category, this gastronomic gem offers a lofty view of Pleasure Island and the Disney Village Marketplace from its 27th-floor perch and rates among Florida's finest restaurants. Large booths, each equipped with a window, make for wonderfully intimate dining. House specialties include duckling, Florida Gulf shrimp, and veal medaillons. The wine list is excellent. Jackets required for men. Smoking permitted. Reservations necessary. Very expensive. D.

BASKERVILLES (*Grosvenor*, Hotel Plaza): It doesn't take a detective to surmise the Sherlock Holmes theme of this memorabilia-laden restaurant, which is notable primarily for its prime-rib dinner buffets. Smoking policy varies by day and meal. First-come seating. Moderate. B, L, D.

CAP'N JACK'S OYSTER BAR (Disney Village Marketplace): This attractive pier house perched over Buena Vista Lagoon is the place to socialize over mason-jar drafts and fresh seafood. The special strawberry margarita's a keeper, as are the peel-and-eat shrimp, conch chowder, clams on the half shell, and crab cakes. Besides offering some of the most reasonably priced meals around, the restaurant also fetches some fine sunsets. First-come seating. Moderate. L, D, S.

GOURMET PANTRY (Disney Village Marketplace): Okay, so it's not a restaurant. But this shop is just riddled with delicious inspiration for casual meals, picnics, and even self-catered boating excursions on Lake Buena Vista's waterways. When we mention the terrific heros sold by the inch, specialty salads, Godiva chocolates, wine, and spirits, we're merely hinting at the soup-to-nuts inventory. Inexpensive. B, L, D, S.

PLANET HOLLYWOOD (Pleasure Island): This new celestial body on the WDW skyline—a branch of the international chain that's ensconced inside a 120-foot-diameter

A Corner Table, Please

For a dining affair to remember, complete with intimate, elegant surroundings, soft lighting, and a memorable meal, reserve a table for two at *Victoria & Albert's* at the *Grand Floridian* or, off property, at *Maison & Jardin*, in Altamonte Springs (862-4410).

Picnic at Sea

At the Disney Village Marketplace, pick up some wine and picnic fixings from the Gourmet Pantry and rent a boat on the marina for an impromptu party.

Brunch and All That Jazz

If it's Sunday, it must be Mardi Gras. Or so the social calendar goes at the *Pleasure Island Jazz Company*, where every week begins (and, depending on how you look at it, ends) with a Mardi Gras Jazz Brunch. At this all-you-can-eat Creole feast, guests are serenaded by a Dixieland band as they chow down on the likes of crab cakes, red beans and rice, chicken Louisianne, and made-to-order omelettes. Two seatings are available; tickets cost $22 for adults and include same-day admission to Pleasure Island. Reservations are necessary (call 828-5636).

sphere—is a fantastic addition to the World's dining lineup. The hordes who assemble to get a look at the interior of this restaurant are rewarded with a mind-boggling three-dimensional collage of movie memorabilia that couldn't possibly be digested in one meal. But there's much more to this fun-filled planet than meets the eye: The menu has creative flair and depth (consider blackened shrimp, Far East chicken salad, vegetable burgers, pasta primavera). Desserts are outstanding (try the butter pecan rum cake or Arnold Schwarzenegger's mother's apple strudel). Smoking permitted. No reservations, alas, just extremely long lines. Moderate to expensive. L, D, S.

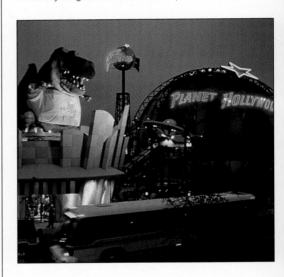

PORTOBELLO YACHT CLUB (Pleasure Island): This polished yet casual piece of nautica is simply one of our favorite places to visit on an empty stomach. Menu standouts include a variety of luscious thin-crust pizzas baked in a wood-burning oven, farfalle primavera, and spaghettini alla Portobello, a seafood medley served over pasta in a light tomato and wine sauce. As an example of the extraordinary qualities of the desserts here, we offer the testimony of a *Portobello* regular regarding the restaurant's rich layer cake with chocolate ganache frosting, chocolate toffee crunch filling, and warm caramel sauce: "Cioccolata paradiso got me through twenty hours of labor." *Portobello* also offers some tempting specialty coffees and an impressive wine list. It's open until 1:30 A.M. Owned and operated by Levy Restaurants of Chicago. Smoking permitted. First-come seating. Moderate to expensive. L, D, S.

Good Bets

CHEF MICKEY'S VILLAGE RESTAURANT (Disney Village Marketplace): It turns out that the Mouse can cook (and if the greenery in this sunny lagoonside dining room is any indication, he's also got a green thumb). The food is all-American. Breakfast is a character affair requiring reservations; at lunch and dinner, reservations suggested. Moderate. B, D.

D-ZERTZ (Pleasure Island): The nightclub metropolis' sweet spot sates late-night urges for sugar and caffeine. Inexpensive. S.

DONALD'S DAIRY DIP (Disney Village Marketplace): Shop here for ice cream and frozen yogurt bargains. Inexpensive. S.

FIREWORKS FACTORY (Pleasure Island, 934-8989): This barbecue spot—housed in a fireworks warehouse that looks to have had a run-in with Murphy's Law—stands out for its impressive beer list, its night-owl noshing, and its lively happy hours. The varied fare is flavorful, though not a total blast. Owned and operated by Levy Restaurants of Chicago. Smoking permitted. Reservations accepted. Expensive. L, D.

BEYOND THE WORLD

Stand-Outs

THE BUBBLE ROOM (1351 S. Orlando Ave., Maitland; 628-3331): Kitschy doesn't begin to describe the camp oozing from the pores of this local legend, where servers called "bubble scouts," a roving toy train, twinkling Christmas lights, and a "tunnel of love" dining booth blend in just fine. Specialties of the house include a 32-ounce "Tarzan-cut" prime rib and an "Eddie Fisherman" grouper fillet. The desserts are both outrageously large and outrageously delicious; the red velvet cake is (rightfully) renowned statewide. Homemade potato chips, called Carolina Moons, are addictive. Smoking permitted. First-come seating. Moderate to expensive. L, D.

Appetizing News

A huge expansion slated for completion sometime in 1997 will not only blur the lines between Pleasure Island and the Disney Village Marketplace; it will also add a few compelling options to the World's dining lineup.

■ *Wolfgang Puck's Café* will mark the L.A. chef's Florida debut and bring creative California cuisine to the fore.

■ The tastes and sounds of Cuba will dovetail at *Lario's*, a restaurant–nightclub created by singer Gloria Estefan and her husband.

■ An eclectic menu with New Orleans taste buds will distinguish *House of Blues*, a restaurant–nightclub part-owned by Dan Aykroyd.

■ Before all this comes to pass, Levy Restaurants will have opened a traditional crab house aboard the *Empress Lilly* riverboat docked here. The casual dining spot, due in port in late 1995, launches a new era for the waterborne venue.

"X" Marks the Spot

WDW visitors have a number of reasonably priced dining options at the Crossroads of Lake Buena Vista shopping center, across from the Disney Village Hotel Plaza. These include *Pebbles*, *T.G.I. Friday's*, *Johnny Rocket's*, *Red Lobster*, *McDonald's*, *Taco Bell*, *Perkins*, *Chevy's Tex-Mex*, *Jungle Jim's*, and *Pizzeria Uno*.

BUBBALOU'S BODACIOUS BBQ (1471 Lee Rd., Winter Park; 628-1212): Call it finger-licking cozy. This teensy shack boasts the best barbecue and tongue-tingling hot sauce in town. Smoking permitted. First-come seating. Inexpensive. L, D.

CAPTAIN APPLEBY'S INN (Two locations including 549 W. Par St., Orlando; 426-8838): While seafood is the primary bill of fare at this country charmer, locals flock here for the superb salad bar, the home-baked cinnamon rolls, and the self-serve cinnamon-stick apples. Early-bird specials. Smoking permitted. First-come seating. Moderate. L, D, Sunday brunch.

CHALET SUZANNE (3800 Chalet Suzanne Dr., Lake Wales; 813-676-6011): Family owned and operated for 65 years, this award-winning lakeside restaurant is among the finest in Central Florida (celebrities arrive by plane at the country inn's private landing strip). With imaginative continental dishes served in a setting straight out of a Bavarian fairy tale, the question is not whether it's worth the 30-minute trip from Walt Disney World but whether you're prepared to put a whole lot of money where your mouth is. Excellent wine list. Smoking permitted. Reservations suggested. Very expensive. B, L, D.

COLORADO FONDUE COMPANY (1016 E. Semoran Blvd., Casselberry; 767-8232): Never associated Colorado with fondue? Here's (great) food for thought. Smoking permitted. Reservations suggested. Moderate. L, D.

LE COQ AU VIN (4800 S. Orange Ave., Orlando; 851-6980): Countrified French cuisine in an enchanting chalet-style setting. Stained-glass windows, private dining rooms, and floral flourishes up the romantic quotient; as for the food, know that local chefs are among this place's most devoted fans. Extensive wine list. Smoking permitted. Reservations suggested. Expensive. L, D.

MAISON & JARDIN (430 S. Wymore Rd., Altamonte Springs; 862-4410): Museum-quality Oriental rugs, Austrian crystal, and mirrors aglow with candlelight set the stage for romance; flamboyant tableside preparations of classic French dishes further entice. Hunger and thirst are well taken care of, too. Smoking permitted. Reservations suggested. Very expensive. D, Sunday brunch.

MANUEL'S ON THE 28TH (Top floor, Barnett Bank Building; 390 N. Orange Ave., Orlando; 246-6580): The "new kid on the block," this penthouse dining room serves downtown Orlando on a platter (if only the celebs and execs would look up from their creatively prepared meat and seafood dishes to enjoy it). Excellent wine list. Reservations suggested. Expensive. D.

Good Bets

ANGEL'S DINER & BAKERY (Several locations including 1345 Lee Rd., Orlando; 291-4832): This new-wave rock 'n' roll diner earns its wings in typical fashion: blue-plate specials, burgers, homemade desserts, and breakfast till 11 P.M. No alcohol served. Smoking permitted. First-come seating. Inexpensive. B, L, D.

CHATHAM'S PLACE (7575 Dr. Phillips Blvd., Orlando; 345-2992): The Florida black grouper with pecan butter is among the finest entrées in town, so it doesn't matter so much that the upscale American menu is a bit limited. The atmosphere is both warm and casual. Smoking permitted. Reservations suggested. Expensive. L, D.

DUX (*Peabody Orlando;* 9801 International Dr., Orlando; 353-4000): "Deluxe" is a good word. So is "epicurean." This is one acclaimed dining spot that actually deserves the applause, both for its outstanding international cuisine (sans duck) and its award-winning wine list. Smoking permitted. Reservations suggested. Expensive to very expensive. L, D.

PEBBLES (Four locations including Crossroads of Lake Buena Vista; 827-1111): Inventive California cuisine meets casual Florida elegance in this yuppie grazing spot, ideal for conspicuous late-night consumption. Fine wine list. Smoking permitted. First-come seating. Moderate. L, D.

STRAUB'S (5101 E. Colonial Dr., Orlando; 273-9330): Locally synonymous with fresh, reasonably priced seafood, it's a special treat from October through May, when Florida stone crab claws are in season. Early-bird specials. Smoking permitted. Reservations suggested. Moderate. D.

Dining Rooms with Knockout Views

- *California Grill* (*Contemporary*)

- *Narcoossee's* (*Grand Floridian*)

- *Cap'n Jack's Oyster Bar* (**Disney Village Marketplace**)

- *Planet Hollywood* (**Pleasure Island**)—No windows necessary here!

- *Rose & Crown Dining Room* (**United Kingdom, Epcot's World Showcase**)

- *Cantina de San Angel* (**Mexico, Epcot's World Showcase**)

- *Coral Reef* (**The Living Seas, Epcot's Future World**)

- *Garden Grill* (**The Land, Epcot's Future World**)

- *Arthur's 27* (*Buena Vista Palace*)

- *Manuel's on the 28th* (**Orlando**)

NIGHTLIFE GUIDE

Those who find the energy to hit the town after a hard day's recreation are rewarded with a whole new world of amusements and entertainments. Among the myriad ways to take advantage of a second wind (and find a third) at Walt Disney World, Pleasure Island is the most obvious. This single-admission complex of nightclubs, restaurants, and movie theaters trumpeted as Disney's playground for adults is just that. It has knockout improvisational comedy, cool jazz, raging dance clubs, and much more, rolled into one neat package that creates a populace of happy nomads. If one pocket of ready-made nightlife isn't enough, there's Church Street Station, old Orlando's version of the block party as institution, about 20 miles up the road. And those are just the prix fixe entertainment menus; à la carte nightlife options abound. The theme parks offer a few notable watering holes for early birds. The resorts in and around the World rally to the adult cause with a tempting slate of lounges and nightclubs to suit every taste. Tally it all up, and you have sufficient incentive to take even the faintest breeze of a second wind for all it's worth: havens for wine lovers and havens for beer drinkers; gems that enchant and gems that rock; places to shoot the breeze and places to shoot pool; desirable digs for singles and desirable digs for couples. The key is knowing where to find them.

In the pages that follow, we present the best nightlife in the World. First, you'll receive a thorough indoctrination to Pleasure Island, complete with a walking tour. Next, an informed briefing on additional clubs and lounges located on WDW property. This second section is structured as a listing. Under the heading "Stand-Outs," we have singled out those places both quiet and jumping that are worth going out of your way for or simply a joy to have nearby. Within the designation "Good Bets," we have corralled the best of the rest—additional clubs and lounges worth checking out, particularly if you're in the area. The last section of this guide completes the nightlife picture by illuminating "Stand-Outs" and "Good Bets" located outside the bounds of Walt Disney World. *Cheers!*

A Sense of Place

Pleasure Island's clubs are described here in the order they are encountered upon passing through the turnstiles.

PLEASURE ISLAND

This bustling metropolis—a six-acre island consumed entirely by nightclubs, restaurants, stage shows, movie theaters, and shops—can be counted on to fill the entertainment void when Walt Disney World's theme parks and golf courses have closed for the day. We'd liken the atmosphere of this most adult venture (guests must be 18 or joined at the hip to a parent to be admitted to clubs, and *Mannequins Dance Palace* disco is strictly 21 and up) to a four-alarm block party. Pleasure Island's vigor and longevity is bolstered by its unique interpretation of the calendar—the place celebrates more New Year's Eves in a year than Dick Clark could know in four lifetimes ("Auld Lang Syne" and confetti cannons join special effects-enhanced fireworks as nightly rituals). It tosses a nod to most every nightlife

niche. And although it's perhaps more fun once you've cased out your favorite hangouts, it is possible to experience all seven of Pleasure Island's nightclubs in one whirlwind night, and this is the course we recommend for first-time visitors.

While the main draw here is certainly the nightly street party that begins once the clubs have opened their doors, Pleasure Island's shops are open from 10 A.M. to 1 A.M., its restaurants serve lunch as well as dinner, and its multiplex cinema gets started before noon. There is no admission fee until 7 P.M., when a single cover charge of $16.91 (good for entry to all clubs) applies to all but restaurant- and movie-goers. Length of Stay Passes and Five-Day World Hopper Passes include Pleasure Island admission. The drinking age in Florida is 21, and proof of age is required at the gate and at most club entrances. Be advised: The *Adventurers Club, Rock & Roll Beach Club,* and the *Neon Armadillo* are up and running at 7 P.M. The *Comedy Warehouse* (whose first show we

Another Round

Caught with your pockets empty on Pleasure Island? Have a chat with the ATM located just past the stairway at the *Rock & Roll Beach Club.*

Pleasure Island Tips

■ The *Adventurers Club* is the only watering hole up and running at 7 P.M. It also is the island's only nonsmoking venue.

■ At the *Comedy Warehouse*, aim for the earlier shows for the shortest queues, and know that it's possible but not likely to get in on the fly.

 ■ To snag a good table at the *Pleasure Island Jazz Company*, arrive about 20 minutes before showtime.

highly recommend for its shorter queues) opens its doors at 7:30 P.M., with the rest kicking in at 8 P.M. Also, while the clubs don't close down until 2 A.M., note that last call is sounded at 1:30 A.M.

Before we take you on a club-hopping tour of Pleasure Island, a few words about the other diversions here are warranted. The exceptional **AMC Theatres** cinema offers more than a little incentive to give aching feet a rest. Current motion picture releases are shown in ten plush theaters, all of them equipped with an advanced sound system called THX that was developed by George Lucas (call 827-1300 for showtimes).

Also, the full-service restaurants on and around Pleasure Island contain some of the best eating to be had at Walt Disney World. Of the Island's own, *Portobello Yacht Club* (an Italian restaurant emphasizing delicious seafood and pasta) doesn't shut down its galley until midnight; *Planet Hollywood*, terrific, but hardly a drop-in affair, takes orders right up to 1 A.M.; and the *Fireworks Factory* stands by with barbecue until about 1:30 A.M. For dining recommendations, consult this chapter's "Restaurant Guide," which includes reviews of all the key noshing spots here and at the adjacent Disney Village Marketplace. (Note: Dinner at the *Portobello Yacht Club* or the *Fireworks Factory* nets you a 20 percent discount off Pleasure Island admission for the night.)

For impromptu snacking, we like the crepe cart located just inside the entrance; of the several clubs that serve food, the *Pleasure Island Jazz Company* is the only one offering salads and other fare beyond pub grub. The *Hill Street Diner* features salads alongside its fast food, while *D-Zertz* sates the sweet tooth. Cues on Pleasure Island's unique shops are offered in our extensive shopping guide in the *Diversions* chapter. For information about transportation to and from Pleasure Island, which is connected by footbridges to the Disney Village Marketplace, consult the "Transportation" section of this book's *Planning Ahead* chapter.

To give you a sense of location, clubs are described here in the order they are encountered upon passing through the main turnstiles. But Pleasure Island is an open invitation to serendipity—truly a club-hopper's paradise—and its varied venues are ideally explored according to mood and energy level. Generally, you'll find that *Mannequins Dance Palace*, poised right inside the gate, is not one best encountered cold. Better warm-ups are the fetchingly upbeat *Comedy Warehouse*, the *Rock & Roll Beach Club, 8Trax,* and the *Neon Armadillo Music Saloon*. For a cooldown or a relaxing interlude, there are two choices: the *Pleasure Island Jazz Company* and the *Adventurers Club*.

A Walking Tour

As you bear down on Pleasure Island, note that the parking lot here is a highly trafficked place requiring pedestrian vigilance. Either take advantage of valet parking or resist the urge to look up at the eye-catching cluster of neon lights and skyward lasers until you've crossed over to the sidewalk where the ticket booth sits. Once here, do all the neck-craning, head-bobbing, and people-watching you please (everyone else is), and be sure to pick up an entertainment schedule.

The main entrance lies directly ahead. After presenting your ticket in exchange for a lovely plastic bracelet, you pass (limbo if you like) under the neon archway and into the pleasuredom itself. The first building on the left houses **Mannequins Dance Palace**, a pulsating den of incredible special effects and current techno-pop tracks that puts a unique spin on the standard club scene with a huge, rotating dance floor. It takes its name from the many mannequins, all related to the dance world, found throughout. The only venue on Pleasure Island reserved strictly for patrons 21 and older, *Mannequins* is a club in the urban mold, and it attracts a dressed-to-impress crowd. The music here is cranked so loud that a jet could pass through virtually unnoticed; yet somehow the place is packed all night long with revelers who actually employ verbal communication in their flirtations. If you can stand the volume, you may take pleasure in the fact that the circulating dance floor gives a little boost to your dance skills and allows for exceptionally easy scoping, whether you're dancing or on the sidelines.

Several explosive modern dance performances are staged here nightly, and on Thursday nights the music runs to retro-progressive. The club is entered (via an elevator) on the third floor, a level that enjoys the same volume as the rest of the club, and offers little beyond a bit of privacy and a perch from which to view the action below.

After-Dark Dazzle

■ Epcot's World Showcase, the only part of the theme park circuit that stays open until at least 9 P.M. year-round, assumes a sparkling beauty at night that rarely fails to enchant. Disney takes superb advantage of this by presenting IllumiNations, a nightly symphony of fireworks, music, lasers, and dancing water fountains that rates among the most spectacular displays the World over. The 20-minute show, generally ignited at closing time, is visible from any point along the promenade.

■ The Electrical Water Pageant, a 1,000-foot-long string of illuminated floating creatures, makes its beautiful yet boisterous way around Bay Lake every night. You can usually view the parade at 9 P.M. from the *Polynesian*, 9:20 P.M. from the *Grand Floridian*, 9:35 P.M. from the *Wilderness Lodge*, 9:45 P.M. from *Fort Wilderness*, and 10:05 P.M. from the *Contemporary*.

■ During busy seasons (summers and holiday periods) when park hours stretch late into the evening, the relaxed atmosphere and, yes, romance, of the theme parks at night is nearly enough to make you forget about the daytime crowds. The Magic Kingdom celebrates its extended curfew with nightly fireworks over Cinderella Castle. Remember the 10 P.M. display as five to ten minutes of pyrotechnics worthy of a Fourth of July finale.

Twice each night during busy periods, the Magic Kingdom's biggest extravaganza, a fiber-optic light parade known as Spectro-Magic, makes its way down Main Street; aim for the later show when prime viewing spots (anywhere along Main Street) are easier to snare, thanks to youngsters needing to go beddie-bye.

■ The last—and best—of WDW's seasonal nighttime entertainments is the Sorcery in the Sky show at the Disney-MGM Studios. Ten minutes of dazzling fireworks set to music from *Fantasia* and other classic films can be seen nightly anytime the park is open late. Best viewing is on Hollywood Boulevard.

Ditto the second floor. As for drinks, *Mannequins* offers a full bar but emphasizes the bubbly, serving Champagne by the glass or by the bottle, from Piper Sonoma to Dom Perignon. This club is popular with both locals and visitors, so be prepared to encounter a line at the door, especially on weekends.

Directly across from *Mannequins* you will see a warehouse-like structure. This is the site of the **Pleasure Island Jazz Company**, the island's newest and most sophisticated entity. Cool, uninhibited jazz and blues are the order at this live-music venue, which runs the gamut from 1930s to contemporary tunes and features both local and national talent. A haven for jazz enthusiasts and a relaxing interlude from the rowdier scenes, the place is dimly lit and dotted with small cocktail tables that encourage intimate conversation.

If you're up for some quality entertainment in a romantic atmosphere; if you're too pooped for anything beyond snapping your fingers; if you're hankering for a jazzy libation, a nice bottle of wine, or a bite on the other side of the fast-food tracks, the *Jazz Company* will take care of you. The menu here covers all bases. For under $10 you'll find the likes of shrimp quesadillas and crème brûlée. Whether you're thirsty or not, check out the drink descriptions. From "the cookie dough of wine" to a red with "enough velour texture to do Ricardo Montalban proud," they're a hoot. Muddy Waters is paid tribute in a terrific specialty coffee with Bailey's, Frangelico, and a hazelnut finish. If it's too hot for coffee, try a Kinky Sax. To snag a good table, aim to arrive about 20 minutes before showtime.

Onward. Make a right turn out of the *Jazz Company*, and you're on due course for the **Rock & Roll Beach Club**. As the club's surfboard stairway comes into sight, you'll notice Pleasure Island's gradually sloping main strip leading off to the left. At the top of the stairs, you enter a rollicking dance spot featuring excellent bands that is much easier on the eardrums than *Mannequins*, and substantially more laid-back (perhaps due to its surfer sensibility). Between sets, some of the wackiest deejays you'll ever see keep the classic rock and current pop coming even as they're bouncing like oversize Super Balls off the walls of the prominent audio booth. While dancing is definitely a big deal here—the dance floor is generally packed, primarily with twentysomethings—there's more to do than twist and shout the night away, and many guests enjoy the three-story club's great music and casual

atmosphere without so much as stepping onto the lowest level. They shoot pool, play air hockey and pinball, and hang out at tables overlooking the dance floor to eat the house pizza, people-watch, and sip a beer. Roving souls should note that the *Rock & Roll Beach Club's* specialty drinks are available in refillable 16-ounce squeeze bottles.

From the *Rock & Roll Beach Club* it's a right turn, then a short walk (you'll pass several shops and then see it on your left) to our next gig, **8Trax**, a place so thoroughly '70s that "YMCA" is a scheduled event (12:30 A.M.). In this rather rocking joint you'll see a lot of people with goofy (lowercase, that is) grins on their faces and hear a continual stream of "Omigod, this song...We have to dance to this one...No way...I completely forgot about this song." Suffice it to say that the *Saturday Night Fever*–style dance floor is not only an extraordinarily popular destination but an infinitely fascinating eyeful. Decor tends toward the psychedelic. Specialty drinks include Brady Bunch Punch. And some off-the-beaten-vinyl-sofa nooks are given over to beanbag chairs and a built-in game of Twister. Note: *8Trax* offers burgers and chicken sandwiches on Friday and Saturday nights, and the small courtyard out back is a good place to have a smoke or sneak a kiss.

Pleasure Island Plastic Cup Rule

It's fun to club-hop on Pleasure Island, but you can't do it with a glass in your hand. Most places are sympathetic and keep a stack of plastic cups near the door. Or plan ahead, and request that your last drink be served in plastic.

Virgin Daiquiri, Anyone?

Soft drinks, fruit juices, and tasty specialty drinks sans alcohol are available at all Pleasure Island clubs. Just ask the bartender.

Moving along, the next club on the horizon (veer left out of *8Trax* and cross the street) is Pleasure Island's biggest enigma—the **Adventurers Club**. This elegant and eccentric parlor takes after the salons of 19th-century explorers clubs, and is decked out with photos, trinkets, and furnishings that document the awfully far-reaching (and far-fetched) travels of its card-carrying members.

On the surface, it's a quiet place, filled with comfortable chairs; the official club drink, the Kungaloosh, is a tasty frozen number with strawberry and orange juices, blackberry brandy, and rum. But penetrate the recesses of the *Adventurers Club*, and you'll notice some pretty odd characters milling about, stumble upon some rather curious corners and goings-on, and ultimately be invited into a hideaway library (where those odd characters put on a rather curious show complete with haunted organ). A few hints to making the most of this intriguing parlor: Grab a stool at the main bar downstairs, and ask the bartender for a raise; read the captions for the displayed photos; and don't miss the mask room. Finally, note that this is a non-smoking venue.

Right next door to the *Adventurers Club* is a thriving patch of bluegrass known as the **Neon Armadillo Music Saloon**. Here, you'll almost always see folks dressed in cowboy boots and Stetsons who have (clearly) come to Pleasure Island with one thing in mind: kicking up their heels on the *Neon Armadillo's* dance floor.

But you need not know a two-step from a tango to appreciate the swinging musicality of the country-and-western bands that perform nightly underneath this club's giant spur-shaped chandelier. Listening and watching's half the fun at this friendly—and highly spirited—two-floor retreat. If you're game to try it, the Country Two Step (vodka and amaretto) is said to get *anyone* out on the dance floor, although we imagine the *Neon Armadillo's* other specialty concoctions could accomplish the same. Certainly, the free line-dancing lessons offered here on Sunday evenings will help things along. The club's snack menu favors such munchables as potato skins (ask for an order of Cow Chips).

Our next order of business is not a nightclub but a forum known as the **West End Stage**, which provides much of the juice for Pleasure Island's street party. Live bands (mostly local, but occasionally big-name acts) perform here nightly, with Pleasure Island's dance troupe kicking in with some pretty slick performances as well.

While you won't find any seating to speak of in the plaza that fronts this stage, you may very well sight full-blown adults dancing under the stars. And unless you are allergic to confetti, this is the place to be when the nightly New Year's Eve countdown reaches its dramatic, sky-brighteningly pyrotechnic climax (showtime is 11:45 P.M.). Sure, the premise is a bit contrived, but it's a lot of fun, a good way to gather some new energy, and you'd be surprised how many couples jump at the chance for an extra New Year's Eve smooch before joining the rest of the crowd in singing "Auld Lang Syne."

In any case, the most strategic spot to take it all in (since you'll be standing anyway) is the queue for the **Comedy Warehouse**, located directly across the plaza from the *Neon Armadillo*. Get there no later than 11:30 P.M. (the next performance is at 12:20 A.M.) to get a jump on any New Year's revelers who might have the same idea. The *Comedy Warehouse*—a perennial favorite—is the sort of club in which you prop yourself on a stool in a tiered studio and hope you don't fall off laughing. The rule here: Drink in sips, because the troupe of five lightning-quick improvisational comedians does brilliant and absolutely hilarious things with assorted suggestions from the audience, and the zingers usually come without warning.

Every performance is different, but you can expect the audience to provide some pretty challenging raw material ("Okay, we need an occupation" nets the likes of "rutabaga farmer"), and count on the troupe to rise to the occasion with spontaneously composed, costumed, and accessorized products (generally songs, stories, and skits). Suffice it to say that when these comics go head-to-head in do-it-or-die improv competitions (and they do), they do not go down quickly.

Beer, wine, and mixed drinks are served, and popcorn is the preferred snack. While the performances here are well worth waiting for, hard-core humorists will often begin lining up a good hour before curtain time for the later shows, making it an increasingly tougher seat to get. A queue attendant keeps count, so you won't wait for nothing. Some additional tips: Aim for the earlier shows, and know that it's possible but not likely to get in on the fly. Also note that this is a nonsmoking venue.

Now That's Improvisation

Picture a shallow coat closet or the central aisle of a bus filled with holiday shoppers, and you have an idea of how much room comics at the *Comedy Warehouse* have backstage when all the costumes and wigs and props are stored.

Along the BoardWalk

WDW guests will gain new nightlife options with the completion of *Disney's BoardWalk*, which is located on the shore of Crescent Lake opposite the *Yacht Club* and *Beach Club*, and is slated to open in mid-1996.

The World has long needed a forum for "Harvest Moon," so we're particularly enthused about the *BoardWalk's* ballroom, a Roaring Twenties–style setup complete with a ten-piece orchestra.

An upscale base for sports lovers is another wish come to fruition here. In addition to the requisite munchables and big-screen TVs, it's equipped with interactive and virtual-reality games.

A third club along the boardwalk raises the energy level of the usual piano bar with dueling ivory ticklers.

Walt Disney World's first microbrewery will round out the new slate of adult hangouts.

The *BoardWalk* venues were unnamed as of press time, and no closing times were available. In other words, check at your resort's Guest Services desk or call 824-4321 before making promises to your dance partner or showing up for "Monday Night Football."

WALT DISNEY WORLD BEYOND PLEASURE ISLAND
Stand-Outs

CALIFORNIA GRILL LOUNGE (*Contemporary*): A fresh 15th-floor affair (the companion lounge to the new *California Grill* restaurant) that offers what amounts to box seats for the Magic Kingdom fireworks in a casual setting that does California wine country proud. The lounge knows its wines so well, it offers a hotline (824-1576). What more could you want? Doors close: 1 A.M.

CAP'N JACK'S OYSTER BAR (Disney Village Marketplace): This pier house jutting out over Buena Vista Lagoon scores with a convivial atmosphere, a mean strawberry margarita, and a circular bar conducive to people-watching. It also offers high-quality, reasonably priced sunsets and beautiful seafood (or is it the reverse?). Note that if you want to sit at the bar, the line out the door doesn't apply. Doors close: 10 P.M.

CATWALK BAR (Disney-MGM Studios): It only sounds like a precarious setting to imbibe. This prop-laden lounge located in the rafters of the *Soundstage* food court is actually the comfiest place at the Disney-MGM Studios. It's dim, cool, a giant step removed from the crowds, and the prop collection features some extraordinary items: sofas and coffee tables you can put your feet up on. Don't forget to get yourself a drink (an iced tea or a screwdriver perhaps?) or something to eat while you're up. Doors close: varies with park closing.

CREW'S CUP LOUNGE (*Yacht Club*): When it comes to beer, the *Crew's Cup* runneth over with 34 worldly brews. Consider the warm copper-accented decor, the scintillating aromas wafting in from the neighboring *Yachtsman Steakhouse*, and the potential for four-cheese garlic bread and New England clam chowder, and you have an even better idea of why we are putty in this lounge's hands. Doors close: midnight.

HARRY'S SAFARI BAR (*Dolphin*): Long live *Harry's* for its house brew, its big-deal appetizers (giant prawns, stuffed mushrooms, and escargot), and its heady Head-hunter (vodka, gin, rum, tequila, and sweet tropical juices). Add draft beers by the yard and a tempting slate of nonalcoholic beverages, and you've got a divine welcome to the jungle. Doors close: 11 P.M.

MARTHA'S VINEYARD LOUNGE (*Beach Club*): Flights of fancy (two-ounce sampler tours of select whites and reds) are the indulgence of choice in this wine lover's paradise. However, the wines may be ordered separately as well, in both full glass and sample sizes. Fine cognac, Armagnac, and port wines are offered. First-rate seafood appetizers and desserts are served until 10 P.M. But do you book the Opus One flight or the Ultimate Chardonnay (Gallo Estate to Far Niente, with stopovers at Grgich Hills and Cakebread)? Decisions, decisions. Doors close: 11 P.M.

MATSU NO MA LOUNGE (Japan, Epcot's World Showcase): A serene setting where—in addition to sake, Japanese beer, cocktails, and green tea—you can imbibe a stunning vista of Epcot. Sushi and sashimi also are served. Doors close: varies with park closing.

ROSE & CROWN PUB (United Kingdom, Epcot's World Showcase): We've always loved this cheeky classic—for its pretty polished-wood and brass decor, its rich Irish, Scottish, and British drafts, and its neighborly feel. So we weren't so surprised during a recent visit to overhear a gentleman asking a fellow behind the bar to please let Jerry (a bartender not present) know that he was sorry he'd missed him. "Next time," he said hopefully. You needn't be a fan of shandies or black-and-tans to appreciate that. Try the miniature chicken-and-leek pie or the Stilton cheese and fruit plate. Doors close: varies with park closing.

TERRITORY LOUNGE (*Wilderness Lodge*): This scenic spot of *Wilderness* is marked by five-foot wood-carved grizzlies that flank the bar and a mural depicting a large weathered-looking map of the western frontier that "unfolds" over the entire ceiling. If you swear you see the image of a certain mouse branded on the backside of a pony, you're right. While this lounge can be swamped with diners-in-waiting during prime meal times, it is more often a pleasantly relaxed setting that inspires lingering. Specialty drinks, hearty appetizers, and a lunch

Whatever Ales You...

Visiting beer lovers should remember these names: *Crew's Cup Lounge* (at the *Yacht Club*, with three beers on tap and 34 worldly brews), *Hubb's Pub* (with several area locations, 39 beers on tap, and 220 bottled brews); and the *Laughing Kookaburra* (at the *Buena Vista Palace*, with 99 labels).

Scenic Cocktail Spots

- *California Grill Lounge (Contemporary)*
- *Cap'n Jack's Oyster Bar (Disney Village Marketplace)*
- *Matsu No Ma Lounge (Epcot's World Showcase)*
- *Narcoossee's (Grand Floridian)*
- *Outer Rim Cocktail Lounge (Contemporary)*
- *Top-of-the-Palace Lounge (Buena Vista Palace)*
- *Toppers (Travelodge)*

WDW Dinner Shows

When it comes to dinner shows, Disney leads the pack. The elaborately themed productions offer set menus with generous portions, generally accompanied by unlimited alcoholic and nonalcoholic beverages, and welcome guests in casual attire.

Reservations are required and may be booked up to two years in advance by calling WDW-DINE (939-3463). Special dietary requests are honored at all the shows, with advance notice. Prices were correct at press time but are subject to change.

The best of the lot (and toughest reservation) is the Hoop-Dee-Doo Musical Revue, held in Pioneer Hall at *Fort Wilderness*. The show incorporates whoopin', singin', dancin', and audience participation in a frontier hoedown. Country vittles include ribs, fried chicken, salad, corn-on-the-cob, baked beans, and strawberry shortcake. There are three seatings, at 5 P.M., 7:15 P.M., and 9:30 P.M.; adults pay $35, plus tax and tip.

At the *Polynesian* resort, hula skirts, ukuleles, and fire dances add to the fun at the lakeside Polynesian Luau, which takes guests on a whirlwind journey

menu that extends through 4 P.M. add to the appeal. But the true toast of the *Territory* is Lodge House Brew, a microbrewed light beer with a hint of honey that's exclusive to the *Wilderness Lodge*. Doors close: midnight.

TOP-OF-THE-PALACE LOUNGE (*Buena Vista Palace*): Show up to toast the setting sun and you're provided with a glass of Champagne, not to mention fine wines by the glass and delectable desserts courtesy of the adjacent *Arthur's 27* restaurant. Miss the sunset and you've still got reason to propose a toast: an enviable view of Epcot's IllumiNations nightly at 9 P.M., and live entertainment (pianist and singer) on weekends. Doors close: 1 A.M.

TOPPERS (*Travelodge*): The place wears several hats—dartboards and pool tables serve the sports crowd, wall-length windows offer prime views of Epcot's Illumi-Nations, and large-screen rock music videos inspire the movers and shakers. Daily happy hours feature half-price drafts and wines. Doors close: 2 A.M.

Good Bets

COTTON CO-OP (*Dixie Landings*): This one's nothing fancy. Just your cozy, unassuming nook that happens to have a lovely fireplace, ready access to hot chicken wings and spicy Cajun onion straws, and a steady gig Tuesday through Saturday nights with a sing-along-inspiring entertainer. Anyway, we've cottoned to the place in general and to the Mississippi Mud Slide (a frozen Chambord-Bailey's blend served in a chocolate-swirled glass) in particular. Doors close: midnight.

GIRAFFE (*Royal Plaza*): Shoot a game of pool, play a round of darts, or dance to the deejay-spun classic rock or progressive music in this late-night place with funky decor. Happy hour is 4 P.M. to 9:30 P.M.; Wednesdays are two-for-one drink nights. Doors close: 3 A.M.

GURGLING SUITCASE (*Disney Vacation Club*): This travel-size bar is too small to warrant a special trip, but it has such a great name we'll take any excuse to mention it. For drinks, we like the one with amaretto, crème de banana, pineapple and orange juices, and a dash of cherry brandy. Tell the bartender you're looking for a Sultry Seahorse. Doors close: midnight.

LAUGHING KOOKABURRA (*Buena Vista Palace*): At "the Kook," a live band perched above the large bar plays Top 40 music for a crowd ranging in age from 25 to 40. If you'd rather listen than dance, snag a spot in one of four seating areas, including a small bar with a skylight on the upper level. Some 99 beers are on hand. Daily happy hour includes a buffet, and ladies drink free on Tuesday nights. Doors close: 2 A.M.

MIZNER'S LOUNGE (*Grand Floridian*): If you look past the house orchestra that sets up shop nightly outside this second-floor alcove, you'll find a mahogany bar with fine ports, brandies, and appetizers. Doors close: 1 A.M.

NARCOOSSEE'S (*Grand Floridian*): You've got to love a lounge that's thoroughly surrounded by Victoriana and nervy enough to serve yards (and half-yards) of beer. Doors close: 10 P.M.

OUTER RIM COCKTAIL LOUNGE (*Contemporary*): A sleek spot that keeps one eye on the monorail and the other on Bay Lake, this generally quiet lounge has a shifting atmosphere. By day, its distinctive monorail ambience graciously cedes to the breathtaking view out the window; when the vista fades to black, the bar's contemporary charms more than pick up the visual slack. In any case, *Outer Rim* is the natural spot to sample Monorail Ale, a full-flavored microbrewed amber made from toasted barley and select Oregon Williamette hops, and available only at the *Contemporary*. Adventurous spirits might also try the ice-cold spirit-soaked fruits, plunked into a cocktail or on their own. Last call for desserts is 11 P.M. Doors close: 1 A.M.

SCAT CAT'S CLUB (*Port Orleans*): Fat Tuesday in New Orleans it's not. *Scat Cat's* could use a (live) jazz infusion. But if you could go for a good Hurricane, this fetching lounge with a French Quarter feel and a popular guitarist ably provides. Doors close: 12:30 A.M.

TAMBU LOUNGE (*Polynesian*): There are mai tais, and there are mai tais served by bartenders who play flip the bottle and blow fire. Doors close: midnight.

from New Zealand to Samoa. The meal, served family-style, features tropical bread, island mixed green salad, ginger chicken, spareribs, seafood stir-fry with rice, and exotic fruit salad. Nightly seatings are at 6:45 P.M. and 9:30 P.M, and the outdoor shows are presented rain or shine, canceled only when temperatures drop below 50 degrees; adults pay $33, plus tax and tip.

The *Biergarten* restaurant in the Germany pavilion at Epcot's World Showcase hosts five nightly shows during which performers in lederhosen or dirndls create an Oktoberfest celebration with yodeling, dancing, and musicians playing everything from accordions to cowbells. Seating here is family-style (eight to a table), and guests have their choice of à la carte menu items that include sauerbraten, veal, roasted chicken, roast pork shank, and fresh fish, accompanied by mounds of red cabbage and roast potatoes, or German noodles. Prices range from $11.75 (for a vegetarian plate) to $20.75, or $28.75 for a *Schlachtplatte* (German-style platter) for two, plus tax and tip—and desserts cost extra.

Screen Gem

Orlando's only art film house answers the mainstream megaplex trend with a single screen on which it presents independent and foreign films; it also hosts an annual Florida Film Festival. The ten-year-old Enzian Theater offers occasional concerts and celebrity guest appearances (Paul Newman serves on the international advisory board). Enzian Theater; 1300 S. Orlando Ave., Maitland; 644-4662.

Dancing on the Water

Dinner-dance cruises on Lake Monroe and the St. Johns River offer a scintillating change of pace every Friday and Saturday night. Excursions include appetizers and a four-course meal, and last about 3½ hours. Three promenade decks allow patrons to dance right under the stars. Reservations suggested; call 800-423-7401.

BEYOND THE WORLD

Stand-Outs

CHURCH STREET STATION (129 W. Church St., Orlando; 422-2434): The ready-made nightlife at this historic downtown district draws locals and out-of-towners alike. While there's plenty of shopping and dining to be done here, the featured attractions are five distinctive clubs whose beautifully restored decor is so flush with antiques the Church Street folks call them showrooms. *Rosie O'Grady's Goodtime Emporium* puts the make on Bourbon Street with live Dixieland jazz and flaming hurricanes. *Apple Annie's Courtyard* could be a Victorian garden but for its bluegrass bands and hefty frozen drinks; Tuesday happy hours include live music and drink specials. The *Cheyenne Saloon and Opera House* boasts Grand Ole Opry–style country-and-western music and tasty barbecue, not to mention an amazing polished-wood setting; Thursday happy hours feature 75-cent long-neck beers. *Phineas Phogg's Dance Club* plays Top 40 hits in a (why ask why?) ballooning museum setting; Wednesday nickel beer happies are an Orlando institution. And the *Orchid Garden Ballroom* is not the waltz palace you might imagine. It's Victorian looking, all right, but the live bands here leave their oboes at home in favor of old-time rock 'n' roll; flaming desserts and specialty coffees are a big deal here. Admission charge for all of Church Street Station is $16.91. Doors close: 1 A.M. Sundays through Thursdays; 2 A.M. Fridays and Saturdays.

THE EDGE (100 W. Livingston St., Orlando; 839-4331): It's the young and the restless who burn the midnight oil in this bastion of anything–but–Top 40 (techno, punk, retro, alternative, and progressive) music. Inside the cavernous warehouse, a deejay rides herd over the (often severely dressed) crowd; outside, local and nationally recognized groups hold court nightly. Cover is $5 Wednesdays through Saturdays. Reduced admission Thursdays for WDW guests. Doors close: no earlier than 5 A.M., later if ten or more people are there.

FRIDAY'S FRONT ROW SPORTS GRILL (8126 International Dr., Orlando; 354-4552): A sporty new link in the *T.G.I. Friday's* chain in which spectators ogle some 66 TVs from bleachers and box seats, and players opt for billiards or electronic dartboards. Happy hour is from 4 P.M. to 7 P.M. Mondays through Fridays, and 10 P.M. to closing daily. Doors close: 2 A.M.

HUBB'S PUB (Several area locations including 6159 Westwood Blvd., Orlando; 354-0777): When a place has 39 beers on tap and some 220 bottled brews on ice, pilsners are sufficient atmosphere. But tell that to *Hubb's*, a local favorite that offers bands, karaoke, and deejay music, plus air-hockey tables, electronic dartboards, and interactive TV. Daily happy hours feature imported drafts for $1.40, domestics for 95 cents. Doors close: 2 A.M.

PINKIE LEE'S (380 W. Amelia St., Orlando; 872-7393): Orlando Magic stars Shaquille O'Neal and Horace Grant can often be spotted catching the live jazz and blues at this tasteful New Orleans–style club (and no wonder, it's located adjacent to the Orlando Arena and the Bob Carr Performing Arts Centre). Sunday gospel brunch. Daily happy hour. Weekend covers vary depending on headliner; some are under $10, others significantly higher. Doors close: midnight Tuesdays through Thursdays; 2 A.M. Fridays and Saturdays; 3 P.M. Sundays (gospel brunch only).

SWEENEY TODD'S (55 W. Church St., Orlando; 839-3444): It's said the friendliest bartenders in town work at this English pub, where dartboards, English and Irish ales (including a dozen on draft), and authentic cuisine such as steak-and-kidney pie draw an upscale, over-25 crowd. Daily happy hours. Doors close: 2 A.M. Mondays through Saturdays; midnight Sundays.

TRELLISES (*Hyatt Regency Grand Cypress;* One Grand Cypress Blvd., Orlando; 239-1234): Every elegant hotel with a lush tropical atrium lobby should have such a classy piano bar. Doors close: 2 A.M.

ZUMA BEACH CLUB (46 N. Orange Ave., Orlando; 648-8727): Where summer-lovin' twentysomethings go to see and be seen. Servers dress the part in bikinis. Wednesday drink specials, Thursday ladies' night (complete with male revues), and Friday happy hour with buffet. Cover is $3 to $5. Doors close: 2:30 A.M.

Orlando Area Dinner Shows

Just east of Walt Disney World in Kissimmee, there are three dinner shows of note. Arabian Nights is an arena-style extravaganza complete with Arabian horses. The meal features prime ribs, and includes salad and dessert. Showtime is 7:30 P.M. (8:30 P.M. in summer); adults pay $34.95, plus tax and tip. Reservations are suggested (239-9221 or 800-553-6116).

The Medieval Times Dinner & Tournament harks back to the Middle Ages with swordplay and a castlelike setting. In keeping with tradition, the food is served without silverware (unless you insist). The meal includes appetizer, soup, spareribs, roasted chicken, and pastry. Showtimes vary seasonally; adults pay $33.95, plus tax and tip. Reservations are suggested (396-1518 or 800-229-8300).

Wild Bill's Wild West Dinner Extravaganza at Fort Liberty stars cowboys and Comanche tribe members. The menu includes spareribs, fried chicken, corn-on-the-cob, and more. Showtime is 7 P.M.; adults pay $31.95, plus tax and tip. Reservations are suggested (351-5151 or 800-883-8181).

25 Candles

When Walt Disney World hits
the quarter-century mark on
October 1, 1996, the occasion
will not go unnoticed. In fact,
more than a year's worth of
special festivities, new shows,
and packages are in store.
Call 824-4321 for an up-to-the-
minute report on goings-on.

HOLIDAYS AND SPECIAL EVENTS

When you consider how infinitely entertaining Walt Disney World is when there's no special occasion on tap, it's hard to believe it can make an even greater spectacle of itself. Yet, the WDW calendar is packed with celebrations and events that do just that. In fact, between holiday extravaganzas and the legion of other festivities staged here, days that are merely infinitely entertaining are few and far between. This calendar highlights some of the holidays and special events that—for their fanfare, their crowd-drawing potential and, in some instances, their package deals—are worth factoring into your vacation plans. For more information on these and a slew of other goings-on, call the number at the end of each listing or 824-4321.

HOLIDAYS

WDW NEW YEAR'S EVE CELEBRATION (December 31): The Magic Kingdom and Epcot stay open until 2 A.M. on New Year's Eve, attracting huge throngs and presenting such unique opportunities as "Auld Lang Syne" à la Space Mountain. Double-size fireworks are launched over both parks, which are still fitted out in full Christmas regalia. (To give you an idea of the magnitude of this celebration, note that the Magic Kingdom's biggest crowd ever was the horde of 93,000 revelers who rang in 1980.) For serious partiers, Pleasure Island unleashes the New Year's Eve spectacular it's been rehearsing for the past 364 nights in a special-admission blowout complete with big-name performers.

PLEASURE ISLAND MARDI GRAS (February 17–20): Pleasure Island makes like the Big Easy in a big way, heightening its usual festive atmosphere with Crescent City jazz bands, Creole and Cajun food, and special Mardi Gras performances in the streets. And it doesn't end with Fat Tuesday. All-you-can-eat Mardi Gras Jazz Brunches are served at the *Pleasure Island Jazz Company* every Sunday.

PLEASURE ISLAND'S ST. PATRICK'S DAY CELEBRATION (March 17): Pleasure Island gets its Irish up with live Irish music, specialty drinks along the lines of the Nutty Irishman, and a four-leaf clover of a food fest.

EASTER SUNDAY (April 7): Main Street becomes a bunny trail in a televised parade that makes for a very hopping Magic Kingdom. More generally, note that the Magic Kingdom, Epcot, and the Disney-MGM Studios have extended hours throughout the Easter season—a time of year in which the World is so crowded you might want to reconsider your timing.

FOURTH OF JULY CELEBRATION: Double-fisted fireworks from the Magic Kingdom (they're set off over Cinderella Castle as well as Seven Seas Lagoon), the SpectroMagic electrical parade, and the Disney-MGM Studios' stunning symphony of music and fireworks (Sorcery in the Sky) are glorious. But you pay a price: This is the busiest day of the summer.

CHRISTMAS: Walt Disney World puts its spectacular Christmas decorations up early, so you can enjoy the World at its most festive during one of its least-crowded times of year—the period from the last Sunday in November until Christmas. The theme parks and resorts are positively aglow with holiday spirit, and it doesn't stop at decorations. There are nightly tree-lighting ceremonies in all three parks. The Disney Village Marketplace offers a Nativity pageant. Epcot invites guests to enjoy a candlelight procession and a chorale celebration of holidays around the world. During the nights of December 1, 2, 7, 8, 9, 14, and 15, the Magic Kingdom reopens its doors to host Mickey's Very Merry Christmas Party, a special-admission celebration including a holiday parade that extends to 1 A.M. To take advantage of the best Walt Disney World has to offer during this time of year, consider booking a Jolly Holidays vacation package. The two- to four-night packages, available from November 26 through December 21, include admission to the Jolly Holidays Dinner Show—an all-you-can-eat holiday feast served forth with a celebration featuring more than 100 singers and dancers. This show, held at the *Contemporary* resort, is available only with the purchase of a Jolly Holidays package. Holiday receptions at WDW resorts add to the fun. The four-night package offers unlimited admission to the three theme parks and Pleasure Island. Call 827-7200 for information.

Joy to the World

To experience all the extra fun and festivity on tap at Walt Disney World during the Christmas season, consider booking a Jolly Holidays vacation package.

Orlando-Area Special Events

A visit to Walt Disney World might coincide with one of Central Florida's annual events. January happenings include the Scottish Highland Games in Orlando and the Zora Neale Hurston Festival in Eatonville. Other notable events are Speed Weeks in February (Daytona); Silver Spurs Rodeo in February and July (Kissimmee); the Winter Park Sidewalk Art Festival in March (Winter Park); the Shakespeare Festival, from late March through early April (Orlando); the Pepsi 400 NASCAR Winston Cup Series Race in July (Daytona); and the Festival of Trees in December (Orlando Museum of Art). For more information about area goings-on, contact the Orlando/Orange County Convention & Visitors Bureau (363-5871).

SPECIAL EVENTS

WALT DISNEY WORLD MARATHON (January 7): As grueling 26.2-mile races go, this young upstart (in just its third running) is uniquely tempting. The course is flat as a flapjack and wends its way through each of the theme parks (hitting the Magic Kingdom at about 8 miles, Disney-MGM Studios at about 21 miles, and Epcot with 1½ miles to go) and past several resort areas before finishing up in Epcot's parking lot. Because it wouldn't be a Disney event without entertainment, live bands, Disney characters, and hot-air balloons inspire the some 10,000 runners to stay the course. For more information on this whirlwind tour of Walt Disney World, call 939-7810.

LPGA HEALTHSOUTH INAUGURAL (January 19–21): No matter that this tournament debuted at Walt Disney World in 1995. The name has stuck because it's the first full-field event of the year—an opportunity for women pros to start the season off with a bang. The Pete Dye–designed Eagle Pines course serves as the sole venue, and a one-day pro-am precedes the exciting three-day competition. For more information, call 824-2250.

EPCOT INTERNATIONAL FLOWER & GARDEN FESTIVAL (April 18–June 2): This flowery event—a fragrant affair featuring some 30 million blossoms—not only makes a glorious perfumery of Epcot; it allows gardeners to learn a trick or two from the folks who care for 10,000 rose bushes and then some. In addition to the animated character topiaries and elaborate display gardens in full bloom throughout Future World and World Showcase, gardening workshops, behind-the-scenes tours, and special dining and entertainment events are featured. Special vacation packages offered in conjunction with this third annual festival include accommodations, choice of horticultural tours, and other amenities. For further information, call 939-7814.

DISNEYANA (September): For serious Disney enthusiasts, this five-day convention is the be-all and end-all. Featured attractions include a Disneyana fair with original artwork and collectibles, behind-the-scenes seminars, and opportunities to obtain signed limited-edition pieces created exclusively for the convention. Past offerings have included Cinderella's (Waterford) Glass Slipper. Topping it all off is a unique auction in which attendees can bid for one-of-a-kind Disney experiences as well as special pieces of Disneyana. This is your chance to be boat captain of the Jungle Cruise or the engineer of the Walt Disney World Railroad. Parts of renovated attractions often end up on the auction block as well. During a recent Disneyana convention, one couple walked off with their very own Dumbo car (for which they paid around $16,000). The event alternates between Disneyland and Walt Disney World, with the 1996 convention being held in Florida. Special vacation packages are available; for additional information, call 560-7232.

WALT DISNEY WORLD/OLDSMOBILE GOLF CLASSIC (October 5–8): In this exciting tournament, celebrating its 26th year, top PGA Tour players compete alongside amateurs on three classic venues of the Magic Linkdom: the Joe Lee–designed Palm, Magnolia, and Lake Buena Vista. The drama builds until the final day, when the Magnolia's fickle 18th hole has been known to twist fates. Tickets are available on site each day of the tournament, with one-day admission ranging from $10 for the first or second round to $15 for the final round. Gallery badges for all four championship rounds are $35 (pay $50 for a Season badge, and you also get reduced greens fees on the Disney golf courses). For more information see the "Golf" section in the *Diversions* chapter, or call 824-2250.

DISNEY VILLAGE MARKETPLACE BOAT SHOW (October): Some 200 brand-spanking-new watercraft from more than 17 dealers hit the Buena Vista Lagoon in this, Central Florida's largest (and only in-the-water) boat show. Offering the first public glimpses of the freshest things afloat, it draws close to 100,000 people. Prospective buyers may take the boats out on the water.

FESTIVAL OF THE MASTERS AT DISNEY VILLAGE MARKETPLACE (November): One of the South's top-rated art shows, it draws upwards of 200 award-winning exhibitors from around the country. Even celebrities come out for this one. A tip: The festival tends to be least crowded on Friday and Sunday mornings. Special Fall Fantasy packages are available.

Art Smarts

The optimum times to visit Festival of the Masters are Friday and Sunday mornings.

Index

A

accommodations, 37-73
  beyond Walt Disney World
    (Orlando area), 68-73
      Best Western Buena Vista
        Suites, 70-71
      Clarion Plaza, 72
      Country Hearth Inn, 72-73
      Grand Cypress, 68-69
      Holiday Inn Express, 73
      Peabody Orlando, 68-70
      Summerfield Suites, 71
  check-in and check-out
    times, 41
  cost-cutting tips, 14
  deluxe resort properties, 40,
    41-53, 68-70
  home away from home resort
    properties, 40, 54-58, 70-71
  moderate resort properties,
    40, 59-63, 72
  most romantic WDW resorts, 34
  off-property lodging
    information, 68
  ranking system for WDW
    resorts, 40
  rates, 40
  reservations, 41, 65, 68
  transportation around WDW, 39
  value resort properties, 40,
    63-64, 72-73
  WDW resort properties, 39-67
    All-Star Music, 63-64
    All-Star Sports, 63-64
    Beach Club, 52-53
    Caribbean Beach, 59-60
    Contemporary, 41-42
    Disney Vacation Club,
      54-55
    Disney Village Hotel Plaza,
      65-67
      Buena Vista Palace, 65-66
      Courtyard by Marriott, 67
      Hilton, 66-67
    Disney's BoardWalk, 42-44
    Dixie Landings, 60-61
    Dolphin, 44-46
    Fort Wilderness resort and
      campground, 55-57

Grand Floridian, 46-48
Polynesian, 48-50
Port Orleans, 61-63
Swan, 44-46
Villas at The Disney
  Institute, The, 57-58
Wilderness Lodge,
  50-51
Yacht Club, 52-53
admission passes, 15-16
  Disney-MGM Studios, 118
  Epcot, 90
  Magic Kingdom, 78
  water parks, 164-166
  where to purchase, 15
Adult Learning Seminars,
  170-171
Adventureland, 89
Adventurers Club, 206
afternoon tea, 70, 192
Alien Encounter, 83-84
All-Star Music resort, 14,
  63-64
All-Star Sports resort, 14,
  63-64
AMC Theatres, 202
American Adventure, The,
  113-114
  shopping, 158
American Express Vacation
  Travel packages, 13
America Gardens Theatre, 114
America Online access to
  WDW updates, 25
Animation Gallery, 160
Animation Plaza, 126-128
Art of Disney, The, 153
Astro Orbiter, 83
ATMs, 14
  Disney-MGM Studios, 123
  Epcot, 95
  Magic Kingdom, 80, 83
  Pleasure Island, 201

B

Backstage Studio Tour,
  126-127
banking. *see* money matters;
  ATMs; Sun Bank
Beach Club, 52-53
  lounge, 209
  restaurants, 189, 190, 193
beaches, 150
Beauty and the Beast Stage
  Show, 124

beer lover's hangouts, 27,
  193, 209
Belz Factory Outlet World
  (Orlando), 161
Best Western Buena Vista Suites
  (Orlando), 70-71
Big Thunder Mountain
  Railroad, 88
biking, 149
Blizzard Beach, 166
  transportation to, 20
Blue Spring State Park, 169
boating, 147-149
  canoeing, 148
  cruising, 148
  half-day (sample schedule),
    26-27
  pedal boating, 148
  sailing, 148
  speedboating, 149
  waterskiing, 149
Body Wars, 104-105, 106
Briar Patch, 156
Buena Vista Palace, 65-66
  lounges, 210-211
  restaurant, 195

C

camcorders, renting, 24
cameras and film, 24
campsites, 55-57
Canada, 109-110
  restaurant, 186
  shopping, 158
canoeing, 148
  Florida State Canoe Trail, 168
car, traveling by, 17-19
  directions to WDW from
    Orlando Airport, 20
  tips for drivers, 17
Caribbean Beach, 14, 59-60
Caribbean Coral Reef Ride, 100
cash machines. *see* ATMs
Catholic masses, 29
Celebrity 5 & 10, 160
Centorium, 158
Charles Hosmer Morse
  Museum of American Art
  (Winter Park), 162
check-in and check-out times
  for WDW resort hotels, 41
China, 116
  restaurant, 188
  shopping, 158
Christmas Chalet, 154

Christmas festivities, 10, 12, 215
Cinderella Castle, 86, 87
Cinderella's Golden Carrousel, 86
Circle of Life, 101-102
City, The, 155
Clarion Plaza (Orlando), 72
clothing, 11
Comedy Warehouse, 207
Contemporary, 41-42
 lounges, 208, 211
 restaurants, 190, 193
Coronado Springs resort (1997), 62
Costume Shop, The, 160
Country Bear Jamboree, 89
Country Hearth Inn (Orlando), 72-73
couples, 33-35
 honeymoons, 35, 48, 49
 WDW most romantic lounges, resorts, and restaurants, 34
 weddings, 34-35
Courtyard by Marriott, 67
Cranium Command, 105-106
credit cards, 14
Cristal Arts, 155
Crossroads of Lake Buena Vista
 restaurants, 198, 199
 shopping, 161
crowd patterns, 12, 80, 95, 123
cruises
 dinner-dance, 212
 Winter Park, 162
Crystal Arts, 156

D
Delta Air Lines packages, 13
diabetics, special needs for, 16
Diamond Horseshoe Saloon Revue, 86, 89
dinner-dance cruises, 212
dinner shows, 210-211, 213
disabilities, guests with, 22, 29-31, 45
 wheelchair rental, 30
Discover, 155
Discovery Island, 168-170
 half-day visit (sample schedule), 27-28
 transportation to, 20

Disneyana (collectibles convention), 11, 216-217
Disneyana Collectibles, 156
Disney Catalog, 157
Disney Clothiers, 156
Disney Institute, The, 171-173
 Villas at, 57-58, 173
Disney Magical Holidays, 12, 215
Disney-MGM Studios, 118-131
 admission prices, 15-16, 118
 Animation Plaza and Mickey Avenue, 126-128
 coming attractions, 120
 Echo Lake area, 128-130
 entertainment, 128-129
 fireworks displays, 129, 204
 getting oriented, 120-122
 guiding principles, 120
 Hollywood Boulevard, 123
 hot tips, 123, 126
 hours, 118
 lounge, 208
 map, 121
 New York Street, 130-131
 quiet nooks, 124
 recommended visiting pattern for first-timers, 77
 restaurants, 179-188
  fast food, 183, 185, 186, 187
  full service, 180, 181, 184, 185
  reservations, 178-179
 sample schedule, 23-24
 shopping, 160-161
 snacker's guides, 130, 188
 Sunset Boulevard, 124-125
 tip board, 123
 touring priorities, 122
 transportation to, 19-20
 walking tour, 122-131
Disney Oscars, 127
Disney's BoardWalk, 47-44, 208
Disney's Racquet Club, 143-144
Disney's Wild Animal Kingdom, 32
Disney Vacation Club, 14, 54-55
 lounge, 210
 restaurant, 191
Disney Village Hotel Plaza, 65-67
 Buena Vista Palace, 65-66
 Courtyard by Marriott, 67
 Hilton, 66-67

 lounges, 210, 211
 restaurants, 195
 reservations, 179
Disney Village Marketplace, 153
 Festival of the Masters art show, 12, 217
 guided fishing trips from, 146
 half-day visit (sample schedule), 27
 lounge, 208
 restaurants, 195, 197
 reservations, 179
 shopping, 153-155
 transportation to, 20
Disney Village Marketplace Boat Show, 12, 217
Dixie Landings, 14, 34, 60-61
 guided fishing trips from, 146
 lounge, 210
 restaurant, 193
Dolphin, 44-46
 lounge, 208-209
 restaurants, 191, 194
Dreamflight, 84
Dumbo, the Flying Elephant, 86

E
Eagle Pines (golf course), 141-142
Easter Sunday, 11, 215
Echo Lake Area, 128-130
Edwin Watts Golf Shops (Orlando), 161
8Trax, 205
Electrical Water Pageant, 203
El Rió del Tiempo (boat ride), 117
emergency medical care, 16
Emporium, 157
Epcot, 90-117
 admission prices, 15-16, 90
 entertainment, 96-97
 getting oriented, 94
 guiding principles, 92
 hot tips, 95
 hours, 90, 95
 map, 93
 recommended visiting pattern for first-timers, 77
 restaurants, 179-188
  fast food, 183, 185, 186, 187, 188

full service, 179, 180, 181, 182, 183, 184, 185
reservations, 178-179
sample schedules, 22-23, 25
snacker's guides, 108-109, 188
tip board, 95
touring priorities, 94
transportation to, 19
walking tour, 95-117
See also Future World; World Showcase
Epcot Discovery Center, 95, 104
Epcot International Flower & Garden Festival, 11, 171, 216
EuroSpain, 155

F

Fantasy in the Sky, 86
Fantasyland, 85-86
fast food. *see* restaurant guide; snacker's guides
Festival of the Masters at Disney Village Marketplace (art show), 12, 217
fireworks displays, 76, 86, 97, 129, 203-204
first aid centers, 16
fishing, 144-147
guided trips, 23, 145-146
half-day (sample schedule), 28
on your own, 146-147
fitness centers, 151
Five-Day World Hopper Pass, 15, 16
Flea World (Orlando), 161-162
Florida State Canoe Trail, 168
Food Rocks, 102, 106
Fort Wilderness, 167-168
half-day visit (sample schedule), 28
resort and campground, 55-57
transportation to, 20
Four-Day Park Hopper Pass, 15, 16
Four-Day Value Pass, 15, 16
Fourth of July celebration, 11, 215
France, 111
restaurants, 179, 183, 185
shopping, 158
freshwater fishing, 145
Frontierland, 87-89
Future World, 96-107
Horizons, 92, 104
Innoventions, 98-99, 106

Journey Into Imagination, 102-103
The Land, 101-102, 103
The Living Seas, 100
Spaceship Earth, 97
Universe of Energy, 92, 106-107
Wonders of Life, 104-106
World of Motion, 92, 103

G

Gardens of the World (learning seminar), 100, 170-171, 173
Germany, 115
restaurants, 183, 187, 211
shopping, 158
golf, 135-142
courses, 140-142
dress, 138
equipment rental, 138
half-day (sample schedule), 26
instruction, 138
rates, 137
reservations, 22-23, 137-138
tournaments, 138-139
transportation, 138
Gourmet Pantry, 154
Grad Nights, 11
Grand Cypress resort (Orlando), 68-69
Grand Floridian, 34, 46-48
afternoon tea, 192
lounges, 211
restaurants, 190, 192, 193-194
Grand Prix Raceway, 84
Great Movie Ride, The, 128
Great Southern Craft Co., 154
Greenhouse Tour, 100, 101
Green Thumb Emporium, 158
guided fishing trips, 23, 145-146

H

Hall of Presidents, The, 86
Harrington Bay Clothiers, 154
Haunted Mansion, 87
health clubs, 151
Hidden Treasures of World Showcase (learning seminar), 100, 170, 173
Hilton, 66-67
Holiday Inn Express (Orlando), 73
holidays, 10-12, 214-215
Hollywood Boulevard, 123
Honey, I Shrunk the Audience, 102-103, 106

Honey, I Shrunk the Kids Movie Set Adventure, 131
honeymoons, 35, 48, 49
Hoop-Dee-Doo Musical Revue, 22, 167, 210
Horizons, 92, 104
hours of operation
Disney-MGM Studios, 118, 123
Epcot, 90, 95
Magic Kingdom, 78, 80
Hyatt Regency Grand Cypress (Orlando), 68-69

I

IllumiNations, 97, 203
Image Works, 103, 106
Impressions de France (film), 111
Indiana Jones Epic Stunt Spectacular, 129
Indy 200 at Walt Disney World, 11
Innoventions, 98-99, 106
International Designer Outlets (Orlando), 162
International Sports Complex (1997), 135
Internet access to WDW updates, 25
Italy, 114-115
restaurant, 182
shopping, 159
It's A Small World, 85

J

Japan, 112-113
restaurants, 182, 188
shopping, 159
Jewish religious services, 29
Jim Henson's Muppet*Vision 3-D, 130
jogging, 58, 148
Jolly Holidays vacation package, 215
Journey Into Imagination, 102-103
Jungle Cruise, 89

K

Kennedy Space Center's Spaceport USA Visitors Center, 172
Keystone Clothiers, 160
King's Gallery, The, 157
Kissimmee—St. Cloud Convention & Visitors Bureau, 68
kosher meals, 181

L

Lake Buena Vista (golf course), 142
Land, The, 101-102, 103
Legend of The Lion King, 86
Legends of Hollywood, 160
Length of Stay Pass, 15-16
Liberty Square, 86-87
Liberty Square Market, 88
Liberty Square Riverboat, 86-87
Living Seas, The, 100
Living with the Land (boat ride), 101
LPGA HealthSouth Inaugural championship, 11, 139, 216

M

Mad Tea Party, 86
Maelstrom, 117
Magic Kingdom, 78-89
    admission prices, 15-16, 78
    Adventureland, 89
    entertainment, 86
    Fantasyland, 85-86
    Frontierland, 87-89
    fireworks displays, 204
    getting oriented, 80
    guiding principles, 79-80
    hot tips, 80, 93
    hours, 78, 80
    Liberty Square, 86-87
    Main Street, U.S.A., 82
    map, 81
    Mickey's Starland, 85
    quiet nooks, 84
    recommended visiting patterns for first-timers, 77
    restaurants, 179-188
        fast food, 183, 186, 187, 188
        full service, 181, 182, 183, 184
        reservations, 178-179
    sample schedule, 24
    shopping, 156-157
    snacker's guides, 88, 188
    tip board, 80
    Tomorrowland, 82-84
    touring priorities, 82
    Town Square, 80
    transportation to, 19
    walking tour, 80-89

Magic of Disney Animation, The, 126
Magnolia (golf course), 140-141
mail order shopping (WDW Mail Order), 157
Main Street, U.S.A., 82
Main Street Athletic Store, 157
Main Street Bake Shop, 88
Main Street Cinema, 82
Main Street Confectionery, 157
Making of..., The, 127
Mannequins Dance Palace, 203-204
map(s)
    central Florida, 17
    Disney-MGM Studios, 121
    Epcot, 93
    Magic Kingdom, 81
    Orlando area, 18
Mardi Gras Jazz Brunch, 196
massages, 151
medical matters, 16
Merritt Island National Wildlife Refuge, 168
Mexico, 117
    restaurants, 185
    shopping, 159
Mickey Avenue, 126-128
Mickey Mania Parade, 86
Mickey's Character Shop, 154
Mickey's Starland, 85
money matters, 14-15, 77, 80
    cost-cutting tips, 14
Monster Sound Show, 129
Morocco, 111-112
    restaurant, 184
    shopping, 159
movies, 17, 212
    AMC Theatres, 202
Mr. Toad's Wild Ride, 86
Muslim services, 29

N

Neon Armadillo Music Saloon, 206
New Year's Eve celebration, 10, 214
New York Street, 130-131
nightlife guide, 200-213
    beer lover's hangouts, 27, 193, 209

dinner-dance cruises, 212
dinner shows, 210-211, 213
Disney's BoardWalk, 208
evening activities, 26-27
most romantic lounges, 34
movies, 17, 212
    AMC Theatres, 202
    Orlando-area stand-outs, 212-213
Pleasure Island, 201-207
    walking tour, 203-207
    in the theme parks, 203-204
WDW beyond Pleasure Island, 208-211
    good bets, 210-211
    scenic spots, 209
    stand-outs, 208-210
nonemergency medical care, 16
nonsmokers, accommodations for, 45
Norway, 116-117
    restaurants, 179, 186
    shopping, 159

O

Oak Trail (golf course), 141
older travelers, 31-32, 94
Olde World Antiques, 157
Once Upon A Time, 160
one-day admission ticket, 15
Orlando/Orange County Convention & Visitors Bureau, 68
Orlando area
    accommodations, 68-73
    directions to WDW from Orlando Airport, 20
    map, 18
    nightlife guide, 212-213
    professional sports, 142
    restaurants, 197-199
    shopping, 161-162
    special events, 216
Osprey Ridge (golf course), 141

P

package tours, 13-14
    Jolly Holidays vacation package, 215
packing suggestions, 11
Palm (golf course), 140

parasailing, 147
Park Avenue, Winter Park,
    shopping, 162
Peabody Orlando, 69-70
pedal boating, 148
Peter Pan's Flight, 85-86
pets, 30
pharmacies, 16
picnics, 195
Pirates of the Caribbean, 89
Planet Hollywood, 154
planning your trip, 9-35
    admission options, 15-16
    America Online access to
        WDW updates, 25
    crowd patterns, 12, 80, 95, 123
    getting around WDW,
        17-20, 39
    important telephone numbers,
        31, 33
    Internet access to WDW
        updates, 25
    medical matters, 16
    money matters, 14-15, 80
        cost-cutting tips, 14
    package tours, 13-14
    packing, 11
    rainy day activities, 28
    recommended pattern for
        visiting the parks, 77
    sample schedules, 21-28
    special needs, 29-35
        couples, 33-34
        guests with disabilities, 29-31
        honeymoons, 35
        older travelers, 31-32
        religious services, 29
        single travelers, 32-33
        traveling with pets, 30
        weddings, 34-35
    weather, 12
    when to go, 10-12
Plaza Ice Cream Parlor, 88
Pleasure Island, 201-207
    Mardi Gras Jazz Brunch, 196
    restaurants, 195-196, 197
    transportation to, 20
    walking tour, 203-207
Pleasure Island Jazz Company,
    12, 196, 204
Pleasure Island Mardi Gras,
    11, 196, 214
Polynesian, 34, 48-50
    lounge, 211
    restaurants, 190-191, 210-211

Port Orleans, 14, 34, 61-63
    lounge, 211
    restaurant, 189
Premium Annual Pass, 16
professional sports in the
    Orlando area, 142
Protestant religious services, 29
pubs, 27, 193, 209

R

rainy day activities, 28
ranking system for WDW resort
    hotels, 40
religious services, 29
Renninger's Antique Center, 162
reservations, 22
    restaurants, 22, 178-179
    for WDW resort
        accommodations, 41, 43
Resortwear Unlimited, 155
restaurant guide, 177-199
    afternoon tea, 192
    best burgers, 189
    best wine spots, 185-186
    cost-cutting tips, 14
    Crossroads of Lake Buena
        Vista, 198, 199
    dietary needs, 181
    dining rooms with knockout
        views, 199
    dinner-dance cruises, 212
    dinner shows, 210-211, 213
    Mardi Gras Jazz Brunch, 196
    most romantic dining
        spots, 34
    newcomers to WDW dining
        lineup, 197
    nonsmoking regulations, 180
    picnicking, 195
    reservations, 22, 178-179
        without reservations, 187
    in the theme parks, 179-188
        fast food, 183, 185-188
        full service, 179-185
        24-hour resort eateries, 194
    in WDW resorts, 189-194
        good bets, 193-194
        stand-outs, 189-193
    beyond WDW, 197-199
        good bets, 199
        stand-outs, 197-199
    other WDW options, 195-197
        good bets, 197
        stand-outs, 195-196
    See also snacker's guides

River Country, 164
    transportation to, 20
Rock & Roll Beach Club, 204-205
Ron Jon Surf Shops (Cocoa
    Beach), 162
RV campers, 56

S

sailing, 148
St. Patrick's Day celebration,
    11, 214
saltwater fishing, 145
Sci-Fi Convention, 11
Sea Base Alpha, 100
Seminole Towne Center, 162
shopping, 152-162
    at Crossroads of Lake Buena
        Vista, 161
    in Disney-MGM Studios,
        160-161
    in Disney Village Marketplace,
        153-155
    half-day visit (sample
        schedule), 26
    in Epcot, 158-159
    in the Magic Kingdom, 156-157
    beyond WDW, 161-162
Sid Cahuenga's One-of-a-Kind,
    160-161
Silversmith, 157
single travelers, 32-33
Skyway to Fantasyland, 84
snacker's guides
    Disney-MGM Studios, 130
    Epcot, 108-109
    Magic Kingdom, 88
Snow White's Adventures, 86
Sorcery in the Sky, 129, 204
Space Mountain, 82-83
Spaceship Earth, 97
special events, 10-12, 216-217
    WDW 25th Anniversary
        Celebration, 12, 214
    weddings, 34-35
SpectroMagic light parade,
    86, 204
speedboating, 149
Spirit of Pocahontas Stage
    Show, The, 131
Splash Mountain, 87-88
sports, 135-151
    biking, 149
    boating, 147-149, 168
    fishing, 144-147
    golf, 135-142

health clubs, 151
International Sports Complex (1997), 135
jogging, 58, 148
parasailing, 147
professional sports in the Orlando area, 142
scuba diving, 169
swimming, 150-151, 164-166
tennis, 26, 44, 143-144
waterskiing, 149
Studio Showcase, 127
Summerfield Suites (Orlando), 71
Sun Bank, 14-15, 80
Sunset Boulevard, 124-125
SuperStar Television, 128-129
Swan, 44-46
restaurant, 194
Sweet Success, 161
swimming, 150-151, 164-166
Swiss Family Treehouse, 89

T

tea, afternoon, 192
Team Mickey's Athletic Club, 155
telephones, 48
area code, 10, 38, 176
important phone numbers, 31, 33
temperatures. *see* weather
tennis, 23, 143-144
clay courts, 44
nighttime, 26, 44, 143
theme park annual pass, 16
Timekeeper, The, 84
Tomorrowland, 82-84
Tom Sawyer Island, 89
Tony's Town Square, 88
tours. *see* package tours
transportation
around WDW, 17-20, 39, 111
See also car, traveling by
Transportation and Ticket Center (TTC), 19, 40
Tropical Serenade, 89
24-hour eateries, 194
24kt Precious Adornments, 155
Twilight Zone Tower of Terror, The, 124-125

2R's Reading and Riting, 154-155
Typhoon Lagoon, 165
transportation to, 20

U

United Kingdom, 110
restaurants, 184
shopping, 159
Universe of Energy, 92, 106-107
Uptown Jewelers, 157

V

Villas at The Disney Institute, The, 57-58, 173
Voyage of the Little Mermaid, 127-128

W

Walt Disney Imagineering Laboratory, 99
Walt Disney's Carousel of Progress, 84
Walt Disney World/Oldsmobile Golf Classic, 12, 138-139, 217
Walt Disney World Guidebook for Guests with Disabilities, 22, 29
Walt Disney World Marathon, 11, 216
Walt Disney World 25th Anniversary Celebration, 12, 214
water parks, 164-166
Blizzard Beach, 166
half-day visit (sample schedule), 25-26
River Country, 164
Typhoon Lagoon, 165
waterskiing, 149
WDW Mail Order, 157
weather, 12, 146
rainy day activities, 28
weddings, 34-35
West End Stage, 206-207
wheelchair rental, 30, 94
Wilderness Lodge, 34, 50-51
lounge, 209-210
restaurants, 189, 194
wines, 27, 65, 185-186, 191

Winter Park, shopping, 162
Wonders of China (film), 116
Wonders of Life, 104-106
World of Motion, 92, 103
World Showcase, 107-117
The American Adventure, 113-114
art galleries, 112
Canada, 109-110
China, 116
drinking spots, 116-117
entertainment, 97
fast food, 183, 185, 186, 187, 188
fireworks displays, 97, 203
France, 111
Germany, 115
hours, 90, 95
Italy, 114-115
Japan, 112-113
Mexico, 117
Morocco, 111-112
Norway, 116-117
quiet nooks, 110
restaurants
fast food, 183, 185, 186, 187, 188
full service, 179, 180, 181, 182, 183, 184, 185
romantic spots, 115
shopping, 158-159
snacker's guides, 108-109, 188
United Kingdom, 110

Y

Yacht Club, 34, 52-53
lounge, 208
restaurants, 189, 192-193
Yankee Trader, 157
You & Me Kid, 155

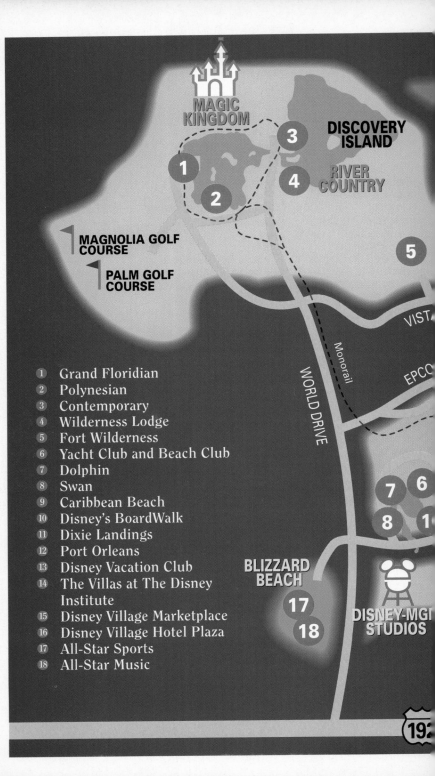

MAGIC KINGDOM

DISCOVERY ISLAND

3

1

4

2

RIVER COUNTRY

5

MAGNOLIA GOLF COURSE

PALM GOLF COURSE

VISTA

Monorail

WORLD DRIVE

EPCO

① Grand Floridian
② Polynesian
③ Contemporary
④ Wilderness Lodge
⑤ Fort Wilderness
⑥ Yacht Club and Beach Club
⑦ Dolphin
⑧ Swan
⑨ Caribbean Beach
⑩ Disney's BoardWalk
⑪ Dixie Landings
⑫ Port Orleans
⑬ Disney Vacation Club
⑭ The Villas at The Disney Institute
⑮ Disney Village Marketplace
⑯ Disney Village Hotel Plaza
⑰ All-Star Sports
⑱ All-Star Music

7   6

8   1

BLIZZARD BEACH

17

18

DISNEY-MGI STUDIOS

192